THE
HARD
STUFF

THE HARD STUFF

DOPE, CRIME, THE MC5 & MY LIFE OF IMPOSSIBILITIES

WAYNE KRAMER

FABER & FABER

First published in the UK in 2018
by Faber & Faber Ltd
Bloomsbury House
74–77 Great Russell Street London
WC1B 3DA

First published in the USA in 2018
by Da Capo Press
Hachette Book Group
1290 Avenue of the Americas, New York, NY 10104

Printed and bound by CPI Group (UK) Ltd, Croydon CR0 4YY

The right of Wayne Kramer to be identified as author of this work
has been asserted in accordance with Section 77 of the Copyright,
Designs and Patents Act 1988

A CIP record for this book
is available from the British Library

ISBN 978–0–571–34126–9

FSC
www.fsc.org
MIX
Paper from
responsible sources
FSC® C020471

My final contribution to this memoir is this dedication.

I'm trying to get it done before my family wakes up and the wonderful chaos of our life begins again. My wife and son have become the center of my universe. We are like the nucleus of an atom, spinning around each other and holding on to what we have together. A force of nature.

To my darling son, Francis; I wrote this book so you would know the road I have traveled to get to you. The world will soon be yours. Take good care of it and take good care of yourself.

To my beloved wife, Margaret; you are the one from whom all good things flow. Without you I would not have this abundant life. I will be eternally grateful for your love, encouragement, belief, and kindness. With you and Francis I am, indeed, a fortunate man.

CONTENTS

PART TWO

PART THREE

PART 1

Happy the youth who believes that his duty is to remake the world and bring it more in accord with virtue and justice, more in accord with his own heart. Woe to whoever commences his life without lunacy.

–NIKOS KAZANTZAKIS, *Report to Greco*

PROLOGUE

The Belle Isle police riot of April 30, 1967, was the first riot I ever played. It was on my birthday; I was 19 years old. The hippie movement had arrived in Detroit that spring, and since the MC5 was a band on the cutting edge of the counterculture, it was only natural that we'd play the motor city's first Love-in.

Belle Isle is a delightful city park in the middle of the Detroit River. The day had progressed peacefully enough, with pot smoking and acid tripping and freaks of all stripes carrying on. When we took the stage, which was in a gazebo near a wooded area of the park, it was the peak of the afternoon and everything was going great. The crowd was pure Detroit, black and white, friends and strangers, and they all moved in close to see the MC5. I resorted to my technique of brushing the crowd back by looking the other way and then crashing into them, as if I was so caught up in the moment that I didn't know what I was doing. It worked like a charm—make some room, motherfuckers, I'm doing a show here! Everyone was having fun, and I enjoyed myself immensely.

The sun went down, and the Detroit Police Department decided we weren't clearing out quickly enough. There was a small confrontation with some drunken Outlaw bikers, and the police threw down on them. The bikers fought back, and the crowd backed away from the mayhem.

Police reinforcements arrived and started bum-rushing everyone off of Belle Isle. We were just getting ready to leave as the cops got into position. They had probably been rehearsing their lockstep, and were overjoyed to have a chance to use it—not that anyone there posed a threat. This wasn't a cadre of highly trained Marxist revolutionaries; we were a bunch of regular folks, stoned-out weirdos and Budweiser-buzzed factory rats, simply enjoying a free concert.

At first, it was a game. When the police line came forward, everyone shrieked and laughed and ran away. But when the first heads got busted, the humor abruptly dissipated. The cops' violence was outrageously out of proportion to the situation. They seemed to enjoy their total dominance over the crowd. They were sadistic.

Wanting to save our gear from being smashed, I hopped into an open-bed pickup truck with some of the instruments. Michael and Fred piled in with me. We drove slowly toward the only bridge off the island, where, to our surprise, a police roadblock had stopped traffic. The sun had gone down, and it was now dark. It was then that the mounted police arrived.

The mounted cops took a galloping start on people who were running away, and clubbed them like they were playing polo. Giddyup! Whack! Pow! Score! Women were screaming, blood was gushing, men were cursing at the cops. The trees were backlit by police headlights and spotlights. Everywhere I looked, another horrific scene was going down like some unholy Chinese shadow puppet show. After traffic started backing up on the bridge, the police finally let us drive off the island.

WE FINALLY GOT BACK to our headquarters at the Artists Workshop, and started putting out calls for help. I made inquiries to hospitals and jails as to the whereabouts of my sister Kathi and our other missing friends. I was outraged at what had just gone down. The line had been crossed; never again would I believe the myth that the police were there to protect and serve.

Later that summer, this became even clearer when the Detroit Police Department enacted one of the worst outbreaks of police violence in American history. It wasn't black people killing white people, any more than it was black people killing cops. It was the police who were doing the killing.

CHAPTER 1

BACK TO DETROIT

My mother was a pragmatist. Of French ancestry, she was born in Detroit on November 15, 1927. Family lore has it that her mother's parents owned property in Paris, but immigrated to Sarnia, Ontario, just north of Detroit. They relocated to the Motor City between the world wars because my grandfather Max was a bricklayer, and there was a lot of new building going on there.

In the '40s and '50s, Mable Evelyn Dyell was a real looker. She was a natural brunette, but dyed her hair blond, and had a great figure. Marilyn Monroe was the ideal, and Mable came close with her voluptuous hips, full lips, and platinum hair set in the latest styles. She understood her sexual power, and had a sly grin and wink of the eye that made you feel like you were the most important person in the world.

But she was also tough. She told me that when she was young, her father abused her, and she wouldn't let anyone abuse her ever again.

Once, later in her life when she was semiretired and living in Florida, a friend's enraged husband came into her beauty shop and threatened her with a pistol. She looked him straight in the eye, and told him to put the gun away before she stuck it up his ass. He did.

She was fearless, and also exceedingly lucky that the guy wasn't crazy enough to shoot her.

Hardened by deep poverty and with eleven brothers and sisters—which meant no one got enough attention or food—she developed a resolute way of getting things done that I'd like to think I inherited. She was from the Great Depression era, and had a harsh life growing up in pre- and post–World War II Detroit. She had persevered through hard times, and her work ethic was written in stone.

My father, Stanley George Andrew Kambes, was of Greek stock and was also born in Detroit on March 16, 1926. His father, George Karoumbus, also came to America as an émigré from the island of Corfu. His surname was Americanized at Ellis Island. My father's father was a chef and owned a restaurant, George's, at Monroe Avenue and Beaubien Street in what is now known as Greektown. His family only spoke Greek in the home and well into his adult life he carried a pocket dictionary to refine his English.

I was born Wayne Stanley Kambes in Detroit on April 30, 1948, at Lincoln Hospital on Twenty-Fifth Street. We lived nearby on West Grand Boulevard. My earliest memory is of a single moment lying in bed with my mother under soft lamplight with my head on her arm, feeling absolutely peaceful, safe, and loved. (I took acid in the sixties, and had a hallucination of being in my crib as a baby. Later I asked my mother if there were baby birds painted on the headboard of my crib, and she confirmed it.) My sister Kathi arrived on May 5, 1952, when I was four. Otherwise my memories of childhood begin when I was around five, and we lived on Harsens Island.

Harsens is a small, marshy island on the north side of Lake St. Clair, in Anchor Bay, about 50 miles north of Detroit, and just across the river from the town of Algonac. The only access to the island was a couple of small auto-ferries. In the winter, days or weeks went by without ferry service because the river was frozen.

The island was a paradise. The woods and swamps were my natural wonderland. In the summers, there was swimming in the river;

in winter, the canals and marshes froze, and I could ice skate all over the island. We lived there for about three years.

My father had served in the Marines in World War II, and fought in the horrific South Pacific campaigns. He was wounded, and had shrapnel in his back and leg. When asked about his job in the Marines on job applications, his response was, "paid killer." He returned from the war a profoundly damaged man.

I remember him talking about his experience only once when I was very young. We were visiting some of my parents' friends, a Filipino woman named Sita and her husband, who was also a Marine. He and my father were drinking, and they got into an animated discussion of battles they'd been in, vividly recounting how the planes were strafing the beach and the shells that were landing around them. They talked loud and late into the night, but I never heard my father talk about the war again.

My mother and father fell in love as teenagers before the war. They were introduced by one of my mother's brothers, my uncle Donald. My mother waited for my father while he went off to serve. My mother said he was "different" after the war.

In those days, they called it shell shock. After he returned, they married and soon he became a full-blown alcoholic. My mother repeated the tales ad nauseam: how he fell over on the bed, passed out drunk on top of me or my sister when she was a baby, and how he could have killed us. The usual litany of bad behavior that accompanies serious boozing. I was aware that he was my father, but emotionally, I draw a blank. I do remember learning to spell my first word, "B-A-R. That's where Daddy goes."

Stan had invested in a few acres of property with one of my uncles, and was building a house for us. We lived in a trailer on the site while he was building. I liked living in the trailer; it was cozy, and I felt safe. One night my father and his buddies went frog hunting, and brought home a couple dozen big frogs for a fried frog leg feast. He dropped the still-living frogs off at the trailer, and went to the local tavern with his pals. The frogs were in a few large paper grocery bags on the kitchen counter. In the middle of the night, they escaped the wet bags and were croaking and hopping all over the living room and kitchen. Big, bellowing, bleeding toads were everywhere. My mother was hysterical. She woke me up from a sound sleep, screaming, "Wayne, help! Do something about the frogs!" I thought it was the funniest thing I'd ever seen. My mom was distraught, and was pleading with me to save her from the frogs. Which, of course, I did. Life in the country was good.

I marveled at my father's building skills. With a few friends, he dug the footings, poured the concrete foundations, and began framing out what would be our new home. He seemed to know how to do anything and everything. In these moments, he was my hero. He'd be sweating out in the sun with his shirt off, drinking beer, and I just thought he was the best. My father was a professional electrician. I thought it was the greatest thing ever when he strapped on his climbing spurs and flew up telephone poles to connect the power to the property.

A hundred yards or so behind our trailer, my uncles had stored the parts for several pre-fab homes: completed wall sections and roofs, interior partitions, doors, windows, lumber, and roofing supplies. They were going to assemble them at some future point and create a housing development on the property they owned. The walls and roof sections were stacked like cards, leaning against each other, creating perfect forts and hideaways for me and my friends to play in. I was probably seven years old.

One morning, I decided we needed a fire in the fort, and got some matches to start one. The house sections were covered with black tar paper, which ignited almost immediately. At first, I thought I could put the fire out. I had a Tinkertoy container, a cardboard tube with a metal bottom. I ran to the marsh, filled it with water, and ran back to the fort where the fire had spread. Another trip, and another. I was running so fast in the muddy swamp that my shoes came off. I was crying; this was getting out of hand, and it was my fault. The cardboard tube was soaked through and disintegrated in my hands. My friends all ran home. The fire grew out of control, and there was nothing else to do but go tell the grown-ups what was happening. I was in a terrible state of overload. My memory blanks out, but I do recall a lot of fire engines and firefighters. It was a really big deal.

The fire went on all day and into the evening. Fire companies from the surrounding communities joined in to bring down the conflagration. My mother told me that I had to meet with some child-psychologist types afterward to determine if I was a pyromaniac. The authorities determined I wasn't dangerous, just a kid who shouldn't have been playing with fire. I felt really bad about all the damage and trouble I caused. One of the firemen showed me the burns he received on his arms fighting the fire. He seemed to be proud of it.

Once my father was hired to wire a hobbyist's massive model train setup. He took me to work with him and I was captivated with the trains. The man's setup had mountains, cities, roads and rivers, dozens of locomotives, and hundreds of cars. It initiated a love of both model and actual trains that has stayed with me my whole life.

My father read a lot, and I couldn't wait to learn to read. He could draw a rocket ship if I asked, and he was an excellent Lincoln Logs constructor. He would sit quietly in an easy chair and read and drink for hours. We all lived in the same house, but beyond that, he is a shadow. I have no memory of him holding me or comforting me. I can't see his face. I don't know his body or his smell. He is unavailable to me.

One day, out of the blue, my mother sat me down to tell me that she and my father were breaking up, and that we'd be moving back to Detroit. My world collapsed. I loved living on Harsens Island. The idea of moving back to the city was the worst thing I could imagine.

Moving day was a nightmare. We left the island on a beautiful summer day, just like so many others. I hadn't known this kind of pain before. I knew that things were changing for the worst, but there was nothing I could do about it. We drove into Detroit, to my Aunt Dorothy and Uncle Herb Farah's large brick house on the northwest side of town. We were pretty tight with the Farahs, and often spent time with them. They would come up to the island in the summer, and I'd have a ball with my cousins, Hal, Michael, Poppy, and Cynthia. I loved being around them. They were loud and raucous, but good kids.

By the time we arrived at their house, the weather had changed dramatically. Tornado warnings were issued, and all of us kids were sent to bed as the wind kicked up. It was a hell of a day. My family was ripped apart, my father was gone, and I was taken out of the world I loved and thrown into my cousins' dark bedroom with the threat of imminent death. Tornados are terrifying. Without a storm cellar or basement, you're at the mercy of the elements. But the Farahs didn't have a cellar.

We survived the storm, and afterward my mother, Kathi, and I moved in with Mable's parents on Livernois Avenue. Grandma and Grandpa lived in a wood-frame duplex that was massive to me. We all lived in the upper unit on the second floor, along with my big strapping uncles, Max and Dennis. I loved waking up in their bed between the two of them with the bright sunlight streaming in the room. I had never felt safer. They were supermen to me. Smart, handsome grown men both with a great irreverent sense of humor. On the other hand, my grandpa was a mean alcoholic and was drunk most of the time. He was loud and a bully, and he scared me when he was around. He'd barge through the house, usually with some drama: a broken finger or black eye from a barroom fight.

A few months later, my mother found a small one-bedroom, second-floor apartment she could afford on Michigan Avenue at Thirty-First Street. It had a room in the front for her first beauty shop. In 1943, when she was 15, she had attended the Dearborn School of Beauty Culture, where she'd earned her license as a hairstylist. She had left school in the eighth grade, and thereafter was self-educated. She named her shop La Belle's Beauty Salon, and there was room for three chairs. It was upstairs from Vi's Sweet Shop, an ice cream and soda fountain with a jukebox.

My sister Kathi and I shared the bedroom in the back of the apartment, which always smelled of permanent wave solution. Mable slept on a hideaway couch in the living room. My sister and I were both assigned small tasks to help out in the beauty shop. One of my jobs was to remove the little perforated papers from the curling rods so they could dry out and then be reused.

Mable was raised in the Catholic Church, and she insisted that I attend Mass at St. Hedwig's nearby on Junction Avenue. She never went with me; she always slept in on Sundays. Kathi was too little, so I went alone. This was a meaningless exercise for me because the Mass was in Latin, and I had absolutely no idea what was going on. Everyone kneeled, so I kneeled; everyone stood up, so I stood up. I didn't know any of the songs they sang, and based on the mumbled singing, neither did they. I did get the idea that love was good, and if I sinned, I would burn in hell for forever.

Mable believed in the American dream; that with determination and hard work, she could achieve a quality life. She had gone hungry as a kid, and she was committed to making sure that her children would never do the same. In fact, she was obsessed with making sure we weren't hungry. She used an egg timer to force my sister and me to finish all the food on our plates. If the food hadn't been eaten when the timer rang, there was hell to pay. Pavlov in reverse. I was in my forties before I retired from the clean-plate club.

In our early days on Michigan Avenue, meals were pretty uninspiring. To her credit, though, we always had something to eat. Campbell's Tomato Soup with rice added to make it more filling was one of my least favorites.

Around this time, I couldn't wait to learn to read. I suppose it was natural for me to emulate my father's love of reading. I wanted to read the Sunday newspaper comics. I'd even read the labels on cleaning supplies. My mother bought a set of *Encyclopedia Britannica*, and I could find information on anything I was interested in. She also had a series of booklets on child-rearing. These I found especially intriguing. I sensed that the books on troubled children had something to do with me, but I wasn't sure what. I also really liked *Life* and *Look* magazines. My mother had them in her shop for the customers, and I'd devour them. Between the magazines and the encyclopedias, I knew there was a big world out there. Somewhere.

Many times, I suffered bottomless fear in the apartment. My mother would work all day in the shop, and at night she worked a shift as a barmaid in a club on Michigan Avenue. She would leave for work after I went to bed, but I'd wake up and worry about where my mother was. I was afraid of what might happen to me and my sister all alone. I didn't know which bar Mable was working in, and I didn't know when or *if* she would ever be home again. This was chilling; my fear was to the bone. I felt a great responsibility to take care of Kathi (who slept through the night like a rock). Nothing bad ever happened, but the damage was done.

One day my father showed up and had a talk with my mother. She told me he'd borrowed 50 dollars for a deal he had going in South America. We never saw him again, and he never paid any child support.

I decided I would beat my father up if I ever saw him again. My mother encouraged this kind of talk, and I cast myself as her avenging angel. She called him a "rat" and a "bum" for running out on us. I vowed never to marry, so I'd never have to go through the pain of a divorce. But except for resenting my father for abandoning us, I was okay, and felt pretty secure most of the time.

CHAPTER 2

HUCK FINN HITS THE STREETS

At age nine, I was more than happy running the streets and alleys around Michigan Avenue and Junction Boulevard. In 1957, the neighborhood was bustling with shops and shoppers. I loved the early mornings when the sun was just rising, the streets and buildings were clean and fresh, and anything seemed possible. Mable did well in the beauty shop, putting in long hours and building up her customer base in the neighborhood. We soon had a TV and a record player. Our refrigerator was bought on credit. It had a small timer box on the floor; we had to keep putting quarters in to keep it running. My mother collected S&H Green Stamps to exchange for toasters and other household items. On Friday nights, I could stay up late to watch *Shock Theater* on television and scare myself silly.

These were boom times in Detroit. The great American promise was coming true. After winning World War II and getting through the war in Korea, everything was coming up roses.

Detroit was a bustling industrial center with good-paying union factory jobs. Work was available, and money was flowing. If something needed to be built, it could be built in Detroit. People were emigrating from the South for jobs at Chrysler, Ford, General Motors, and at the many small machine shops that made components for auto manufacturing.

But black people who came north for jobs and better living conditions found that Jim Crow's northern cousin was alive and well in Detroit. Motor City racism was institutionalized from the top tiers of industry down to its poorest neighborhoods. Despite this, people kept coming.

The earning power of steady work created a city that was the crown jewel of American capitalism with an unlimited sense of possibilities. I was proud of the fact that great American cars were built in my hometown.

People took care of their homes and lots, and the streets and alleys were well maintained. There were excellent public parks and libraries. Bus service was good, and electric buses used the overhead wire power system until the '60s. The city hummed with productivity and growth. Major streets were filled with thriving retail businesses, and bars and restaurants dotted the neighborhoods.

There were movie theaters all over the city. The Crystal Theatre was just on the next corner, and further down Michigan Avenue was the Kramer Theater. At age nine, I spent many happy hours in these air-conditioned palaces, soaking up everything Hollywood dished out in the late '50s. I was obsessed with the science fiction film *Forbidden Planet*. The idea that the robot could be a friend appealed to me.

I went back to see the film a third time at a Sunday matinee. I was enjoying the movie when a teenager tapped me on the shoulder and asked me to "loan" him a quarter. I told him I didn't have any money and I got up and moved down front where a bunch of loud young men were laughing and cutting up. I figured I'd be safe from the boy and his partner, but the usher said I had to move to the back. When I did, the two older boys followed and started bracing me again. By then, I was getting scared, and since I had seen the movie already, I thought I'd escape. The two boys came out of the theater behind me, cornered me in the vestibule of a store and started roughing me up. They towered over me. Terrified, I broke free and ran home. I didn't tell my mother because I was ashamed that I hadn't fought back. My shame was deepened by the fact that I'd had a jackknife in my pocket, but I'd been too afraid to use it.

Mable sent me back to fight kids who messed with me plenty of times. She demanded that I even the score. I would get righteously angry and head back ready to go to war, but usually when I returned to the scene, the kid I was looking for was gone. It almost never worked out as she wanted it to.

Growing up in Detroit, I could ride my bike all over the place. Everything was a great adventure. I spent a lot of time out on the streets by myself. My mother was working, and the city streets weren't considered dangerous.

I met a kid at school, Tommy Pope, who invited me to his church. There, I discovered the Southern Baptists. First Temple Baptist was huge; a large population of white southerners who'd relocated to Detroit had brought their religion along with them. The church was bright, sunny, and open; not medieval, dark, and gloomy like the Catholics at St. Hedwig's. The minister spoke in regular English instead of Latin. I could understand what he was saying, even if most of it didn't connect. But most importantly, the congregation was very enthusiastic. They were happy to be there, which was appealing to me.

After church let out, my friend explained that if I were "saved," I wouldn't have to burn in hell when I died. I had been sure that was where I was headed because of my growing obsession with girls' breasts, hips, lips, and everything in between. I knew I was sunk, but maybe this was a way out.

I told my mother that I was going to Tommy's church. Her response was, "As long as you believe in something." Mable was working two jobs, and by Sunday she was exhausted. She didn't much care where I went to church, as long as I went somewhere.

After giving it some thought, one Sunday, I went up the aisle in front of the whole congregation. There must have been 500 people there. The preacher put his hands on my forehead and hollered, "Save this child, Lord!" I don't know if the Holy Spirit entered me, but I shook to my bones.

Later that day, I was baptized in a pool up front that had a tile mural of John the Baptist and Jesus at the river's edge. No one told me what to expect; I just put on the robe they gave me, wearing only my briefs underneath, and climbed down into the baptism pool. The minister put a folded-up handkerchief over my mouth and nose, leaned me back over his arm, and dunked me under. I thought the guy was going to drown me. I swallowed some water, and sputtered it out when he let me up for air. Sopping wet, I climbed out of the pool, and he moved on to the next person. I hadn't brought any dry undies to put on afterward, so I had to put on my clothes over the wet underwear, which was pretty uncomfortable.

Following the service, there was a long receiving line in the vestibule where everybody welcomed me to the new "born again" life. All the women hugged me, and I was so overwhelmed that I cried.

After a week or so of heavenly purity, thoughts of what was under girls' skirts returned, and I was moved to fondle my penis again. What the hell was going on? I'd thought all this evil behavior was done.

I questioned Tommy. He said that this was called backsliding, but that it didn't matter because I had been saved. "Huh? What do you mean, it doesn't matter?" He didn't understand my question, and I didn't get his answer. I felt like a fool. I was embarrassed. I had followed his lead, and I'd been betrayed. Now I hated his church and his God, and all this religious bullshit. If thinking bad thoughts and doing bad things didn't matter, then none of it mattered. It was all a lie. God's forgiveness was a ruse invented by church people. The real world didn't work that way.

I rejected God, Jesus, religion, faith, prayer, heaven, hell, and everything that came with it. If you could be sentenced to eternity in a lake of fire for sinning, how could it be possible to escape such a fate by having someone yell over you and then getting dunked in a pool? Then go back and sin again and keep a clean slate? It defied logic and insulted my intelligence. I was furious about the whole business. I never really understood what adults were talking about when they tried to explain religion to me, because none of it made any sense. I understood the consequences of bad behavior. If I did wrong, there would be punishment in the here and now. I knew the difference between right and wrong; my mother had drilled her honesty and hard work ethic into me. She was egalitarian and a living example of self-determination and self-efficacy, but there was never a supernatural element to it. All this God/church/hell/heaven stuff was inconsistent to a degree that I couldn't live with.

Soon I had an opportunity to commit a real sin. It was in my mother's beauty shop that I first started to steal. I knew she kept cash in the desk drawer, and I was convinced there was no way she could know exactly how much money was in it. How could she keep track? There must have been 15 or 20 one-dollar bills. I would sneak out of bed, creep into the shop in the middle of the night, and lift a few one-dollar bills from the desk. A few bucks in the hands of a nine-year-old was a fortune, and made me a big man out on the street. You could buy a lot of Snickers bars and Dubble Bubble gum with money like that. I could buy plastic swords, yo-yos, marbles, slingshots, peashooters, and more.

I started boosting from stores out on Michigan Avenue as well. If I browsed around long enough, I was able to lull the employees into ignoring me so I could lift small items and pocket them. My mother was just too busy and too tired to monitor my comings and goings. There was power in stealing. It became my thing. I knew it was wrong, but I did it anyway.

Walking the city streets at night in 1958 was not a big deal for a kid. I walked the 20 or so blocks home after the Boys' Club of Detroit on Livernois Avenue closed at 8:00 PM without a second thought. I liked being out at night. The neon signs lit up the sidewalks with a magical glow. I felt safe; this was my kingdom, my play land. The Jet Coney Island diner was halfway home, and I'd buy an order of toast with butter and jelly for ten cents. This was a real treat after a long afternoon of sports, games, and swimming at the Boys'

Club. It had a big Seeburg jukebox, and from it I first heard the glorious deep tones of Duane Eddy's electric guitar on "Rebel Rouser." There was something compelling about that sound, like it was from another dimension, and was speaking a secret language just to me. It hit me in my groin.

There was a song I had been hearing on the radio about a fellow called Johnny B. Goode who played an electric guitar and people came from far and near to hear him play and some day he would be famous. I found out the artist's name was Chuck Berry. He played so many notes, he just dazzled me. The notes came out of his electric guitar at a velocity that grabbed my attention in a way that nothing in my young life ever had before. It sounded unearthly. Magical. Powerful. I wanted to be that guy in the song. And I wanted to play the guitar like that, too.

My mother had a teenage friend who lived a few doors up from us. Annie would babysit me and Kathi on occasion. Annie was very cute; I used to watch her getting undressed from the rooftop of the building next door. I was hoping I'd catch her removing her bra, but I never did. Annie had some rock & roll records. One in particular was mesmerizing: "Ready Teddy" by Little Richard. Like the Chuck Berry record, it grabbed me so hard that I would stop at Annie's apartment on my way to school in the morning, just to listen to it a few times before heading out. That music powered me up for the day.

I saved up my 25-cent-a-week allowance to buy my first 45 rpm record. It was Jimmie Rodgers's "Honeycomb." I was convinced that the song had a hidden message in the lyrics where he compared his girlfriend to a honeycomb. I thought the lyrics were referring to sex, which was taboo, and enticing. He was hinting at something that was mysterious and I wanted to know more. I was getting drawn into the power of rock & roll. It was suggestive, motivating, and mystifying all at the same time. There were things I knew in a practical sense, but there were also things I didn't know yet that pulled me forward.

I wasn't planning my path in life, but I knew that music was more important than people around me gave it credit for. It was like they were all sleepwalking, and I was the only one who was awake and seeing the markers. They were living in black and white, but with music, my life was in color.

We moved a lot. Every year. My mother was always looking for a bit better apartment in just a bit nicer neighborhood. It was her pursuit of the American dream: the "great good place."

Mable had a boyfriend named Herschel. He would come over to our apartment with his guitar and sing to my mother, and he drove a Cadillac, I didn't connect with Herschel at all. We were too different: He was from the South and grew up on a farm. I was growing up in the big city.

I did, however, see Herschel use the power of music to win my mother over. This affected me deeply. Here was a guy I didn't like, and I couldn't understand what my mother saw in him, but she was falling for him. I was jealous of the affection I saw in her eyes as he sang to her. I thought he was getting between me and my mom. At the same time, I was intrigued with the seduction I was witnessing in my living room. I didn't know what was going on, but it made an impression on me. I was only ten, but I could see how it worked.

THEN ONE DAY, Mable came home with Herschel. They wanted to tell me some good news. She showed me her left hand and the ring on her finger. I didn't get it. Nice ring. So what? "We're married," she said. She was smiling, and he was grinning like the cat that ate the canary. I didn't want to believe this. No one had asked me what I wanted. "You married the wrong guy!" I wanted to scream at her. This was a major disappointment, and I was angry.

Herschel was not my first choice of her boyfriends. I preferred "Big Chet" Kowalski. Chet was a gangster, and I was in awe of him. He wore a black leather jacket, had been to the penitentiary, and spoke in a language that mystified me. He talked in slang and street-talk. Once, describing a fight with another man in a bar, he said, "I was getting hot with him," as in angry. He always brought my mother presents: electric blankets, perfume, silverware sets, all in boxes. "Fell off a truck at the loading dock," he'd explain.

Once, Chet took me with him over to the east side, where he had some business with a guy who owned a pawnshop. We passed a young black man with no shirt ranting and raging out in the middle of the street. "He's on dope," Chet explained. We went into the pawnshop and there was a ruckus out on the street. The man with no shirt broke the pawnshop's window, and Chet sent me into the back of the store and said to stay put. Then he and a couple of his guys went out front to deal with the situation. I was terrified, waiting in the back room. A short time later, Chet came back to get me, telling me that everything was ok now. I felt safe with Big Chet.

The Boys' Club of Detroit ran a summer camp for city kids. It was located up on Harsens Island, where I used to live. After my mother got married, I signed up and went off to camp. The trip up was great, riding in a bus full of boys hollering their brains out. The best part was when a boy sitting in the front got carsick and puked out his window, only to have the puke blow back into all the windows behind his. We went nuts.

Every morning, each cabin would form two lines, military-style, for the march down to the chow hall for breakfast. One boy played a marching beat on his snare drum, and we walked in time all the way down the hill. I was knocked out with the power of the beat. It pulled all of us boys together in lockstep. I had never felt so in sync, so connected with others. These signs were undeniable; I needed to start putting some energy into music.

It wasn't lost on me that thousands of young girls were screaming hysterically for a guy named Elvis Presley. Their adulation was, on a massive scale, the same thing I saw in my mother's reaction to her guitar-slinging suitor. I was getting the picture now. This was important in a way that other, day-to-day things weren't.

When I got home from camp, I looked up the kid with the snare drum and invited him—and his drum—over. He was generous enough to let me try his drum. Wow, what a sound! The snare drum was beautiful to me. Loud. It had the power to make people pay attention to you. That fall, I signed up for drums at school. Detroit public schools offered instruction in the range of popular marching and symphonic band instruments. I got my rubber baloney pad and a pair of sticks, and began learning the rudiments.

Then I got sidetracked by the guitar. I had been fooling around with Herschel's when he wasn't playing. It became the key to the locked room with all the answers. Eventually Herschel bought me a Kay acoustic. It was a piece of crap guitar; the action was so bad, I could hardly hold the strings down. An F chord was almost impossible to play on it. Despite all that, it was my portal.

My mother found a teacher who would come over once a week for guitar lessons, for $2.50 an hour. The teacher was swarthy, smelled like garlic, and was impatient with me. I started learning simple songs: "Twinkle, Twinkle Little Star" and "On Top of Old Smokey." He kept stressing reading music and counting out time. It was easier for me to learn by ear and play from memory. The reading process was too slow for me; I wanted to play now.

Playing the guitar quickly became one of my top pastimes, along with all the other things city kids did to amuse themselves. Like exploring the city. There would be daylong treks across town to find a particular area of dense foliage or "jungle." Discovering a shuttered paint factory or slaughterhouse was always fun. Abandoned buildings were exciting, and train yards were also great. I never did much train hopping, but I knew a boy who lost a leg below the knee from hopping a train. He had a prosthetic leg, and could hide a pack of cigarettes inside it, which was cool.

I kept an eye on Elvis. He was upsetting grown-ups, but all the kids went crazy for him. Especially the girls, who were gaining in importance for me. I even got to kiss a girl at a birthday party. We were in the dark, and it was the most intense thing I had ever felt. I needed to do more of this.

I kept up with my guitar lessons, and endured hell when I forgot and missed one since my mother had to pay my teacher anyway. But I liked playing the guitar. I enjoyed the sounds, and it gave me a little extra status when other kids heard me play.

CHAPTER 3

CORRINA, CORRINA

Over the next year or two, from ages ten through twelve, I started to become aware of changes in my body. The other boys in the neighborhood who were my age were going through this too, and it was the subject of a lot of talk. "Having a boner" and "jacking-off" were fascinating subjects. Three or four of us would get together in someone's bathroom when their parents were at work, and the older guys would smoke cigarettes and spit and display their "boners." I had no frame of reference for any of this. I wasn't sure if this was bad or not. Everyone seemed to be enjoying himself, and I didn't feel threatened. We were just kids, and it was a new adventure. I had just moved into the neighborhood, and was content to be part of the gang.

It didn't take me long to figure out that masturbating felt great. I experienced feelings I had never known before, and I practiced a lot. I also had enormous shame and guilt about it, because I was sure my mother would be devastated if she discovered that her son was so perverted.

When I was ten, I discovered a magazine that was perfectly at-tuned to my interest in horror and science fiction movies. I lived for the next issue of *Famous Monsters of Filmland*. I was fascinated and terrified by horror on TV, film, or in print. The behind-the-scenes on movie set stories were just the best, such as Boris Karloff eating a sandwich in full Frankenstein makeup. I was both repelled and attracted to horror at the same time. The fantasy world of horror films was a way to deal with the reality of death. The idea that you could die but then return as a vampire or stitched-together monster seemed like a way to beat death. A loophole to avoid the inevitable.

I had a friend from the neighborhood, Mickey Duran. He was different from most of the other boys I knew. He turned out to be gay, but that wasn't in play then. We were too young for our sexual preferences to have any bearing on anything. Mickey had an intelligence and curiosity that most other kids didn't have. I had a fertile imagination, and I'd make up scenes for us to play out. I would imagine us as sailors on a disabled submarine on the bottom of the sea, stuck in a survival compartment (the bottom bunk of the bunk bed). I'd use a diving mask and snorkel to fashion a periscope and we would improvise our rescue. Mickey's big sister was also very interesting to me, but for a different reason.

Corrina Duran was a "fast" girl. She must have been 17 or 18 years old to my 10. She was tiny and sassy, and had a short haircut that brought out her pixie looks.

I think Mable related to Corrina's nonconformist attitude. She hired her to babysit my sister and me. Corrina was affectionate to me in a big-sisterly way, and I felt safe with her. She swore and found humor in everything. She would have her girlfriends over while she was watching us, and they'd smoke and talk and cut up when no adults were around.

I overheard them talking about boys and this thing called sex. I asked her to explain it to me, and she did. She was very honest in a practical, real-world way. I knew nothing; my mother had never had any kind of birds and bees talk with me. So, when Corrina told me that everybody in the world had sex, I was flabbergasted. I was sure it was a deep, dark secret act that only little boys did on the toilet.

The idea that it was widespread behavior, natural, and actually okay was great news. She said that almost any woman I saw on the street did it. This was inconceivable to me. And that they did it with guys meant that someday I could be one of those guys. Unbelievable! It was too much to hope for.

I asked her, how does a guy get a girl to agree to do it? Obviously, this was something that took a great deal of convincing. Surely, no girl in her right mind would actually want to do this despicable act? Corrina explained that yes, in fact, girls wanted to do it, too.

She said that there was a whole sequence of events that started with being friends, and then, when the time and place were right, kissing was the start. I knew what a kiss was; I kissed my mom and aunts. But this was a different kind of kiss. She said it felt good in a different way. And girls really liked to be kissed this way. It got them "in the mood." Then, you advanced slowly. You should kiss her neck and blow softly in her ear, all the while rubbing her shoulders and back. I eagerly drank in this information.

This was the most important news I had ever heard in my life. As you continued to kiss and rub and blow, you moved your hands over to her breasts. If she let you go this far, you were in a good position, and you just might go all the way. I had heard from the neighborhood boys about the anatomical alignment of penis and vagina—although we used more colloquial terms—so I was able to fill in the rest of the sequence without Corrina getting any more graphic. People actually had sex! My guilt and shame over masturbation was firmly locked in place, and this new knowledge didn't do much to ameliorate it. But at least I had a sense of it all fitting into the larger picture of how life worked.

I had a special relationship with Corrina. She was a mentor to me as I passed from adolescence into puberty.

After that, I was on a mission. There was a girl in the neighborhood that some of the boys said would let you do it to her. Some of them had. Sue was 16. A teenager, the most exotic of all creatures on earth. Adults were from another planet, but teenage girls were within my orbit.

Sue lived around the corner from me. I stalked her for a few days, and then introduced myself with the offer of a babysitting job. I was cunning and determined when it came to getting what I wanted, and I was deeply motivated. I told my mother about the nice neighborhood girl that might be available to babysit for Kathi and me. The time came, and Mable went out with Herschel, leaving Kathi and me alone with Sue. Kathi went to sleep early.

I was in love with the new movie *The Blob*. I found a recording of the theme song by the Five Blobs and bought the 45. The B-side was "Saturday Night in Tijuana." I thought this was perfect seduction music, and I played it repeatedly on the record player. We had a convertible couch in the living room, and I suggested that we open it so we'd be more comfortable watching TV. She was agreeable to my suggestions, and sat next to me. I was wearing my kimono robe. I figured it was attractive, and easy to get out of if things went right.

I started on the technique that Corrina had laid out for me. I began kissing, rubbing, and blowing. I'm sure I was awkward, ill-timed, rushed, and juvenile. How could I not be? I'd never done this before. Fortunately, Sue didn't take offense, and in fact was responding as Corrina had predicted. I was shocked and inspired.

After a few minutes, she stunned me by saying, "I'd let you do it, but my daddy's downstairs drinking and I'm afraid of getting caught." At that point, we lived on the second floor in a duplex apartment over a neighborhood corner bar. I was quick to offer an incredibly reasonable plan. "We could lock the door at the bottom of the stairwell. Even if we didn't do that, we can hear him coming up the stairs in enough time to straighten up." She agreed and pulled down her pants, and put me inside her. No foreplay. No more kissing. We just jumped to it. I had no idea what I was doing. I was ten years old, in uncharted waters. This was something that I was clearly not mature enough to handle, even if I was physically able to have an erection.

I couldn't believe my good fortune. I was proud of the fact that I was doing it, but was terribly confused by it, too. I didn't actually know what to do. I lay still inside her and marveled at how much this felt like masturbating. She said I did it different than the other boys who went in and out. I said that I had my own way, but now we should probably stop before her father came up. No orgasm. I didn't know how to go any further. Her father did, in fact, come up to check on us a few minutes later, but we had folded up the couch and were innocently watching TV.

My guilt and shame were overwhelming. I carried it with me all the time. "What if Mom finds out what I did?" I didn't want to disappoint her. She worked so hard, and I wanted to be her hero. But I was guilty of something so bad that I could burn in hell forever now. The Baptists and the Catholics had done their work, but the real fear was disappointing Mable.

I never got with Sue again; it was too much for me. I went back to my love of music, comic books, horror magazines and movies, riding my bike around the streets, and generally being a Converse sneaker–wearing kid. I didn't have sex again until I was 17 years old—a long dry spell.

CHAPTER 4
LINCOLN PARK

Now that Mable and Herschel were married and had combined incomes, they started looking for a house to buy. I had lived in apartments for years, and the idea of a house of my own was a dream come true. They found a deal they liked in the community of Lincoln Park. The suburbs south of Detroit were known as "Downriver." A new subdivision was going up, and the location, price, and style of house worked. The house featured three bedrooms, living room, dining room, kitchen, bath, with a full basement on a corner lot, and a big backyard. Paradise! All I cared about was having my own room and a basement where I could have a model train setup and play my guitar. America elected John F. Kennedy as president, and the future looked bright.

We moved in when I was 12, and I started the sixth grade at Priest Elementary School, a 30-minute walk from home. I got along well with the kids, except for the occasional fistfight with boys with whom there seemed to be no other way to resolve our differences. I didn't mind fighting, and I won as many as I lost. These contests were usually over quickly without any real damage done.

Art class was my favorite. I had always liked to draw, and was good with my hands in clay, or doing woodcuts in asphalt tile. I drew a lot of trains, and I'd copy comic book characters. I loved playing sports and tried out for a PONY-league baseball team, but didn't make the cut because I was goofing around too much for the coaches' liking. Pickup games of baseball happened all over the neighborhood, and I enjoyed the physicality of it all, as well as bike riding in the summer and sledding and ice skating in the winter. I was a pretty good ice skater. I played a little hockey, but enjoyed figure skating to music more. I slipped and fell on my face once, drove my front teeth through my lower lip, and got 12 stitches to close the wound. I excelled in gym class at school and loved Scatterball. I had good reflexes and could almost always outlast all the other players.

I played my guitar at home, and through a neighborhood guitarist I met a new music teacher who lived close by. A low-key, gentle man, he had a studio in his basement. He started me on major and minor bar chords, and rhythm and melody playing. I asked him to teach me to play like all the instrumental groups I was hearing, and mostly like Chuck Berry. He couldn't quite do that, but he was still a good teacher. I studied with him for the next year. The guitar was taking more of my time and interest, and I started looking for records to buy that featured the guitar.

PLAYING MY GUITAR, science fiction movies, drawing, and sports with my friends were the good things in my life at the time. The bad thing that overshadowed everything was that Herschel abused me. When he first moved in with us, he liked to hold me down, tickle me and then tweak my penis, laughing hysterically as if this was good family fun. The smell of his aftershave and the heat of his body were overwhelming. The muscles in his arms were like steel to me. I would scream and cry, violently trying to fight him off. It was perverse, and it was torture. I would battle back as best I could, but my punches didn't have enough power to make a difference. I would be sweating, breathing hard, and thrashing to get free of him. He was a grown man. I was a boy. This backwoods depravity was horrific, and it increased my revulsion of him.

My mother would laugh along, and seemed to find it highly amusing. It was anything but. I couldn't understand why she wasn't protecting me from this monster. I couldn't believe this was happening to me. No one ever said anything about it afterward, and it happened far too many times. It was family fun—if your family lived in the ninth circle of hell.

Much later, when I was in my forties, I found out that Herschel's sexual deviance was much worse with my sister Kathi. This miscreant profoundly harmed her. Like with me, hers would start out with tickling, but then it would move to touching her vagina and fondling her while he held her in his grip. Later, he forced her into fellatio, and she had to endure his cunning, horrific abuse. Now that we're both adults, we've discussed it, and we have to live with its dreadfulness. We have long wondered how Mable could have been the victim of sexual abuse by her own father, and yet have allowed the same thing to happen to her children. I buried these experiences and never brought them up to my mother as an adult. They were just too painful. Kathi confronted her once in her teens and again later as an adult, and both times Mable retreated into denial. Facing her own abuse as a child and then the abuse of her own children was beyond her. The pattern of hiding and denying sexual abuse repeats generation after generation if it's never brought out in the open. These are experiences we will never get over. I will never forget, and my sister sure as hell never will, either.

I FOUND A MUSIC STORE on Fort Street that sold records, musical instruments, and gave lessons. Town & Country Music had a Rickenbacker franchise, and had all the latest models in stock. One of the fringe benefits of taking lessons there was that I could play the new Ricky's through an amp. After a while, the teacher would set me up with the guitar, leave the room, and let me play whatever I wanted. Then I got another teacher who was a professional player who worked in the clubs. He'd regale me with stories of things that happened at gigs, which was intriguing. Local musicians would come in and hang out with the instructors, talking about music and gigs. At 13, I transitioned from seeing myself as a solo Elvis-type performer to wanting to be a band member. When my dog, Ben-Hur, was run over and killed in the street in front of my house, I found a place for my feelings by playing my guitar alone in my room.

I had been playing the guitar for a few years, and I could play pretty well. My ongoing problem with most music teachers was that they always tried to teach me to sight-read the standards: Gershwin, Cole Porter, and so on. I wasn't interested in any of that old cornball stuff; I wanted to play rock & roll. I wanted to know Chuck Berry solos. I wanted to be able to play like the Ventures. I wanted to play "Apache" by Jorgen Ingmann. I started listening to Barney Kessel and Kenny Burrell, but I had trouble figuring out where all those notes they played came from.

I decided to start answering ads in the Sunday papers for "Guitar Player Wanted." There was so much live music work available in Detroit that there'd be two or three columns of those ads. Groups were active all over Detroit and the suburbs. There was a thriving nightclub scene, and most featured live music. After going on a few auditions, I started to get a feel for what the competition was like. I knew I was too young to work in nightclubs, but I wanted to join a band, and this seemed like the quickest way.

To land a position, you had to be able to play songs like "Hideaway" by Freddie King, and some Ventures stuff. I could play some of the tunes, but not all of them.

I kept running into the same two guys at the auditions: "Big Ray" and "Little Ray," who were both a little older and beat me out every time. I was in over my head.

Common sense dictated that rather than joining someone else's band, starting my own band was going to be the route to take. This was an exciting idea, and I obsessed over it. My schoolwork notebooks were filled with drawings of guitars and drums, and bands playing onstage. Lists of band names, song ideas, logos.

I started asking around for kids who played musical instruments. I went through a series of neighborhood connections, but at first couldn't find any serious partners. And instruments were a problem. Who actually owned any? Finally, I found some like-minded boys with their own gear, and we got down to business. We practiced in our basements and garages. We were truly a garage band. Kids from around the block would hear us playing, and would come over on their bikes to see what the noise was about. We played "Ramrod" by Duane Eddy, "Red River Rock" by Johnny and the Hurricanes, The Ventures' "Walk, Don't Run," The Rebels' "Wild Weekend," and others. We worked on our choreography, practicing when to jump up, and when to crouch down or spin around. Who went up front, and who moved back. The moves were almost as important as the music.

I had started to develop a performance style even before I could play the guitar. A natural ham, I'd entertain my mother and her girl-friends with Elvis impressions, using a broom as my guitar. I learned this by standing in front of the mirror in my mother's bedroom, holding the broom and lip-synching to records. Jody Reynolds's "Endless Sleep" was one. The dark mood of the song fit my romantic self-image perfectly. This evolved into entertaining the neighborhood kids out under the streetlights at night.

Now that I was beginning to be able to actually play an instrument and had a gang to do it with, there was little doubt about where I was headed.

Sometimes Herschel would invite a few professional musician friends over for a jam session. I would be asleep, and would wake up to hear live music coming from the living room. Mable let me get up to watch. I was amazed at the way they could go from song to song without having to talk about what they were going to do. I was intrigued by how Don Chessor, a guitarist, could solo and invent a melody on the spot. They'd play for about an hour, then go in the kitchen and drink whiskey, then play another set. When they were on break, Don said it would be okay if I played his guitar, a sunburst Fender Jazzmaster. Someday, I vowed, I'd have a guitar that cool.

Don and I became friends. I volunteered to do his yard work, just to get to know him better. The paragon of cool, Don played in bars, and did electronic repairs as a second job. I couldn't believe how many songs he knew.

When I was 14, my mother sat me down one day to talk about me being a musician. "I want you to do what you want to do with your life. I want you to do what makes you happy, but being a musician is a very hard life. To be a professional musician means that you'll be working in bars and nightclubs at night, and sleeping during the day. Plus, musicians are around drinking and drugs, and loose women. It's a hard life."

If I wasn't committed before we had our talk, I was afterward. The things she warned me about sounded great to me.

IN 1962, Mable got pregnant with my sister Peggy. She was born on October 10, 1962. Peggy was very premature, and the oxygen in her incubator compromised her eyesight, blinding her. Mable was stoic and took the news with acceptance, grace, and love. I didn't really know how to feel about it and just rolled with it all. I naturally loved my new little sister, and liked rocking her to sleep. She was a very sweet baby. I knew she had some challenges ahead, but I was a teenage boy and was going through my own major growing pains.

Besides, I was in a state of constant crisis because my relationship with Herschel couldn't have been worse. I loathed him, and he didn't get me at all.

That fall, I was nailed for shoplifting from a discount store at the Lincoln Park Mall. A buddy, a girlfriend, and I were stealing just for the hell of it. I grabbed some model car parts, and my girlfriend stole a facecloth. We had just exited the store when a plainclothes dick grabbed us and brought us back inside to the security office. They made us call our parents and tell them to come and get us. Herschel was home, and he came to collect me. In the car, he asked me why I would do something like that, and I told him I didn't know. We rode home in silence. When my mother came home from work and heard the news, all hell broke loose. She went into an explosion of disbelief that her son could do such a thing. Stealing! I couldn't mount any kind of defense, and I just had to take it. This became a pattern. I'd get into another mess, she'd lose her mind for a few days, and then it would pass.

There were three more days of gloom when my grades took a nosedive. I couldn't focus on school anymore. If I had a great teacher, one who actually took an interest in the class, I did well and got good grades. But more often, the teachers just punched in and collected their pay.

I had big trouble with an eighth-grade teacher. Mrs. Edwards was a mean-spirited disciplinarian with no interest in educating kids. Earlier in the year, she was physically abusive to me and I defended myself. On the last day of school before summer vacation, I went out in our backyard and scooped up some dog turds. I put them in a box, wrapped it like a present, and wrote, "To Mrs. Edwards. What we think of you," on it. Later that day, she saw me putting it on her desk and gave me a big smile, as if all was forgiven. Just then, another boy lit an entire pack of firecrackers in the classroom.

Pandemonium! Noise and smoke blew into the hallways, and kids were screaming and cracking up. I ran out of the classroom and watched the panic from the stairwell. Mrs. Edwards came at me, convinced that I'd set them off. She dug her nails into my neck and arms, and I swung on her. Another teacher ran over and dug her nails into my earlobe, almost severing it. Blood was pouring as Mrs. Edwards marched me to the office.

After an hour of pleading that I hadn't set off the firecrackers, she relented and let me go home. I went out riding my bike, enjoying the first day of summer vacation. After a while I went home, and as I was eating a snack, the doorbell rang. I looked out the window to see Mrs. Edwards, her husband, and my guidance counselor, who was holding the gift-wrapped box of dog shit. Herschel let them in. We all stood there in silence looking at each other. They left, and

Herschel was dumbstruck again at my behavior. He was totally un-equipped for parenthood.

When Mable got home and heard what happened, the earth tipped on its axis. She wept, she screamed, she hit me repeatedly. She sat down with her head in her hands and said, "First it was stealing, then it was lying, then it was bad grades—and now, this!" I felt bad that I'd made my mother feel so bad, but I didn't cry. And I didn't regret it.

Later that night when I got ready for bed, she came into my room and saw the claw marks and scratches all over my shoulders and neck, and the deep wound to my ear. She went off again, this time at Mrs. Edwards for abusing me. The next morning, she took me to the school board offices and demanded the teacher be fired for what she'd done. I was proud of her.

That fall at Huff Junior High School, I wanted to join a sports team. I had always enjoyed sports, and although I wasn't a stand-out athlete, I was adept and had some physical talent. Having always been a good swimmer (Mable got Kathi and me swimming lessons at an early age), I went out for the swim team. I passed the tryout, joined the team, and attended practice every day after school. I learned the butterfly, and that became my event. I swam the 50-meter fly and the fly leg of the medley relays.

During this time, I was aware that a serious international problem was brewing. I watched the news on TV, and there was no mistaking the gravity of the reports of Russian nuclear missiles being deployed in Cuba. I knew what the atomic bomb was, and that the use of these kinds of bombs would mean that the entire world could be destroyed. No one tried to mitigate my fears; Mable's business had expanded to a third salon and she had her hands full running them, and Herschel was no student of world affairs. I was just starting to see what grown-up life might hold, and I didn't want the world to blow up. My concerns grew as the crisis escalated daily. I had no one to talk to about this; it was like only Walter Cronkite and I understood how serious the situation was.

In the final days of the showdown between Kennedy and Khrushchev, I went to sleep with the certainty that a nuclear attack would happen any minute. I envisioned a giant flash of light off in the distance in the night sky, followed by a shock wave sweeping through the neighborhood, destroying everything. It was so real I could taste it.

The rumor was that Detroit would be a likely target, as it was the manufacturing center of the country, and they'd want to destroy our capacity to build weapons. The city was known as the "Arsenal of Democracy" for its production of tanks, planes, artillery, and jeeps during World War II. I had never been that scared in my entire life. When the crisis passed, I felt reborn. With that behind us, I was committed to rocking.

Around this time, I discovered hot rods and drag racing. I began reading all the current hot rod magazines, and built model cars. Drag racing was popular in the Detroit area, with weekly meets at the Detroit Dragway. The radio ads were exciting; the announcer screaming, "Sunday! Sunday! At Detroit Dragway!" with the piano intro from Ray Charles's "What'd I Say" blasting out underneath. I went whenever I could convince an adult to take me. I was exhilarated by the super-loud sounds of high-performance engines, the smoke from the tires, and the announcer calling out the winning times all under the lights at night.

I had become friends with a kid in the neighborhood named Ricky Derminer. Ricky was a drag racing fan, too, and we liked each other. He introduced me to his brother, Bob, who was four years older than me. Bob was pretty far-out by Lincoln Park norms. He had tight kinky hair, wore black horn-rimmed glasses, and had a gap between his two front teeth. He ignored fashion; he was iconoclastic, even then.

Bob considered himself a beatnik. He listened to jazz, and he also painted. He stayed in the basement of his parents' house four blocks from mine. He was the first natural intellectual I'd ever met, and he knew about things that I was interested in. We would have marathon talks. I still hung out with Ricky, but his big brother became the object of my interest. I had a lot of questions about why things were the way they were. Bob had radical ideas about life and God, art, science, history, and culture. He was the first person I'd met that had a handle on this stuff, and he didn't blow me off as being too weird for asking about things that most people didn't seem interested in.

Bob also exposed me to Zen. With his gentle and humorous teaching style, reincarnation, nirvana, and the wheel of karma made more sense than anything I had been exposed to up to this point. Buddhist thought was palatable to me. It was a philosophy and a way of life with a moral code that held you accountable beyond the fear-driven Catholic burn-in-hell-if-you-sin. I was ready for some new cosmic answers.

The ideas that Bob was exposing me to aligned with my sense of accountability, and didn't insult my intelligence. At last someone could explain complex ideas and ethics to me without expecting me to buy into unerring stupidity.

I had all the big questions: Where do we go when we die? Where did we come from? Why are we here? What is eternity? Is all this a big accident, or is it part of a secret plan that no one is talking about?

The Catholic Mass confused me. There were too many things to believe that were impossible: life after death, walking on water, virgin birth, and all the other fantastical myths the faith was predicated on.

But Bob's Zen stuff made more sense. It was better poetry to me than anything I'd heard before.

CHAPTER 5

THE SIREN'S CALL

Aside from hanging out with Bob, who I liked a lot, finding guys to form a better band with was my mission. I *needed* to be in a real band. A schoolmate told me he knew a kid named Fred Smith who played bongos. I figured a band could use a bongo player. I hunted him down, we had a chat about it, and he seemed interested. Fred's family was from the South, and they also had a guitar.

I spent summer vacation of 1963 going over to Fred's house and teaching him parts on the guitar. We would play "Underwater" by the Frogmen and "Red River Rock." I showed him the chords to "Walk, Don't Run," the rhythm guitar part to "Honky Tonk," "Wild Weekend," "Wipe Out," and everything else that I could. He was a natural player, and learned the songs with real enthusiasm. It was fun to play with him. I continued to play with other kids; mostly with Billy Vargo. Billy was an only child, and his parents bought him everything he wanted. He had a top-of-the-line Fender Jaguar guitar and an Ampeg amp. Later when he was 16, they bought him a '32 Ford hot rod with a V8 engine. Billy was a good guy, generous with his stuff, and happy to practice playing music together. I christened the band The Bounty Hunters. I got the name from Conrad Kalitta's dragster that was popular around then. The name combined my two loves: loud, fast, high-powered drag racing machines and music. I loved drag racing so much, I took a job selling ice cream at the Detroit Dragway just so I could attend the races every Sunday afternoon.

There was a special championship race at the Dragway one hot summer Saturday night with a live band that played between time trials and eliminations. The band was the Royaltones, and their vocalist was Del Shannon. I couldn't believe my good luck. There they were, not five feet in front of me. They played on the return road, separated from the fans by a flimsy snow fence. They looked and sounded fantastic: matching red sport coats with a monogrammed "R" on the breast pocket, slick dance steps, and matching Fender guitars, bass, and amps. They sounded great, and Del sang all his hits. This was heaven on earth, and a confirmation of all that I knew to be right and good and possible.

BY 1963, Fred and I had been playing guitars together for a while. On the side, I was practicing with the Bounty Hunters, with Billy Vargo and a succession of other players. Fred was trying to get his own thing going, and we talked a lot about doing something together. His older sister Margie could sing, and we thought about a group with her and some other players we knew. Finally, we joined up together. It wasn't exactly what I wanted to do; my idea was to have a band more like Booker T. & the M.G.'s or the Royaltones. I wanted one guitar, bass, piano/organ, and drums. I figured we could play the widest variety of music with that lineup, and thus get the most work.

Fred had a wicked sense of humor, and we always had fun together. We were teenage boys discovering the world. One summer, he grew two inches taller than me. He was a skinny kid, and used to wear a sweatshirt under his regular shirt because he though it made him look bigger. We both fell in love with Ian Fleming's James Bond novels. As boys, we would wrestle each other to exhaustion. Testing each other's will and strength. We made a pact to defend each other if we got into trouble. It was a lot of teenage macho posturing, but we meant it. We talked about girls a lot, too. We were different, but we met in the space between us and found in each other a durable counterpart, sharing real affection and respect.

By this time I had been playing in various lineups and had played friends' parties; school events; street dances; Elks, Moose, Eagles, and VFW halls all over the Detroit area. I loved everything about being in a band. This was what I wanted to do more than anything I had ever wanted in my life. Playing music for people was a magical, mystical experience.

My relationship with Bob Derminer grew as well. We talked endlessly. I was his acolyte, and he was my mentor. Bob was a talented artist and would draw weirdo shirts for kids. He would create a monster driving a hot rod in magic marker on a sweatshirt or T-shirt, and kids would pay him for it. Since I could draw, too, we joined forces and set up at a picnic table that summer in Gregory Park. We made some money together and it was fun.

I tried to convince him that being in a rock & roll band was the coolest thing going. I raved to him about how much fun it was when you were up there on the stage and the crowd was dancing to your music, and the colored lights were bright and the sound was blasting, and you were sweating your ass off doing your dance steps. He wasn't buying any of it. He thought it was passé, corny teenage shit. He was into Charles Mingus, Sonny Rollins and Cannonball Adderley, John Lee Hooker and Muddy Waters. He wanted to be cool in the beatnik sense. We had an agreeable disagreement on the subject.

In the fall of 1963, I was in science class when an emergency announcement came over the school PA system that JFK had been assassinated. I started laughing uncontrollably. The truth was, I was as shocked and horrified as everybody else; it just took me a while to absorb the news. Over the next few days, my mother and I watched events unfold on TV. We were watching live when Jack Ruby shot Oswald in the police garage in Texas. Mable had just said that "somebody is going to do something to him" when it happened. I couldn't believe my eyes. It was unreal, as if this was a movie—but I knew it was real. Kennedy symbolized a positive future to me. Since he was young, I believed he was a different kind of president than Eisenhower and all the older generation. He was my president, and he'd been shot dead. The reason for his killing was incomprehensible to me, and nothing I heard from the authorities changed that.

In 1964, I turned 16 and acquired the most valuable possession of my youth: my driver's license. I bought a motorcycle by selling magazines door-to-door all summer. While out riding one night, I ran into Bob Derminer at a White Castle burger joint. He was a little drunk and playing a harmonica. I knew he was musical because he had a cello and a flute at home that he'd scammed out of the Lincoln Park High School band, and he could make jazzy sounds with them. He asked me if I had ever heard of this band from England, the Rolling Stones? Of course, I knew all about them. I owned their records, and I was learning to play their stuff. "You still doing your band?" "Yeah, you should come over and check us out." "I will." The Rolling Stones had changed his mind about rock & roll, and now he was into it. I knew he would dig rock if he gave it a chance.

He showed up a few days later, and heard me and Fred play some things we were working on: Chuck Berry stuff, instrumental tunes, Stones, Beatles, and so on. I told him about my idea for a band with one guitar, bass, drums, and an organ; I didn't really want to do two guitars. Fred was going to switch over to playing bass as soon as we figured out how to get our hands on one. "No, you and Fred play guitar really well together, you should stay with him on guitar." Then he decided that he wanted to manage us. "I'll have you guys in diamond stick pins and eating steak in six months." We were willing to listen to what he had to say.

Of course, Bob had no idea how to manage a band, and the whole thing fizzled out before it started. But we liked him a lot. His absurdist sense of humor appealed to us in a *Mad* magazine sort of way.

I didn't know any bass players, and this was a problem in putting a real band together. Bass just wasn't as popular an instrument as drums or the guitar. None of us had any money, jobs, or credit. After all, we were just 16. But I had an idea.

I knew Bob was musical, so I suggested that he become the bass player. I'd teach him. I had been playing for six years at that point, and knew my way around the guitar a bit. Bob convinced his dad to finance his instrument and picked up a pawnshop bass and amp, and we set to work. It was slow going. There is no way to skip steps in learning a musical instrument. It takes dedication, time, and effort. Practice, practice, practice. The trouble was, Fred and I could already play, and we wanted to be out playing gigs. The whole scheme blew up one night when we had scheduled a rehearsal and someone called up with a last-minute gig replacing a band that had canceled. I said sure, we'd do it, but Derminer refused. He was adamant that we just rehearse as planned. Fred and I wanted to play the gig, so we did it without him, and he quit the band.

We met a drummer named Bob Gaspar, and he joined us. Fred and I dug his playing. He was a rock-solid hitter from neighboring Southgate. After Derminer quit, Gaspar recommended his buddy Pat Burrows on bass. They had worked together in other bands. We met him and really dug his style. The four of us started playing all over the area. Any place that would let us. We had been calling ourselves the MC5—short for Motor City Five—for a while, even though we only had four players. That was a little hard to explain, but we liked the name. MC5 sounded like a car part. Give me one of those four-barrel carbs, a 4-56 rear end, four shock absorbers, and an MC5.

As a band, we really started to rock. Burrows and Gaspar were as driving a rhythm section as you could find, and Fred and I were locked in on guitars. There was an unspoken competition between guitar players around the Downriver music scene. All over the suburbs of Detroit, bands were starting up. Parents had good-paying jobs, and instruments could be bought on time-payment plans. Every high school had a band or two. Teen centers all across the area had dances with live bands every weekend. It felt like all of a sudden, a new, vibrant scene was happening. It was friendly, competitive, and we were right in the middle of it.

The British First Wave hit like a tsunami, and we were learning the new material while still perfecting our American rock & roll. I wanted to know the most Chuck Berry solos note for note. I was always scoping out the other guitarists and asking them to teach me the solos I didn't have yet. I learned from a kid at school that you could use a plain, unwound string for a G string and really bend it for a cool effect on the guitar. This was a major breakthrough.

Fred developed into a superior rhythm guitarist. He really found his niche, and went for it wholeheartedly. We would play Chuck Berry progressions for hours. If you played them correctly, your forearms would cramp, so getting the muscles in our forearms toughened up to be able to play the figure correctly without tiring was the goal. We just loved what we were doing, and the sound propelled us forward. The joy of the rhythms and the pure physical release in the volume was thrilling. It was a way to say, "Listen to this, world! Listen to us!"

It was now 1965, and Martin Luther King Jr. led a civil rights march from Selma to Montgomery, Alabama. The Los Angeles neighborhood of Watts exploded in violence, claiming 35 lives. Malcolm X was assassinated in New York City, and U.S. troops in Vietnam increased from 75,000 to 120,000.

In the spring of that year, a documentary film, *T.A.M.I. Show* (Teenage Awards Music International), was released to theaters and drive-ins across America. Naturally, I tracked all things rock & roll, and as soon as I saw the ads in the Detroit newspaper movie guide, I made plans to see it. It looked pretty damn good: The Beach Boys, Chuck Berry, The Barbarians, The Blossoms, James Brown, Jan and Dean, Gerry and the Pacemakers, Lesley Gore, Billy J. Kramer and the Dakotas, The Miracles, Marvin Gaye, The Supremes, and The Rolling Stones. All performing live at the Santa Monica Civic Auditorium.

My mother lent me her car, and I went alone to the Southgate Drive-in and had my mind blown. I was flabbergasted by what I saw and heard. I was so knocked out that the next day, I called bassist Pat Burrows and demanded that he come with me the next night, so I could watch it again with him.

We were both so moved by what we witnessed on-screen that we returned again the next night. By the fourth night, we were broke, but convinced the ticket booth guy to let us in to watch it again because we had already paid three times to see it and plus we were starving musicians (we had all of our band gear there in the back seat of the car) and this film was the most important thing we'd ever seen. The guy was cool and let us in that night and again the next night, until the movie's run had finished.

I went back to see this film six nights in a row. Here it was: The complete roadmap of everything I wanted to do with my life. The past, present, and future. With repeated viewings, I was able to deconstruct the subtlety and nuance of each act's genius. Not just the big-ticket items like James Brown's unstoppable band, whose drummer, Clayton Fillyau, was able to punctuate every move James made, but the sly grin an "exhausted" Brown revealed while sitting on a riser resting from the superhuman dancing demonstration he'd just delivered. Then he'd jump up, reenergized by the supernatural forces of sanctified "holiness" rhythm and blues, and outdo himself while his band scorched the earth with their version of "Night Train."

I was mystified by the powerful, sanctified performance ritual of Brown's cape act, with the spirit overtaking the utterly spent singer, driving him onward to give more and more. Was this real? Was this an act? Was he having a psychotic break? Whatever it was, I couldn't take my eyes off of him; I wanted to be him.

And as if that wasn't enough, from England, the Rolling Stones! Still relatively unknown in the States, the rumors about them being uncouth louts and social misfits all worked brilliantly. They were the perfect counterbalance to the dark, driving mysteries of James Brown and the Famous Flames. The Stones were playful and wicked, and rocked the stage like no other act on the bill. And they played electric guitars! They could really play, and their music had drive. It swung. What James Brown was doing would take more study, but the Rolling Stones were accessible right now. I could play what they were playing. The Stones opened the door to the high-energy guitar rock that was the future as I understood it.

And there were other great acts in this show. My main man Chuck Berry played his ass off. The Motown artists slammed. Lesley Gore was intense. Gerry and the Pacemakers and Billy J. Kramer and the Dakotas were lightweight, but since they represented the British First Wave, they were cool enough. I was more interested in their gear, the guitars and basses they played and the amps they used: Vox mostly. The Beach Boys were big favorites of mine, and they played and sang well, too. This film set me up for the next few years of my life as I tried with all I had to reproduce it for myself. Pat and I bonded, sitting there in the dark watching this overload of live performance art and having it seared into our brain cells forever. Now the way ahead was clear. I had just witnessed everything I knew to be right in one film, and I knew what I had to do: get out there and make it happen.

Fred came to me at one point and said a band needed a weirdo, someone with strange and different ideas. I agreed with him in principle, but who? "What about Derminer? Let's get him back in the band as the singer. Now we have Pat on bass, so what do you think?" I was reluctant after the way he flaked out on us the last time, but I still went along with the idea. I liked Bob's weirdo ideas, too. I asked him, and he was happy to return to the band.

We were now "the five." These were very exciting days. The Beatles and Stones joined Motown to rule the Detroit airwaves, along with the rest of the British First Wave. I loved them all. It all seemed to fit together: my attraction to the instrumental groups and Chuck Berry, Derminer's blues music (John Lee Hooker and Muddy Waters), plus the modern music coming out of Motown. Our band being right in the middle of the mix was superb. We were on the cutting edge of the new generation. We played record hops, private parties, and the occasional bar gigs. Weddings, beer bashes, whatever. As a band, the five of us really started to rock. Burrows's and Gaspar's bass and drums swung hard and propelled the sound forward, and that set up a platform for Fred and me to really develop our guitar-playing style together. Now we had the final missing element: a stand-up front man. With weirdo ideas.

Fred and I discovered a paperback book, *Our Own Story* by the Rolling Stones, in a drugstore. We both were mesmerized by the brilliant bullshit Andrew Loog Oldham had invented to market the Stones as the anti-Beatles. We bought it all, hook, line, and sinker. Rebel, yeah that's me. Plus, the Stones were making some of the hardest-driving, creative music we'd ever heard, so we analyzed everything they did and learned as much as we could from them. The Animals and Them were big influences, too. Derminer was inspired to embrace rock when he heard these English dudes singing the blues music that he had been into for so long. He had been a champion of the blues for years before any of us.

We proclaimed that the music we liked had to have "drive." The forward motion that a solid rhythm pounded out. Very Detroit.

Our gigs were urban adventures. I would borrow a car or get a friend to drive us to our engagements. We took our Lincoln Park, rhythm-heavy, guitar music all over the Detroit area. There was always the excitement of meeting girls or witnessing a huge fistfight, and the thrill of getting up in front of everybody and playing music for them. To win them over was the goal, and usually we did.

We met a WKNR deejay who called himself "Swinging Sweeney." He was a jerk, but he wanted to manage us. He had a partner in former beauty queen and championship archer Ann Marston. They were having a secret affair, and were attempting to be in the artist management business together as a cover story. We hated Sweeney but loved Ann. She was a beautiful grown woman, and we all wanted to sleep with her. She would toy with our teenage libidos, but never crossed the line. She even got us booked to open for the Dave Clark Five at Cobo Hall. Fifteen thousand screaming girls. It was a real rush of power to wave to one side of the arena and have a thousand teenagers scream back at you. That was the hysteria connected to pop music stars back then. My idea was to get our picture taken backstage with the Dave Clark Five, and by association we would become a successful band. We finally got the shot set up and had a chance to chat with the British superstars. Mike Smith was genial and funny but the bass player, Rick Huxley, was a dick. Pat asked him about his favorite amp and he was as condescending as possible, dismissing Pat with a sneer and a mumble about "the Vox foundation something or other . . ." The photo didn't have any effect on our careers, but the thrill of hearing thousands of kids screaming as we ran out onstage was intoxicating. Probably the most intense sensation I had ever felt. It changed me; I needed more of this.

We had been promised the opening spot on the Rolling Stones' first concert in Detroit by another deejay, Dave Schafer, who we played hops for. This was an even bigger deal for me; going from the Dave Clark Five to the Rolling Stones was the perfect transition to the inevitable fame ahead for the MC5. At least that's what I thought.

That booking fell through at the last minute, and I was devastated. I had bragged to all my friends that I was playing with the Rolling Stones, and we had practiced hard to learn a bunch of new songs because we played a lot of their songs. When we were canceled, it broke my heart. It was my first bitter taste of defeat, but not the last. The disappointment really took a toll on my spirit. This hurt. I was still as determined as ever, maybe even more so, but I developed a distrust of success, knowing how quickly it could go away. We were aced out of the gig by another local band that featured an 11-year-old drummer. Plus, the kid's father knew the promoter, and that was that. I was so angry that I attended the concert, and egged our replacements when they came on.

CHAPTER 6

TEENAGE LUST

Lincoln Park is a working-class enclave. Everybody worked. The auto industry was thriving, and the unions were strong. A family could survive on one paycheck and put money in the bank. The community was growing and prospering. Lincoln Park, like many other Downriver communities, was also a racist stronghold.

I was born miles away on the near west side of Detroit. My first memories of other kids were brown and black kids. I wasn't taught prejudicial ideas. My mother never filled my head with racist language or attitudes. She was concerned that people were fair with each other and that no one took advantage of us. She insisted that I defend myself if attacked, but never deliberately harm others. These were simple rules that my sister and I took to heart.

We lived with all kinds of people. Kids were kids. They might be a different color, but so what? We all went to the same schools, lived in the same neighborhoods, and played like all kids do. Our parents all worked in the same factories and had the jobs that held families together. Of course, there were black neighborhoods and Mexican neighborhoods close by, but they were just different, not worse. Elsewhere in Detroit were Irish, Italian, Slavic, Russian, Greek, and Polish neighborhoods, too.

In 1965, my mother opened her third salon and it was the first interracial beauty salon in Detroit's history. My sister and I walked the streets of the city passing out handbills for the big opening. We were very proud of her.

But Herschel had deeply regressive ideas about race. He was from the South, and was a bigot and racist to his core. My mother ignored his racism. Telling me, "He's a good man." As time went on, this caused a great deal of conflict. More than once, when he proclaimed his disappointment that the South had not won the Civil War, I would get into a fight with him. He would tell me, "If the South had won, I'd have me ten big-butt niggers out there working in the yard." I was furious with his racist beliefs, and found him incomprehensibly ignorant. Later, after I grew a little bigger, these arguments would become physically violent.

He fashioned a disciplining instrument from a piece of wood with a leather belt looped around the end. After a certain age, I stopped crying when he hit me with it. Actually, the way the thing was built, it didn't really hurt too badly. I think the energy from his swing dissipated through the handle to the leather strap, so by the time the strap struck me, it wasn't so intense.

One time when I got sarcastic with him, he chased me down the block and hit me in the back with a shovel he was using to dig in the yard. I laughed at him. He was an ignorant, loutish man, and I despised him. We once had a fight over how many planets were in the solar system. "Ain't but seven," he argued. I mocked him. We just could not relate to each other. He was country, I was city.

Herschel turned out to be a serial womanizer, and one of his girlfriends called my mother one fine day and confessed. Their marriage didn't end well. I got home from school that day, and all of his clothes were in a pile out on the sidewalk. My mother was on the warpath. She told me about the call, and my reaction was, "Good riddance to bad rubbish!" I would finally be free of this cretin. After a while, my mother called a friend for advice and calmed down. She returned the clothes to the closet, and hired a lawyer.

The lawyer hired a private detective to follow the adulterer and document his activities. Soon Mable had all she needed, and she served him with divorce papers. Kathi and I were overjoyed to see him go. This was another confirmation that marriage was never going to be an option for me. It was too ugly, too painful.

The house in Lincoln Park was sold and we moved out. We moved a few miles away into a rental in the adjoining blue-collar suburb of Taylor. I changed schools *again*.

It was 1965, Lyndon B. Johnson was in the White House, Gemini 4 was launched, and I was 16 years old with an electric guitar, a driver's license, and a motorcycle. On the teenage status meter, this was high voltage. I played in a band and rode my motorcycle in a black leather jacket (Euro-tunic style, not Marlon Brando). I was in full effect. School was still an unavoidable slog, but I promised my mother I'd finish high school because it was a big thing to her. She'd left school in the eighth grade to get a job, and really wanted her kids to do better. I was never motivated to quit school.

College never came up. Working in a factory was talked about a lot. Getting a good union job on the line. That was the goal among my friends and family; it was as if that was the only realistic option.

My main educational objective was to entertain my fellow students. I had perfected the skills of a class clown, and did it with enough subtlety that most of my teachers laughed along with us. I had been playing the guitar for a number of years now. I could play chords and solos, and had a pretty good ear for picking up things from records. I was playing in bands, and music was taking over my life.

I asked the music department if I could join the band, but they didn't have a guitar chair in the school orchestra. I spied an upright bass in the corner of the rehearsal room, picked it up, and started playing it. I knew the strings were tuned the same as the four lower strings on the guitar, and that the fingering positions were basically the same, so it wasn't that strange. The music teacher was so impressed that he said I could add a music class to my schedule, and just come in and practice the bass in a studio room by myself. I would bring in blues, jazz, and soul records, and figure out the bass parts.

I had been seeing a girl from Allen Park named Sharon. She was very pretty in a big, sturdy way: tall, blond, and a very sexy dancer. She had four teenage brothers, and they were basically a gang that ruled anywhere they went. Their father was a long-distance truck driver, and her mom had lost control of the boys years ago. Their house was a social center. I liked them all, and hung out with them. They had motorcycles, too, and we would ride all over the Downriver suburbs raising hell. Fred, Bob, and I played a few of their house parties.

These parties usually turned into giant brawls spilling up and down the street. If a group of guys came to the party and rubbed one of the brothers the wrong way, fighting would start. These were massive group fistfights with a lot of black eyes and swollen knuckles. They were also frightening as hell. A feeling of chaos and uncertainty would knife into my stomach when the fighting started. I was fascinated by the brutality, but I never joined in on these all-out donnybrooks. It wasn't my thing.

I found it difficult to fight if I wasn't angry with the person I was up against. These slugfests were too random, too out of control. I wasn't drawn to violence like many of the guys were. Plus, I saw myself as different from other people. I was a musician. I was usually playing my guitar when the shit would jump off. Later, I experienced plenty of these dance floor–clearing fights playing in the Downriver clubs, and usually we would just keep playing unless it got too out of hand.

I'd had my share of fights in the streets and alleys of Detroit when I was younger, and had a few more later as a teenager in Lincoln Park. Fighting was a part of boyhood then. These fights usually had to do with some kind of insult. Being thin-skinned, I couldn't take being made fun of. And if a kid gave me some lip or provoked me, I'd go off. I would get very angry very quickly and explode. If I couldn't get at them then and there, I would find them later on the street and we would fight.

It was much harder to fight after I had cooled down, but I felt it was something that had to be done. I would build it up in my mind all day, and plan out what I was going to do. My heart would go up in my throat, and I'd get kind of dizzy when I swung on someone. I always wanted to throw the first punch. From then on, it was war, but instigating the action was never a natural act for me. Plus, I didn't want to get really hurt, and there were lots of guys around that were bigger and tougher than me.

Also customary in the Downriver area was teenage guys riding around in cars on weekend nights, looking for an excuse to beat someone up. If you and some friends were walking down the street minding your own business, or carrying on like teenagers do, a car could pull up and a gang of guys would jump out and just throw down on you with fists and feet flying. You had to keep your eyes open for it.

SHARON FROM ALLEN PARK never slept with me, and after the prom, we broke up. Other girls from school were not resistant to my advances, and I started to hit my stride. These girls had no problem touching or being touched. Making out in the back seats of cars was great stuff. I still get turned on if I smell hairspray combined with a new-car smell. My motorcycle was one of the keys to seduction; the magic carpet to carnal pleasures.

I had a few girlfriends that were sexually active and enthusiastic about it. I'm surprised that none of them got pregnant. These encounters were simple and innocent. We were healthy young people discovering how our bodies worked.

I even started having something approaching friendship with a couple of these girls. I was discovering that girls weren't just for sex; they were actual people, too. Girls were a major mystery to me as a kid, and realizing that they wanted to have sex, too, and that some of them were smart and fun to be with was a revelation. Woo-woo!

I was also developing a closer relationship with my sister Kathi. Even though the four years between us seemed immense when we were little, we were now becoming friends, and we were interested in a lot of the same things. Plus, we had been through a lot together over the years.

I started meeting girls at gigs, and found them easy to talk to and easy to bed. I had struggled like all young men trying to figure out the right rap, the right clothes, the right crowd, but I'd never cracked the code. I was never part of the social scene at any of the schools I'd attended. All of a sudden, my teenage awkwardness disappeared. I didn't have to promote, finagle, or talk anyone into anything.

I had my own social world. I had a driver's license, and it didn't matter where I lived because I had my own friends. School cliques diminished in importance. I was driving in the diamond lane now.

CHAPTER 7
GREAT BIG AMP

We left Taylor and moved back into the city of Detroit. My aunt Dorothy and uncle Herb owned a big brick house in northwest Detroit, and they sold it to my mother on terms that she could handle. My final year of high school was in Detroit's Cooley High.

I was barely there that final year, 1966. The MC5 was now a working band. We rehearsed in my basement, which became our clubhouse. Mable was very supportive, and would feed everyone when we were rehearsing. She was raised in a big family and loved having the house full of people, raising hell, and having a good time together. Mable had taken in our little cousins, Leonard and Mitchell, when their family went through a hard time, and she liked to have her girlfriends stay with us. Many did over the years. She would also take in foster kids from time to time. It was fun to have so much action around the house.

Mable hired a wonderful woman named Marie to clean and cook for us. One day, I was practicing, and Marie stuck her head in my room and said, "What you're playing sounds like colored people's music." I had been listening to Little Milton and trying to reproduce his style. I thanked her sincerely.

There was a terrific music store a couple of blocks from our house. Capitol Music was run by a great guitarist, Joe Podorsek. Many of the Motown session musicians hung out there. I was in awe of them. They were the best players in the world. It was there that I met Ted Nugent and many other guys who would go on to be part of the Detroit rock scene. I met Motown bassist Bob Babbitt at Capitol Music. Joe was a mentor to all us young cats. I bought my first high-quality guitar from him: a sunburst Gibson ES-335.

Fred moved in with us for a while. He had dropped out of high school the year before, and was staying out all night and disobeying his parents to a degree that his father couldn't handle. His father disciplined him, and the results were black eyes and bruises.

In those days, everybody looked the other way when child abuse showed up. People just didn't talk about it. It was one of those dirty little secrets that families perpetuated from one generation to the next. Mable was furious about his mistreatment, and offered to take him in. She took Fred's abuse personally, and got visibly angry when she saw his bruises. Why didn't she react this way back when she was married to Herschel and he and I fought?

Fred had developed a taste for alcohol. He had been drinking for the last couple of years, but it seemed harmless enough to me. We were very close, and he would regale me with tales of his adventures when he went out with the hard-drinking crowd. It was a little too much drama for me. I waited till I was older to eclipse him in the bad behavior department. Fred was antiauthoritarian before we knew what the word meant.

There was a guy from Southgate we knew, Bruce Bennington. He was a nice guy and a little bashful, but he had a good job on the line at Ford and he liked our band. He owned a beautiful, new, purple Ford LTD, and he'd drive us to our gigs in it and hang out with us. We had no jobs, no money, and no amps. I owned one, but it was a small 15-watt Epiphone with one input that was way too un-derpowered to use on a gig. I was always borrowing amps and other gear from friends, which was a major problem. Bruce was generous, and often bought us cheeseburgers after the gigs. Fred and I convinced Bruce to be our manager, and to take out a loan to buy us a complete set of Vox amplifiers—the latest thing from England. Many of our idols in the British First Wave used them, including the Beatles and the Stones. Vox amps were more powerful than anything in the States. When Bruce agreed, and the date was set to go pick up our new gear, I thought it was the breakthrough to success that I had been waiting for; nothing could stop us now. The amps were fantastic. They were huge, black, and evil looking; 100 watts of tube power. The day we picked them up from the music store was like Christmas and my birthday combined. We set everything up in Bruce's basement, jammed, and had a party.

We were supposed to make monthly payments on the amps from the profits from our gigs. That never happened, although we used that gear for the next two years. It enhanced our reputation and our sound. There were no other bands in Detroit that had amps as cool as ours, and now none could be as loud as we were, either. We rehearsed and rehearsed. We were playing Rolling Stones songs, which led us to deeper blues material. Derminer was always into John Lee Hooker, and we'd make up our own arrangements of different blues tunes. In an attempt to get more work, we also learned as many pop tunes from the radio as we could: Motown, The Kinks, The Who, James Brown, we still did all our Chuck Berry songs and Sam the Sham and the Pharaohs' "Wooly Bully." We really wanted to work.

In the fall of 1966, a neighbor from across the street heard us rehearsing, and hired us to play his dental fraternity's class picnic. It was on Boblo Island, an amusement park south of the city in the middle of the Detroit River. You could only get there by paddle steamer. The island was a mini-vacation spot for hardworking Detroiters.

This was a great gig for us. It paid a few hundred bucks, and we were very excited. Our friend Emil Bacilla drove us down to the dockside in his Volkswagen minibus. Emil was the MC5's first roadie, but he was way more than that. Emil, Bob Derminer, and artist Gary Grimshaw formed the original beatnik movement in Lincoln Park. I was their junior member, and I brought the rock & roll. A budding audiophile, filmmaker, and photographer, Emil was the first to take a serious interest in the band, and he helped us in any way he could. He took photos, recorded our shows, shot early movies of us, and became a lifelong friend.

We met the riverboat early in the morning, loaded our gear, and sailed to the island. The deal was to play three concerts in three different locations. This turned out to be a major drag; the six of us had to move all those heavy speakers all over this sizable amusement park. Then when we'd get set up and play, no one gave a shit. All the college kids were chasing each other around the island looking for places to hook up. Our big gig was turning out to be an ass-busting, anticlimactic farce.

On the return trip to the city, there was an old-timey music ensemble playing on the boat. This was a plum gig for the old Local 5, American Federation of Musicians guys, who were playing standards from the big band era. I saw a golden opportunity.

The boat was full of college kids, and they were in the mood to party and were a captive audience. I approached the bandleader and suggested that he and his guys take the night off, and let us play the trip home. Since they'd still get paid, he agreed, and we set up our gear. I knew we had exactly what the kids wanted to hear.

We opened with "Louie Louie," and the roof came off the sucker. The kids hit the dance floor and never left. We rocked up the Detroit River the whole way back to the city. The college kids danced and partied like crazy. We played our arrangements of "Shake a Tail Feather," "You Really Got Me," and more. It was sweaty and happy; our best gig to date, and a real confidence builder for us as a band. We connected deeply with the audience. It was pure and innocent; just musicians playing the music they loved for their crowd, who loved being rocked. It made me feel like I was part of something worthwhile. I was building a band that could really move people. I was with my guys, and we were totally together and unstoppable.

I was entirely committed to making the MC5 a success. In 1966, my last year at Cooley High, I would come home from school every day, open the phone book, and call anyplace that a band might play: teen centers, churches, schools, nightclubs, VFW halls, bowling alleys. I did everything I could think of to get exposure for the band. I knew that no one else could do it or was interested in the nuts and bolts of it, so I naturally gravitated to the leadership position. None of the other fellows in the band even had an inkling that this stuff needed to be done. I knew that if something was going to happen for us, it wouldn't be by magic. I had to *make* it happen. We all had a say in the creative side of the band, with Bob and me at the lead, and Fred usually adding his solid agreement. But any business direction or effort was all on me. I did the heavy lifting, and I signed the contracts.

The bookers and club managers I knew were all telling me to learn the Top Ten, as it was called: the top ten songs on the radio charts. This was what the bands that got steady bar work did. There were scores of clubs with live music all over the city in those days. The factories were still going full time, three shifts a day, seven days a week. Our problem was we didn't want to be a bar band that played other bands' songs from the radio. We wanted our own songs on the radio, and to play concerts like our idols. The result was a house divided. Burrows and Gaspar wanted to play top ten and work the clubs for the immediate money; while Bob, Fred, and I wanted to develop our own original music and take over the world with it.

I had been experimenting with new sounds on the guitar, feedback and distortion. Bob was starting to write lyrics. I was listening to what some of the British guitar players were doing, and learning from them. Pete Townshend and Jeff Beck were doing the most advanced things with the electric guitar, and I was way into it. I discovered feedback for myself when I set my guitar down at rehearsal with the volume up and left the room. I heard this unholy howling sound coming from the basement, and then a crash. A jar of nails sitting on a shelf had vibrated off and broken on the floor. I told the guys, "I've discovered the power to change the universe: feedback." I could reproduce most of the things I heard the English guitarists play, and I was developing my own ideas about the sound of the electric guitar. I practiced a lot; it was both my obsession and my refuge.

At the time, bassist Pat Burrows was being forced to make a decision. Pat was torn between his love of bassist James Jamerson and our avant-garde agenda. Fred and I conspired to force him out of the band. We bad-mouthed him behind his back because we wanted tall, thin guys with long hair who looked like the Rolling Stones or the Who.

The final straw came when Pat showed up at rehearsal with his new Fender Precision Bass, just like Jamerson's. He had traded in the Höfner-style bass we'd chosen for him, and he was as proud as could be of his new instrument. But we castigated him for it, and he stormed out of rehearsal. Gone. The truth was that I would have done whatever I thought it took to succeed. I didn't appreciate Pat's expertise; I just assumed that anyone could play the bass with soul, swing, and drive. My disrespect for Pat and his talent would come back to bite me in the ass.

I had another guy waiting in the wings: the new bass player would be Michael Davis. I'd met Michael through Derminer; they both stayed in the same apartment building in the Cass Corridor downtown. Michael was a few years older than me, and he was beautiful—tall and thin, and a talented painter.

He served as a tutor for me in the ways of the world. A charming lady-killer, he had lived in New York City for a couple of years and knew all about drugs. I was an eager student. Michael, like Derminer before him, was not a bass player by his own volition. I decided that he would be the capstone in the band so, like Derminer and Smith, I'd teach him. He could play and sing Bob Dylan tunes on the guitar, so I figured it wouldn't be that much of a stretch to learn bass. We became fast friends as he transitioned from beatnik art student to MC5 bassist. I enjoyed his company immensely.

Then Bob Gaspar quit. He had to choose between our crazed avant-rock music and a steady job in a bank, and he went with the bank job. I had underappreciated his skills on the drums. He was a rock-steady backbeat hitter with great timing, feel, and energy, but I thought all drummers could do what he did.

I went on the hunt for a new drummer. We tried a few different guys, but none were willing to commit. I remembered a guy I knew, Dennis Tomich, from Lincoln Park, and he came out to audition. We were working a four-nights-a-week gig at the Crystal Bar, a terrible dive on Michigan Avenue where we played to an empty room most nights; maybe a neighborhood drunk or two nursing their beers. It was a lousy gig, but we were excited to have the job anyway. Dennis played a night or two with us, and we decided he'd be fine. We had a ceremony onstage to initiate him into the band. He was presented with the official MC5 toilet plunger to commemorate his membership.

Derminer decided to reinvent himself. From now on, he would be known as Robin Tyner. Tyner was the name of his favorite jazz piano player, McCoy Tyner. He also said that I should change my name to Kramer. I liked the idea; Kramer was more mainstream, less clunky than Kambes. To me, Kramer sounded more like an American consumer product. Like cheese or vacuum cleaners. "Yes sir, these new Kramer vacuums are top of the line."

But there was a deeper reason I went with the name change. This was the perfect way to finally get back at my spineless father for running out on us. He would never know that his son had become a famous musician, because I would have a different name. To hell with him! Now he could never share in my glory. Later, when I turned 17, I went to court and legally changed my name to Kramer. Now he would never know. Revenge was mine.

Tyner also added a fictional "Bartholomew" to Fred's name: Frederick Bartholomew Smith. It had a nice Euro-ring to it. Later Fred revised it to Fred "Sonic" Smith. New drummer Dennis Tomich was christened Dennis "Machine Gun" Thompson, and for a minute Michael Davis became "Mick Davies." Tyner was a very creative dude.

Not long after the name change, I smoked my first joint in the parking lot before one of our record hop gigs. I knew Rob and Michael smoked pot, and I wanted to try it. From what I understood, there was no hangover like with liquor, and my mother wouldn't be able to smell it on my breath. We were waiting in the car for show-time and they broke out a joint. The reefer messed up my sense of time, and I was obsessively checking my watch every couple of minutes. The absurdity of my preoccupation with being on time was cracking us up. Everything took on a hysterical note. We were laughing our asses off. After that, I was sold on marijuana.

HAIR WAS A BIG ISSUE. The new, long-haired British bands set the style and we all started to adjust accordingly. Fred, Dennis, and Michael all had good hair. I kept my greaser style pompadour as long as pos-sible but finally came over. Since my hair was curly I had a problem. I would plaster it down with Dippity-Do, and when it dried my hair would be straight for a short time.

Rob had an even bigger challenge. His hair was kinky and he was desperate for a way to straighten it. He and I finally went to a black barbershop where he was offered the "Tony Curtis" style or any number of variations on that theme. He told them, "No, no, no, man. I want it like the Beatles' hair." The barbers assured us they could straighten his hair. He then endured a chemical relaxant treatment, which burned his scalp. He handled it like a soldier, but in the end his hair looked like a helmet and he hated it. One day soon after, he showed up at rehearsal with it all cut off and a small, beautiful natural Afro. He discovered that his hair was perfect the way it came out of his head and we all agreed that he looked fabu-lous. Rob Tyner was the first white boy with an Afro. I also gave up on the Dippity-Do and went with my natural curls. Problem solved.

OVER THE YEARS I developed relationships with local deejays from the radio stations. There was one in particular, Jerry Goodwin, who was much hipper than the rest. One Sunday afternoon I phoned him up while he was on the air. I was happy that he took my call. He in-vited me to call again, and I did. We talked music on these calls. He invited me down to the station one Sunday afternoon to see the way it worked. Jerry became a mentor for me. He was the first person to explain how a band got to go on tour; what record companies did, and how they did it; who paid for what; and how records got on the radio. Where else was a kid like me to get this information?

Jerry was a godsend. We played record hops for him and other deejays all over town. The MC5 would be announced on the radio all week for playing some sock hop on the Keener Deejay Caravan. I figured it was good promotion. The hops' format was that the deejay did 30 minutes of records, and then the band did a 30-minute live set, alternating back and forth. The band always finished off the night. One Saturday night in '66 at Southgate High School, Jerry introduced us, and before he could get off the stage, Fred and I turned on our Vox AC 100 amps full blast. We hit an open E chord, and moved toward the speakers, creating a cacophonous feedback that froze Jerry midstride. Rob then stepped up to the mike and started screaming at top volume.

The 500 kids in the gym stopped dancing and stood staring at the stage, wondering if the world was coming to an end. We kept up the feedback and added as much energy to the performance as we could. Tyner was sticking his microphone into the PA speakers, creating an unearthly feedback howl while improvising lyrics. After several minutes, all the kids started heading toward the doors. I don't think it took ten minutes to clear the place out. We just kept on jamming for the whole 30 minutes, while Jerry kept the one security cop from pulling the plug. After the gig, we sat in our van smoking a joint. We told Jerry that we had been listening to John Coltrane and Pharoah Sanders, and that we wanted to take our music in a different direction. We called what we were doing "avant-rock." Tyner even wanted to change the band's name to Avant Rock, but he was dissuaded from that idea.

Jerry said it made sense to him. A jazz drummer, he was hip to John Coltrane and Miles Davis, and saw music changing. He told us we had a tough row to hoe finding venues for our new music, but if we just stuck with him and played his hops, he'd try to find a club for us to play. He loved our hard-rocking stuff right along with our weirder avant-garde ideas.

Late in 1966, Jerry introduced us to his friend, promoter Russ Gibb, who had just returned from San Francisco with stories of the dance-concert halls on the West Coast. By that time, Jerry had shed his shirt and tie, and had become a card-carrying, reefer-smoking, long-haired freak doing one of the first free-form shows on the then-new WABX-FM. Gibb, a middle school teacher during the day, was also working at the station. He asked Jerry about finding a house band for his new Grande Ballroom. It was the perfect time for Gibb and the MC5 to join together.

IN MY LAST SEMESTER of high school, the only class that mattered to me was art. I had done some acrylic paintings and a life-sized sculpture of Fred Smith's head, featuring his long hair just covering his eyes and his defiant sneer. My other classes were nonstarters. I didn't attend the graduation ceremony because we were booked to play high school parties all week. Some were all-nighters where the kids were basically locked in the school building overnight and everyone went wild. There was no way I was going to play till six AM and then go to my own school. After all, I was a musician.

Michael and I became get-high buddies. He had a connection for a high-potency African ganja that we bought for $10 a matchbox. We spent my first summer out of school smoking that stuff.

That summer, we drove up to Port Austin, at the tip of the thumb of Michigan, where I'd played a gig the summer before and met up with two hip young college guys trying to be promoters. This time they let us crash at their place, where we met a couple of blondes and tried to seduce them. I failed with mine, but I think Mike succeeded. We fell asleep on the beach and woke up with sun poisoning burns on our arms, backs, and legs. We were sick for two days before we could drive back to Detroit. Thank God we had the reefer; it was the only medicine we had to treat the sunburn and nausea.

I pursued my blonde back in the city, and found out that she was from the wealthy suburb of Grosse Pointe. I pressed her pretty hard to sleep with me, but she wouldn't give in. I lent her a book, *The Cradle of Erotica*, a history of sexual expression in Africa. Our relationship ended abruptly when her parents found it. They found the subject matter unacceptable for their sweet young thing.

That fall, my mother sat me down to tell me that while I'd had a nice summer running all over the place with Michael Davis, now it was time to get a job and start contributing to expenses around the house. If not, I would have to live somewhere else. The trouble was, I wasn't interested in getting a job. I was going to be a professional musician; nothing else mattered.

I moved out the next week. I was finished with someone telling me what to do and when to do it. If I wanted to sleep in late and stay up all night, that was what I'd do. I wanted to be in my band and smoke weed first thing in the morning. I was done with rules, schedules, and responsibilities. "Free at last, Free at last, thank God a-mighty, We are free at last!"

Rachel was a young woman I knew who had a nice two-bedroom apartment near the Motown studios on West Grand Boulevard. She was sweet and single, and I convinced her to let me move into her spare bedroom. After a while, we started sleeping together and that worked out beautifully for a while. I was an oversexed 17-year-old who could rock all night long, and she was a young career woman in the big city. Neither of us was looking to get married. It was lust, not love, and after a while I moved out.

The MC5 got our first feature story in the *Detroit Free Press*, and released our first single, an original song, "One of the Guys." On the flip side, we recorded Van Morrison's "I Can Only Give You Everything." Our original plan was to record our version of Van's song "Gloria," but another band, The Shadows of Knight, got theirs out before us.

We were being "managed" by a trio of small-time music business hustlers. One was Cliff Gordon, a promo man for MGM records in Detroit, and the other two didn't seem to have jobs. One of them,

Larry Benjamin, later became something of a character in Detroit, and the third was Arnie Geller. Their label was AMG Records (Arnold Mark Geller).

They booked the session at Tera Shirma Studios, and we went in one morning for our three-hour recording session. As soon as I got my amp in place, I started warming up and trying to get my tone the way I wanted it. The engineer came over and told me that my sound was all wrong. That it was all distorted. My response was, "Yes, it's distorted. That's the way I want it to sound." He told me, "You rock & roll punks are all the same. That sounds like shit. What you want is to sound clean and sharp, like at Motown." He was referring to the sound of the guitars recorded at Motown's Studio A, where they recorded the guitars directly into the board, no amps or mics in the signal chain. The guitars went through the board's pre-amp, and the tone was as clean and pristine as it could possibly be.

That wasn't what I was going for. I wanted a distorted sustain like I was hearing on new records by the Yardbirds, The Stones, and The Who. I set the amp the way I wanted it, and we got to recording. In those days, sessions went quickly. We recorded two songs playing together live as a band in a couple takes, and then set up for vocal overdubs. Tyner went out and sang the lead, and Michael and I did the background harmonies. We then did the mix, packed up our gear, and got out.

As we were loading our stuff, Edwin Starr was rehearsing his band in the waiting room for the next session. He was sitting at the piano singing the tune and showing the players how it went, and they were talking about who should be playing what parts. He was very business-like running down the song, and I was impressed. The song was "Stop Her on Sight."

The MC5's relationship with these managers didn't last long. A few weeks later, in the fall of 1967, we were in the middle of a business meeting with them, and they were telling us we couldn't sing about drugs or politics or what successful managers they were. Their landlord stuck his head in the door and told them they were being evicted for not paying the rent on the office. That was hilarious.

Then, to make matters worse, after the meeting Larry Benjamin asked us if he could cop some reefer from us. That was a clear signal that it was time to move on. They were nice enough guys, but clearly there was no future for us with them.

The MC5 played everywhere we could, and we built up a devoted following over the next year.

CHAPTER 8

"BURN, BABY, BURN!"

On January 14, 1967, the Human Be-In took place in San Francisco's Golden Gate State Park, setting the stage for the Summer of Love. On March 26, in New York City, ten thousand young people gathered for the Central Park Be-In. On November 9, 1967, *Rolling Stone* magazine published its first issue. American troop levels reached 450,000 in Vietnam. The Beatles had released *Sgt. Pepper's*, and Mohammed Ali was stripped of his heavyweight title for refusing induction into the U.S. Army.

The Summer of Love didn't make a stop in Detroit.

Playing the Belle Isle riot on my nineteenth birthday was a turning point for me. It marked the end of my youthful naiveté about the character of the Detroit Police Department and those in authority in general. Witnessing police brutality with my own eyes, seeing the blood, hearing the anguished cries of the young people being beaten mercilessly changed me, and now the same violence was happening across the country. The divisions between my generation and my mother's were now starkly clear. The way America treated people of color and limited economic means, the war in Southeast Asia, the irrational drug laws and oppressive sexist norms held by the establishment fueled my defiance. A line in the sand had been drawn, and I knew which side I was on.

After the Belle Isle carnage that spring, I'd rented my own apartment on Alexandrine Street in the Cass Corridor for $10 a week. The two-room studio came with its own toilet and a hot plate to cook on. The MC5 had landed the house band gig at the Grande Ballroom, which paid $125 per night. We usually played Friday and Saturday nights, so my share was $50 a week. I thought I had life perfected, but when I got back to my quiet little apartment, I suffered the most intense loneliness. I hadn't been this alone since I was a little boy on Michigan Avenue, and those memories were too uncomfortable to bear.

I decided I needed a girlfriend. I was intrigued by a very smart and cute Armenian brunette from the neighborhood. Her name was Eve, but everyone called her "Little Chick." In the beginning, I didn't take her seriously because she seemed to be playing the role of a naïve adolescent in a young woman's body. She spoke with an affected, squeaky, childlike tone of voice that put me off.

One day, Eve and another girl stopped in at our rehearsal to pick up Michael, and we got into an argument over a movie. I couldn't convince her that my take on the film was the correct one, and she displayed a wit and intelligence that knocked my puny ideas out of the park. She understood the characters in the film, the story arc, the meaning of the conflict, and more. I was really out of my league on the subject; I'd had no idea she was that smart. There was a substantial person inside the goofy façade, and I went after her. Fortunately, she liked me, too.

The news reports were predicting a "long, hot summer," and I had an uneasy feeling about it, given the recent police violence across the nation. On July 23, 1967, my pal Frank Bach and I were driving back from Whitmore Lake in his old red Ford panel truck, which stank of motor oil and reefer. It reeked, and so did we. We had attended a picnic organized by Russ Gibb, with Tim Buckley and some other musicians from the Grande Ballroom. I liked Tim; we shared a passion for music, and talked endlessly about politics, music, and girls. I was intrigued with his performances the last few nights at the Grande. He was working with a conga player, and they seemed to go into a trance-like state on a couple of songs, with Tim's vocals becoming a primal scream–like exploration. Neither of us had achieved much recognition yet, but both felt that the future was looking very bright. It had been a beautiful Michigan summer day, with warm but not oppressive temperatures up at the lake.

Frank and I were driving back to our apartments as the sun was going down. We were on Grand River Avenue, one of Detroit's main commercial arteries, since we thought Frank's truck might blow up if we ran it at freeway speed. Suddenly we noticed a fire in the distance—a big one.

"Check it out!" Frank said. The flames were climbing above the tops of some of the four- and five-story buildings that lined Grand River. Fire engines and flashing red and blue emergency lights were all over the streets.

"Man, that's a big one!" I said, as I finished the last hit on a joint.

As we got closer, I noticed a couple of brothers running across the street carrying TVs and other appliances. At first this didn't make any sense; I couldn't put together what was happening. Then a couple of guys ran by with a bolt of carpeting. "Hey, Frank, what the hell?" I said.

Traffic slowed to a crawl, and I saw whitewashed signs on store windows: "Soul," "Black Power," "Soul Brother." Many of the shops had broken windows, and goods were strewn on the sidewalk with people rummaging through them, taking things, and running in all directions. Just then, I realized what this was.

There was a sinking feeling in my heart. Everything that I knew and depended on was coming apart at the seams. The structure of daily life as I had known it was breaking down. America had been in a spasm of urban violence for the last few years: Philadelphia in '64, Watts in '65, and Cleveland in '66. Newark had just exploded in July, where at the conclusion of six days of rioting, 23 people were dead, 725 were injured, and almost 1,500 were arrested. All but two who were killed were African American. Now it was here in Detroit, my city, on streets I had grown up on and traveled my whole life. And it was on, full-force.

The world had detonated while Frank and I were up at the lake, and now we were dead center as the shit hit the fan. I wasn't afraid of the people running down the street carrying TVs; they were preoccupied with the tasks at hand. And at that point, I wasn't afraid of the police too much either. They seemed to be in a state of confusion as to what they should be doing. They weren't chasing anyone on foot; instead, they were staying in their cars. My fear was focused on the breakdown of regular life. The disintegration of the normal social order was something I had no frame of reference for. It was exciting and terrifying all at the same time.

As we made our way further downtown, we came upon a phalanx of police cars in the lane next to us. In each car were three or four cops with shotguns angled out of the windows. We decided to get off Grand River Avenue and take side streets back to our apartment building on Alexandrine. We took the expressway as a short cut. It was deserted, and smoke blanketed everything. Two new convertibles came screaming past us, each with a young brother at the wheel. We gave them the "power to the people" fist-in-the-air salute, and they returned it. "The chickens have come home to roost," Frank said, referring to Malcolm X's prediction.

We came off the freeway, and at the first intersection there had just been a collision between a police car and an old Ford. The detectives were viciously clubbing a black man with nightsticks as they pulled him from his wrecked car. I was shocked at the brazen beating; the degree of violence was overkill. It was sickening and unnecessary—the guy wasn't even fighting back. Since there was nothing we could do, we drove around the scene and continued home.

We made it back, and all of us who lived in the dozen or so apartments in the building assembled in the attic unit that belonged to one of the guys. Our neighborhood, the Cass Corridor, was a bohemian/ghetto area surrounding Wayne State University. It was no big deal to smoke weed, have long hair, or play music loud at night around here; it was a live-and-let-live type of neighborhood. We all knew each other, and there was a nice community vibe. A few musicians, a couple of single girls, and a dope dealer or two lived in my building. It was a nonstop party, and life had been sweet, up until today. Everybody was freaked out about what was happening. We gathered around a little black-and-white TV, and got up to speed from the local news.

The city was unusually calm at first; just a few sirens in the distance. The TV reporter was saying that late Saturday night, the police had raided a "blind pig," an afterhours club or speakeasy at Twelfth Street and Claremont. The patrons had resisted the police.

That was all it took; just a spark.

BUT THAT SPARK hit a pool of gasoline that had been collecting for a long time. Racism had been a part of Detroit's social fabric since the city's founding. When rural southern blacks came up to Detroit in the postwar period for auto-factory jobs, they were last-hired and first-fired. Black workers were routinely assigned the worst, most dangerous jobs, and decades of abuse by white foremen had created an atmosphere of intolerable frustration and occasional violence on the shop floors. The unions didn't help the plight of black workers; instead, they usually sided with management to quell any friction.

Through the '40s and '50s, Detroit's African American communities had endured "urban renewal" projects where whole neighborhoods were bulldozed in the name of progress. But for them, there was no progress. Poverty was systemic and widespread. People of color weren't getting their slice of the prosperity that Detroit whites were enjoying. Unemployment for young black men rose to 25 percent, and city fathers were quick to blame Detroit's problems on the poor. Virulent racism on political, social, and economic levels combined to make the Motor City a tinderbox.

In the '60s, the Detroit Police Department was as bigoted and thug-like as any in America. A notorious, much-feared crew of vice squad cops called "The Big Four" spearheaded the heavy-handed tactics. The three detectives and one uniformed officer driving black sedans were avoided by anyone in their right mind. Their attitude was, "We're the biggest, meanest squad in town, and we'll do what we please—including arresting, beating, and even killing someone, if we feel like it." Working prostitution, drugs, and gambling, they were entirely corrupt. These thugs, armed with badges and guns, were at the center of the raid on the Twelfth Street club that fateful night.

Think about it: this afterhours, private club was the one place where friends in the black community could go and relax. The club members were dancing, partying, and celebrating the return home of two local Vietnam War vets. Then who barged in? The lily-white vice squad. And they were assholes about it, knocking people around in the process. They arrested over 80 people, but nobody was going quietly. People were sick and tired of having their asses kicked by the police, and finally they bucked.

The situation got out of control when the cops started to assemble their prisoners on the street to wait for more paddy wagons. Understandably pissed off, people hanging out on the street started pitching a bitch. Someone threw a bottle that smashed a police car window. Chaos erupted when the prisoners wouldn't get into the wagons, and people on the street started interfering with the cops, who were outnumbered. The cops changed their plans and backed off to wait for reinforcements. This was their second big mistake.

As the cops started to leave, more bottles and bricks started flying. In a flash, all hell broke loose. The remaining cops jumped into their cars and retreated. They called for backup, and in the interim, the anger felt by the crowd grew exponentially. When the cops didn't regain control, they were further emboldened. The spark had found its fuel. Fires erupted in businesses all over town, and looting began.

By noon on Sunday, the Michigan National Guard had been called out. Police from all over the state were racing into Detroit. State police as well as small-town cops from all over southern Michigan and northern Ohio were reporting for duty in big, bad Detroit.

You could exit the attic apartment of our five-story building through a window, walk out on the roof, and see in all directions.

We watched from the roof as the fires increased and the gunfire moved closer. Around midnight on Sunday, something was happening down the street at the corner of Alexandrine and Second. Cop cars had rolled in with sirens and lights off, then cops and National Guardsmen spread out in the dark. They moved in around the building on the corner. From our high perch, we watched intently at what was unfolding. Shots rang out, then it was quiet. The cops got back in their cars and took off. Later we heard that they'd shot and killed a 23-year-old maintenance man who had gone up on the roof with a mop and a bucket of water to protect the building from sparks. They claimed he was a sniper. This murder was a harbinger of the horrors to come.

I called my mother, who was living over on the northwest side. She asked me if I had any guns.

"What would I need a gun for"? I asked.

"What about the rioters, the coloreds?" she said.

I explained that I wasn't worried about them, but I was worried about the police. They were the ones doing all the shooting.

I stayed up all night with my friends, watching from the roof as the sirens, smoke, fires, and gunfire increased. It was unlike anything I had ever experienced: uncertainty, mayhem, a total breakdown of order. It was appalling and breathtaking.

The next day, Monday, a smoky haze settled over the city. You couldn't escape the smell of burning buildings and the sound of sirens in the distance. The gunfire came in waves of varying intensity, sometimes with a pop, pop, pop! Then quiet, followed by a barrage of fire. After a while, you got used to it. It sounded like the soundtrack from a World War II movie. It was the sound of my city at war.

Governor George Romney declared a state of emergency. The sale of gas, booze, and guns was outlawed, and a curfew set. By then, over 2,000 rifles and handguns had been stolen from area gun shops. TV newscasters said that traditionally the second night of a riot was the worst. The rebellion had now spread all across town. Cousins called cousins, friends called friends. The reaction of the

Italian, Irish, and Polish neighborhoods was predictable. They all got out their hunting rifles and handguns, waiting for the marauding hordes of blacks to invade. They never came, but what did happen was that the police and National Guardsmen shot first, and thought about it later. The National Guard responded to unconfirmed reports of sniper fire with massive firepower. Poorly trained young guardsmen with little supervision drove Jeeps with .50 caliber machine guns mounted on top, and they used them. Children were slain by these heavy-caliber weapons that could easily pierce brick walls.

The people of Detroit who had been on the short end of the stick for so long lashed out at everything that represented the generations of racism and poverty they had endured. They took their revenge on slumlords and neighborhood businesses that they'd resented for years. In spontaneous rage at an America that didn't include them, they even set their own neighborhoods afire. The Detroit Fire Department could not keep up with the inferno, and soon whole blocks were burning out of control. The usual rules that held everything together were suspended, and my city became a twilight zone of violent irrationality.

There were no organized groups of revolutionaries building roadblocks. There were no cadres of militants sniping at the police. These were regular folks who'd been pushed too far for too long. When the fire department pulled out, the fires spread, and block after block burned. Solid, working, middle-class black neighborhoods were destroyed all across Detroit.

By Tuesday, President Lyndon Johnson had called out the U.S. Army's 82nd Airborne. By Wednesday, 4,700 paratroopers and 360 state police joined 8,000 National Guard on the streets of my hometown.

U.S. Army tanks drove down Woodward Avenue. Armored personnel carriers and U.S. Army trucks with troops in the back patrolled the neighborhood. The city was blanketed in smoke, and the sounds of gunfire continued; steady single shots punctuated by heavier weapon bursts. This went on all week.

ON FRIDAY, I moved into a house over on Warren Avenue, about six blocks away. I had been planning this move before the rebellion, and I saw no reason not to go ahead with it. The new place was a whole house that I would share with a few friends who were music fans. I needed a space to rehearse the MC5, and this was perfect.

It was also near the home of poet John Sinclair, founder of the Artists Workshop. John was an imposing figure, at least 6'3". He was larger than life, with a twinkle in his eye and an infectious laugh. Boisterous and genial, he took center stage in any room he entered. His wicked smarts and sense of humor left me in awe. Tyner and I were huge fans of John's, and thought of him as a mentor. John's place was at the corner of the John C. Lodge Freeway and Warren Avenue, just down the block from my new abode. His building was a two-story commercial structure that covered the whole corner with three storefronts on each street. This was where the Artists Workshop, a rehearsal and performance space, was located. On the corner was the Detroit office of the Committee to End the War in Vietnam. On the Warren side was the office of Detroit's popular underground newspaper *Fifth Estate*. Upstairs was a dental office that John and Leni Sinclair, their baby daughter Sunny, artist Gary Grimshaw, and others had converted into living quarters.

It was a great place to hang out. Sinclair had a massive jazz and blues record collection, and music played nonstop. It was here that I first heard the wondrous sounds of Sun Ra, Albert Ayler, Cecil Taylor, Archie Shepp, and so many others. I was in heaven there. John and I would smoke reefer, listen to music, and have deep philosophical, political, and cultural discussions. I loved his informed and visionary analysis, and considered him a champion of everything that mattered to me.

During the insurrection his place was raided by the police, who'd taken exception to the "Burn, Baby, Burn!" sign John put on the roof. The scene in his living room had been a serious confrontation, culminating with John, holding his newly born daughter, telling them to "either shoot me or get the fuck out of my house." Fortunately, having nothing to arrest John for, the police and army retreated.

At my new place that Saturday night, we all went to sleep with the city starting to calm down after a week at war. Suddenly there was a massive crash as the front door was busted in. "Everybody up! Everybody up with your hands in the air, or you'll be shot!" The house was filled with men screaming orders. I heard our German shepherd yelping as it was beaten in the stairwell.

Eve and I were startled to see soldiers and police in our bedroom pointing shotguns at us. "Get up and out into the hall!" the state police officer barked. We always slept naked, so I got up off our mattress on the floor and pulled on some jeans. Eve asked the cop to leave so she could put on her clothes. He refused, and grinned as she got dressed at gunpoint. Out in the hall, we all had to lie facedown with shotguns and rifles pointed at our heads, while the cops figured out what they were doing.

They saw a telescope that one of the guys owned in the front upstairs window, and concluded that we were snipers. Searching our house, they found a bow and arrow, and connected us to a reported bow-and-arrow attack on firemen. Bow-and-arrow attack? Really? One of our guys dealt weed, and he'd saved up the seeds for planting. When the raid started, he threw the brown paper bag of seeds out of the window onto the roof in front. A guardsman found it, but didn't know what it was. His superior's response was, "Call that colored officer in here; he'll know what this is." The black policeman said, "This here is marijuana seeds."

We were all put in handcuffs and led out of the front door to see an army tank pointing its cannon at our house. *A fucking U.S. Army tank.* By now, our neighbors had gathered around to watch as the police hustled us into an armored personnel carrier for the trip downtown to police headquarters and central booking. Our neighbors liked us, and they started asking questions and voicing their concerns about what was going down. This reaction made the cops nervous, and they got us out of there quickly.

Central booking at 1300 Beaubien Street was a war zone command center. It was still very warm out, and everyone was dripping sweat. Army and police smoking cigarettes and drinking coffee, hanging around, resting and regrouping. Bloodied prisoners were waiting to be booked. Three of my male roommates and I were taken upstairs to the cells. There was a lot of confusion in the building, with guys yelling and radios crackling. Walking past cells full of mostly young black men who were bloodied and understandably pissed-off was damn scary. They put us in a cell by ourselves. Later in the afternoon, investigators questioned us, and we complained about the arrest and the unprovoked invasion of our house.

The charges were dropped, and by sundown all of us were released. We were small potatoes; the cops had their hands full of real death and destruction. Walking free out of Detroit Police headquarters that evening was one of the sweeter moments of my youth. We all whooped and hollered as we ran down the street.

The horrendous result of a week of lawlessness and police murder was 43 dead, over 1,100 injured, 2,000 buildings burned down, and 7,200 arrests. It was also the beginning of Detroit's long slide down into the abyss. After the uprising, whites fled to the suburbs in increasing numbers, leaving people of color behind in a smoldering and shattered city.

One of the worst results was that Detroiters started arming themselves. It seemed as if everybody bought guns. As time went on, this turned Detroit from the Motor City to the Murder City. Before the rebellion of '67, if two neighbors had a beef, at worst, they would have a fistfight. But after that, someone usually got shot or killed.

The criminal world had access to guns on a whole new scale, and as a result, as jobs declined, violent crime skyrocketed. In 1967, there were 271 homicides; by 1974, that number had risen to 714. Over the next ten years, Detroit would go from a working-class boomtown of union jobs and solid brick houses and endless possibilities, to the American murder capitol. By the mid-1980s, it was an empty shell of a great city, ruled by crime and despair. A city of leftover workers with no work, no hope, and no future.

CHAPTER 9

COME TOGETHER

After the insurgency, I rented a larger apartment five blocks away in the same building on Canfield Street that Tyner lived in. Fred and Mike didn't have a place to live, so they moved in with me, along with my pal Frank Bach and my girlfriend Eve.

Having Fred and Michael living in my apartment, and Tyner living downstairs, had some advantages. Getting the MC5 together to rehearse was always a major challenge. Fred refined passive-aggressiveness to a high art that made getting him to rehearsal on time way harder than it should have been. None of us had any money or owned cars, so living in the same apartment building eliminated one huge step in the process.

On January 24, 1967, Detroit police arrested 54 people, including John Sinclair, in a raid of the Artists Workshop. This was John's third arrest for possession of marijuana. The same narcotics detective, Warner Stringfellow, had engineered John's arrests. He held a vendetta against John because John had written a scathing poem about him after the first bust. I knew this latest bust was trouble, but I tried not to think about it too much.

I came up with a plan for creating a management team for the band. I was very impressed with Barry Kramer (no relation), a hip entrepreneur in the neighborhood who owned a record store over on Cass Avenue called Mixed Media. He seemed to know the business side of pop culture. Russ Gibb, who was running the Grande Ballroom, was also very sharp, and had the best place to play in town. And most importantly, the deepest thinker and visionary I knew, John Sinclair.

My idea was to get all three of them together in a three-way partnership to manage the MC5. Not too grandiose, huh? Of course, there was no way in hell these very different people could work together to make my plan real. I was shooting for the moon and beyond. Barry would go on to found *Creem* magazine, and Russ remained the Grande's promoter while continuing his career in education. But John agreed to manage the band, and I couldn't have been happier.

John told me he was friendly with Grateful Dead manager Rock Scully. When John confided that he didn't actually know anything about managing a rock band, Scully revealed that he didn't know anything, either. But these record company suits were throwing money at the San Francisco bands, and Scully wanted the Dead to get some. He was making it up as they went along. I guess that was good enough for John, and he started in on the business of managing the MC5.

John, Leni, Grimshaw, Tyner, Emil Bacilla, and a bunch of other musicians, poets, and general freaks had joined together in an anarcho-syndicated concept that they christened Trans-Love Energies. It was a sort of movable feast of media resources, technology, and multipurpose facilitators. This was the entity that would manage the band. It was a utopian concept of communal efforts for the good of all. All I knew was that I needed help running things, and now the MC5 had management. From the jump, I had been doing everything that needed doing, and I'd maxed out my limited power. I was very happy to have John as a partner.

John and I would stay up all night talking about everything and everybody. I admired his vision and analysis of how the world worked. We talked endlessly about how things got to be the way they were. John had the ability to articulate feelings that I only knew on a gut level. I knew that life was unjust and unfair, but he could explain in granular detail how and why. We talked about music and culture, too, and I was the beneficiary of his vast detailed knowledge of jazz and the musicians that created this greatest of all American art forms. John also turned me on to The Fugs and I love them. They played with the MC5 at the Grande and hanging out with Ed Sanders, Tuli Kupferberg, and Ken Weaver nearly killed me from laughing so hard. Their influence on me was deep.

One of the first things we did was move everyone in together at the former Artists Workshop building at Warren and John C. Lodge. John and his Trans-Love crew found another building in the neighborhood, and they all moved over there, freeing both the residence and the workshop space downstairs to be converted into the MC5's rehearsal studio. I worked like a dog, stapling egg crates on the walls to soundproof the huge space. I got blisters from that fucking staple gun. The band was predictably absent for most of the drudgery; nothing new there. This setup was perfect; all we had to do was go downstairs to rehearse.

We had a bunch of bolts of cloth that had been liberated during the July 1967 rebellion, and I used some of it to completely seal out any light from my bedroom window. I didn't want to know if it was day or night. I wanted to sleep when I wanted to, and play music, get high, and have sex the rest of the time.

I had been reading about a new artist on the scene, guitarist Jimi Hendrix. I bought *Are You Experienced,* and Tyner and I were both deeply impressed. This new guy was doing something close to what we were doing and he was doing it very well. We loved him. He confirmed that we were on the right track.

THE TIME IN the rehearsal room at our new headquarters on John C. Lodge started to pay off. We could stay in there, smoke reefer, talk, plot, and scheme. We started coming up with new song ideas and production concepts. We were listening to a lot of free jazz, and we'd experiment with the concept night after night. We freaked people who came by to jam out because we didn't play in a key or tempo. It was just far-out, and further out. I wanted to know what Albert and Archie, Sun Ra, and Coltrane were hearing out there. Physical endurance wasn't a problem; we were young, and loved playing music together for hours on end.

I was the only guy in the band who had taken any formal music lessons, and I could get my ideas across by saying, "Do this part eight times, then do the other part four times." We all knew verse, chorus, and bridge construction, and that was fine for our purposes. Discussing free and experimental music was an exercise in metaphor and cosmic double-speak. Tyner was very articulate when he had an idea to communicate. And it was in this period that Fred Smith really blossomed as a guitarist.

Up until now, Fred was the world's greatest rhythm guitarist. He took great pride in his rhythm playing. Back in Lincoln Park, we had both mastered the painful technique of Chuck Berry rhythm playing, and Fred applied that same persistence to everything he did. But something changed. One day he came into the rehearsal room and started playing like Eric Clapton. I was amazed. Seemingly overnight, he had learned the modern blues style that all the English guitarists were employing. He was just playing his ass off. He must have been woodshedding on his own. All I know is, one day he was a bona fide soloist, whereas the day before he wasn't.

Our friendship and musical partnership reached a new level during this period. We played guitars together so much that we could reach a state of ego-loss where we played simultaneously, without regard to who played what role. Playing dual rhythms and dual solos, we were able to improvise together endlessly and effortlessly. We had musical conversations with our guitars. No other current two-guitar groups could do this at the energy level that we could.

This time period, from fall of 1967 through the winter of 1968, was the most idyllic time for the MC5.

Everything that I had worked for since I was 14 years old was coming together better than I'd planned. Finally, we were all living together. Hanging out together. Getting stoned together. These were the people I most wanted to be with, and I was with them 24–7. I would go over to Rob's room and see if he wanted to write some tunes. We would set up a little amp in the kitchen, I would play guitar riffs, and he would come up with lyrics. Rob and I wrote "Kick Out the Jams" in the kitchen, smoking a joint. I had been working on some guitar figures, and I played them for him. He heard something he liked and said, "Whoa, play that again." This was how we learned how to write songs together.

Now that we had a manager we respected and who really understood us and the music we were trying to create, the division of labor improved. I didn't have to spend hours on the phone; instead, I could concentrate on the music. John rose to the challenge and became an excellent manager, charismatic and persuasive. He arranged for us to be represented by the hot booking agency in town, and pretty soon, the work was coming in. In the past, we'd had trouble building professional relationships because we were always late. Club owners and promoters wouldn't hire a band back if they showed up late, and we did that all the time. Now that we lived together, getting everyone out the door on time was much easier.

Russ Gibb hired us to open for Jefferson Airplane at the Ford Auditorium and Bruce Bennington showed up with a court order and two Detroit police officers to repossess the amps we never paid for. Russ negotiated with him, and for a couple hundred bucks Bruce let us play the show with the gear and then took it all afterward. The next day, John arranged for us to buy new gear with a local music store whose owner was a fan.

John got a van, and had Grimshaw paint our logo on it. Now that he lived with John and was part of our crew, Grimshaw started designing our artwork, logos, and graphics. He also started creating the posters for the dance/concert shows at the Grande Ballroom.

John would tell us when to be ready to depart, and we would all get ready to go to the gig together. The van became an extension of the party we were having at home. John had one of the first in-car music systems installed in the van with good speakers in the back so we could listen to the music we wanted to hear. John would program great music for the drives to the gigs. We listened nonstop to free jazz and rhythm and blues. We started getting more and better gigs, too, playing teen clubs and high schools, dances and concerts. We played anywhere they would book us. On one run, we played 18 nights in a row.

Because we were rehearsing so much, our performances got better every week. We always had new songs and new ideas for making the show more exciting. The money from the steady work allowed us to pay rent, buy food, reefer, instruments, and exotic materials to make original stage clothes. Every week, the fans saw improvement. We were building excitement, and these gigs were like giant energy releases. We couldn't wait to hit the stage. In fact, it occurred to me that it would help add excitement if we actually *ran* out to plug in our guitars and get the show going as fast as possible.

We were surrounded by teenage girls and young women at these gigs, and I was a kid in a candy store. I was relentless in my pursuit. We promoted casual sex as part of our "politics." Around this time, we came up with our first three-point program: Dope, Rock & Roll, and Fucking in the Streets. We thought this was hilarious, and so did the fans. Our cachet went up. I would seduce girls wherever I could: in the van outside the venue, in the dressing room, in a closet, a hallway, anywhere. I was ready to go. I hit my pinnacle one night at an after-show party, where I had sex with five different women.

We started to build a good regional reputation with the promoters of the day. There was no sophisticated touring circuit then; you got a gig, and you went out and played it. We played well, the crowds went crazy, and word got out about the MC5. Offers started coming in from Cleveland, where Russ Gibb had opened a Cleveland Grande. We barnstormed our way all over the Midwest: Chicago, Cincinnati, Buffalo, Lansing, Battle Creek, Indianapolis, Milwaukee. We would play anywhere they would let us, and we had a ball doing it.

CHAPTER 10

THE HUMAN BEING LAWNMOWER

The draft had become a subject of serious conversations among young men my age. Everybody wanted to know what could be done to avoid it. My mother wept at the prospect of me going to war, but true to her generation, she said I had to go. I didn't see it that way. As Rob Tyner put it so well, "We're standing before . . . *the human being lawnmower.*"

Everybody I knew agreed that the war was unjustified, immoral, and illegal. Our discussions were down on the ground and personal. Ron Asheton and Dave Alexander from the Stooges had just had their physicals. I needed to know what happened: What did you do? Did you get a 1-Y? A 4-F? Because of their long hair and appearance, they both endured extra pressure from army personnel to conform to their orders, but both proved incapable of doing so and were eventually sent home with deferrals.

Many gained exemptions by attending college or getting married. The need for bodies was ramping up, and it seemed that guys with means found a way out that others didn't have access to.

I was terrified at the prospect of entering the army and being put into a situation where I might have to kill another person, or be killed. This didn't make any sense to me. The more I learned about the reasons we were in Vietnam, the more I knew it was wrong. This wasn't World War II; there was no Hitler or Mussolini. Just who exactly was our enemy?

There were reports of Shell Oil interests in the region. Is that what we were killing and dying for? There was talk of fighting the communists, but communism was a political system from the other side of the world. Where was the threat? No one believed the rationalizations that politicians were spewing, and later the Pentagon Papers revealed the truth. The communists were not invading Detroit.

It didn't take a genius to figure out that all the reasons we were being given didn't add up. And I wasn't alone in my realizations because hundreds of thousands of Americans were taking to the streets to oppose this immoral, illegal war. I had no quarrel with guys that went. Many of my high school friends did. My argument was with the government.

I knew the day was coming when I would be scheduled to report to the U.S. Army's Fort Wayne Induction Center for my physical.

I prepared by going on a ten-day meth binge. I liked speed, and used it from time to time, staying up for days on end writing songs and practicing guitar. I was afraid of what might happen to me at Fort Wayne, so I did speed to fortify myself. After a few days without sleep, methamphetamine produces severe side effects. When I had to fill out forms to determine what my job in the army would be, I had difficulty writing. I couldn't keep the pencil in between the lines. I was also paranoid to the point of psychosis, and hallucinating badly. I tried to explain that I was a musician and I knew about amps and band gear, but not about wrenches, jeeps, or guns.

They had us strip down to our underwear, but since revolutionaries didn't wear underwear, I got in line naked and that caused an uproar. I was told to put my Levi's back on and get back in line. "Yes sir!"

As the day went on, I kept being removed from the line because I was having difficulty following directions. I wasn't defying them; I just couldn't keep up. Do this, stand there, show me your papers, go in that room and take that test, and so on. An irregular heartbeat showed up, probably from the meth. I failed the hearing test. I almost fainted when they drew blood. I was crashing bad from the speed, and my anxiety was off the charts.

After a few hours of testing and probing, I was given a purple card and told to wait on a bench with some other guys. I sat down and couldn't help but overhear the fellow next to me talking about going to Fort Bragg, North Carolina. I asked what was he talking about, and he said, "We're all leaving in a few minutes for Fort Bragg. The bus will be right here." I choked out, "What?" He said, "You got a purple card? Yeah, man, all us purple cards is leaving now."

Panic set in. We were on the second floor, and I weighed jumping through the window to the street below, but decided that would be way too painful. *I'll just nut up, I'll go off.* I had never tried to get hysterical before, and I discovered it wasn't that easy to do.

Finally, I decided to inquire about the accuracy of this guy's info. I went over to an officer sitting at a desk, and asked him if everyone with a purple card was leaving for Fort Bragg. He said, "Give me your papers." He leafed through them, said to wait here, and went and got another guy.

They both looked at my papers, and then they sent me to see the psychiatrist because I had checked the box next to the question asking if I had homosexual tendencies. The doctor asked me about it, and I explained that I had learned through taking LSD that I didn't have to limit my displays of affection to just the opposite sex. And I loved my friends—both male and female.

He checked a box that said I was unacceptable to serve in the U.S. Armed Forces under current standards, and sent me out. My panic subsided.

They walked me to a desk, where an enlisted man asked if I wanted to sign up for mental health care from Wayne County Social Services. I thanked him for his concern, but declined the offer. Then, he asked if LSD made music and lights come alive; he had heard it was cool. I asked if I could go now.

I went home to crash. My teeth had become loose over the days of grinding and speeding, and I was probably certifiably psychotic. In a couple of days, I was back to my regular self, and saw the world in a completely different light. I was not going into the army, and I wouldn't be going to Vietnam. I wasn't ashamed and I wasn't proud; I was just relieved that it was now behind me. For the first time in years, I was free to imagine what my future might be.

CHAPTER 11

KICK OUT THE JAMS

Our place on John C. Lodge and Warren was getting impossible to live in. The office downstairs, the Detroit Committee to End the War in Vietnam, was firebombed. We had suffered a grab-and-run robbery of our rehearsal room, in which we lost my 57 Les Paul, Fred's Gretsch Tennessean, and Michael's Fender Precision Bass. Rightwing extremists firebombed our van on the street outside, and a serial rapist was attacking our wives and girlfriends. Plus, we were constantly being harassed by the Detroit police. Given the situation, we decided to move up to the peaceful college town of Ann Arbor, Michigan, 40 miles west of Detroit.

One of our friends, Lawrence "Pun" Plamondon, was serving time in the county jail. He read in the Black Panther Party's newspaper that Huey Newton put out the call for a group of white radicals to join them doing "parallel but separate" work in the white community. With this news, Pun and John and Leni Sinclair founded the White Panther Party as an anti-racist, cultural revolutionary group. It was a logical extension of our reefer-fueled political ideas, and was done in the spirit of agitprop theater. John wrote up a "Ten-Point Program" to fight for a clean planet and the freeing of all political prisoners. Rob Tyner remarked that the Black Panthers looked pretty cool in their black leather jackets and berets, and we started incorporating their look into our style. The last thing we were was a serious political entity, but being White Panthers was a way to vent our very real frustration with the slow pace of change in America. Being White Panthers gave voice to our contempt for the policies and actions of the government, the police, and the older generation.

In August 1968, on WFMU's *Cocaine Karma* radio show, John Sinclair met Elektra Records' director of publicity and "house hippie," Danny Fields. Sinclair told Fields about the MC5, and invited him to come to Detroit to see the band in action. Fields did, and was intensely impressed. He called respected rock journalist Jon Landau and left the message, "I have found it! Call me!"

Danny came out to Detroit to see the band perform a few more times, and he made an offer to sign the MC5 to Elektra. This was the deal I was looking for, with a very hip label that had pockets deep enough to market the band properly. I was very excited about the possibilities, and I liked Danny a lot.

Danny asked me if there were any other bands like the MC5, and I told him no, there were not. But he should hear our brothers, the Psychedelic Stooges. Iggy and I had been friends for years, and I was happy to help his band get signed to Elektra. Back in the early days when he was playing drums in the Prime Movers blues band, I tried to recruit him to play drums in the MC5, but he had another idea in mind. That concept became the Stooges, and I thought they were as artistically and musically revolutionary in their own way as we were. We all listened to the same free jazz and blues records, jammed together, and smoked reefer together. Iggy Pop was completely original and a compelling live performer. What was not to like? Danny loved them, too. Iggy and I hung out often, and I enjoyed his quirky, idiosyncratic view of the world. His observations were always insightful and poetic. He also had a great absurdist sense of humor that matched up with my own. At one point, he got way into macrobiotics, a new super-vegetarian diet, and got very skinny. Onstage he was brilliant; his dancing was primal and beautiful, and the Stooges' sound was massive and rhythmic. I was very proud of them.

ON SEPTEMBER 29, 1968, just before midnight, I was leaving the band house, also known as White Panther headquarters, on Hill Street in Ann Arbor, when I heard an explosion in the distance followed by police sirens. There had been bombings all across the country that year: a few in Ann Arbor at U of M buildings connected with the Vietnam War, and several in Detroit that mostly targeted police cars. After I listened for a while in the dark, one of the guys rolled up on his bicycle. His partner was standing by the curb to greet him, and they shared a kiss and a hug. I was standing on the front porch when they turned to enter the house. Big smiles on everyone's faces. I said, "What was that?" He answered "I don't know, CIA?" To which I replied, "Right on, right on." We exchanged the raised fist salute, and I went on my way into the night.

Between the MC5 and all the people I lived with, we all talked nonstop about politics and culture. It ran the gamut from reefer-addled absurdist humor to very real concerns, fears, anger, and frustration. I admired the vanguard players in the revolution, the Black Panther Party, and saw them as a beacon lighting the way forward. I believed we were all involved in the same struggle.

I embraced many of the most extreme ideas and actions of my day. It was both frightening and exciting. I felt like I was part of something bigger than anything that had ever come before. I believed that because of our LSD-driven insights, we were an evolutionary break from the past. The news was filled with reports of young people the world over taking radical action. Students in Paris had taken over the Sorbonne, as they had at Columbia University in New York and in Mexico City, where government troops opened fire and killed hundreds of students and civilians. Protests erupted all across Europe, from London to the Balkans. The Black Panthers defined the ethos of the day, and I was on board. I was a romantic anarchist.

The cultural landscape had shifted so radically that I felt my mother's generation was left in the dust of history. This was our time, and we had no respect for the mess we'd inherited from the preceding generation. Civil rights, the war in Vietnam, police oppression, outdated sexual mores, drug laws, the threat of nuclear annihilation, feminism, the environment, and all the other issues of the day inspired extreme rhetoric and actions.

The unknown impact of being raised on violence in television and movies, unconstrained by reality, and using the language and symbols of guns and bombs was something I hadn't thought through completely. In the cop shows and western movies, you get shot and it's like, "Oh damn, they winged me. I'm okay." The reality of being shot is a whole different thing. I had a fantasy of "shooting it out with the man." It all sounded so romantic and macho. This idea was irresistible, but it was dangerously ignorant.

I poured my frustration and commitment into the MC5, the songs I was writing, the intensity with which I played my guitar, the way I performed onstage, and our connection with our audience. The most important thing was our solidarity and unity; that we were together in mind, body, and spirit. It was us against them.

IT WAS DECIDED to record the MC5 live. This was an unorthodox and perhaps revolutionary idea. Most bands of this era produced three studio albums, and then did a live record. We were going to do the opposite. It was born out of the reality that the MC5 had limited experience in the recording studio, and taming our musical recklessness was going to be a complex and laborious task. Not to mention expensive and maybe even detrimental to capturing the raw excitement the band was known for.

Our strength was our live performance. This was where we had focused our energy, and if it could be captured on tape, it would be a radical and fitting introduction for the group on the world stage. I agreed with the decision, and the wheels started turning.

Halloween 1968 was chosen for the live recording at our home venue, the Grande Ballroom. We christened the date "Zenta New Year's Eve." Zenta was our marijuana-inspired religious order. It grew out of a silly, stoned-out riff created by our Master of Ceremonies, Brother J. C. Crawford (the Oracle Ramus), and his partner, David "Panther" White (the Oracle Remus).

Elektra flew in Wally Heider's new mobile 8-track recording rig from California. Heider had been instrumental in recording the San Francisco sound in the late '60s. Bruce Botnick was our recording engineer/producer. I asked Heider what he thought of my band, and he responded diplomatically, "I think you guys will make a lot of money."

We had a long sound check in the afternoon where we worked out some bugs and got the sound right. We recorded a few songs in the empty ballroom, and tried our best to get the guitars in tune. Tuning had always been a problem. Bruce sat out in the room and made a few suggestions. Everything seemed to be going well.

That night, the excitement in the Grande was through the roof. It was all happening for the MC5 and our loyal fans. We were going to make recording history.

The crowd started clapping and stomping their feet like always in anticipation of the show starting. J. C. Crawford stepped up to the mic to deliver his rabble-rousing intro. His introduction of the MC5 that night was truly a great piece of performance poetry, combining elements of Danny Ray's great intro for James Brown, brother Dave Gardner's southern-fried stream-of-consciousness humor, White Panther militancy, and a dash of sanctified gospel revival meeting. He often improvised, and I never knew what he was going to say, but he was always brilliant. That night, he was dazzling.

When he brought us on at the climax of his bit—"I give you a testimonial . . . the MC5!"—the place exploded, and I slammed into the opening guitar figure of "Ramblin' Rose."

Disaster struck. My low E string slipped badly out of tune, throwing me completely out of my groove. I was so hyped up about the performance, and now my guitar sounded like shit. I felt like a fool pretending that everything was going great.

I soldiered on, but the pressure of this being *the night of the recording* only made everything worse. I was self-conscious about what I was doing, and no longer in the moment like I needed to be. As the set went on, more errors occurred from others in the band. Even though the crowd cheered and whooped and hollered, I knew this wasn't a great MC5 performance. I enjoyed the appreciation of the audience, but I wasn't fooled by it. I knew when the music was sounding good and when it was not. This night, for me, it was not.

The MC5 was a mercurial band. Our strengths were in our songwriting, live excitement, adventurous guitar playing, and our direct connection with our fans. Our weakness was our inconsistency. We could be absolutely brilliant one night, and a train wreck the next. It made for higher highs, but lower lows. That night, my solos were not as inspired as they might have been. There were other flaws in our performance. We front-loaded the set list. We came on full bore, and left ourselves no headroom. Dialing it back was a level of sophistication we hadn't achieved yet. It made us great and limited at the same time.

We recorded a second night at the Grande, and waited for rough mixes to come back from Bruce. I woke up a couple of weeks later to the sound of the mixes being played full blast downstairs on Sinclair's system. Everyone in the house was happy about what they were hearing. It was unanimous that the record was great.

I didn't share this feeling, and discussed it with the band and Sinclair. Elektra CEO Jac Holzman had assured me that if I wasn't happy with the recordings, we could record again. But after running my reservations up the chain of command, the consensus was to go ahead with what we had.

An additional session was needed because most of the vocals were not recorded well enough. We were all way off mic on the backing vocals, so this time we all smoked some joints, got close together around the mic, and sang like maniacs along with ourselves to the previously recorded tracks, embellishing what we had recorded and adding more uncontrolled lunacy to the tapes.

I visited the Elektra offices in New York to see mock-ups of the album's artwork, and loved what they were doing. The art department was experimenting with a new technique of semitransparent photo overlays of our live performance. These roughs were ingenious and dramatic. Sinclair composed the liner notes, and we waited for the final product.

Again, I was underwhelmed. The cover ended up looking like an amateur paste-up collage of unflattering images mushed together. It was flattened out with no depth of field, unlike the mock-ups I'd seen earlier.

The faces of the kids in the audience all looked airbrushed, like they were department store mannequins. That was because they *were* airbrushed. Elektra's legal affairs department feared that if they published photos of the kids without releases, they might be sued, so they had the art department alter them. To me, it looked awful. The cover photo of Tyner was terribly uncomplimentary. And, to add insult to injury, Elektra art director Bill Harvey put a shot of *himself* up in the corner.

Even so, when the record came out, it shot up the *Billboard* charts to a high of #30. Things could not have looked better. For a minute.

The writer Lester Bangs eviscerated us in *Rolling Stone.* I was tripping when I read it:

April 5, 1969

About a month ago the MC-5 received a cover article in *Rolling Stone* proclaiming them the New Sensation, a group to break all barriers, kick out all jams, "total energy thing," etc. etc. etc. Never mind that they came on like a bunch of 16 year old punks on a meth power trip—these boys, so the line ran, could play their guitars like John Coltrane and Pharoah Sanders played sax! Well, the album is out now and we can all judge for ourselves. For my money they come on more like

Blue Cheer than Trane and Sanders, but then my money has already gone for a copy of this ridiculous, overbearing, pretentious album; and maybe that's the idea, isn't it? . . . Most of the songs are barely distinguishable from each other in their primitive two-chord structures. You've heard all this before from such notables as the Seeds, Blue Cheer, Question Mark and the Mysterians, and the Kingsmen.

Etc, etc, etc.

That was a bummer. Ironically, Lester Bangs later moved to Detroit to work at *Creem* magazine. He recanted and regretted that review, and became one of the MC5's most ardent supporters and a personal friend until the day he died. Plus, I have always liked the "16 year old punks on a meth power trip" line.

CHAPTER 12

THE FILLMORE FIASCO

By December of 1968, we had played shows all over the Midwest, from Cleveland to Cincinnati, the Chicago Democratic Convention riots, all over Michigan, and dozens of nights at the Grande Ballroom with every local, national, and international band of the day.

We had made a few trips to New York, and had a fine time whenever we played there. Danny Fields would take us to Max's Kansas City, and we would order steaks and get drunk, usually creating a major ruckus in the back room. These were some of the most fun times I'd ever had in the band. We could be like a pirate crew and, with our unbridled energy and joie de vivre, we could produce an amazing amount of good cheer. Once, when we didn't have enough money to pay our bill, J. C. Crawford conducted a fake raffle, exhorting donations from all the other patrons in the back room. He raised more than enough money to cover our bill and generously tip the wait staff, too.

I met Jackie Curtis, the famous Warhol drag queen, at Max's. She flirted with me shamelessly. All in good fun.

I was meeting a lot of new people in Manhattan, and the world was opening up for me. Everything I'd hoped for was falling into place.

Elektra Records wanted to premier the MC5 in New York, and the best venue in town was the Fillmore East. I knew something about the scene in the Lower East Side from friends, and was sensitive to the local politics but I didn't really know the details of what was happening.

The East Village Motherfuckers, an arm of the International Werewolf Conspiracy, were hard-left militants based in the neighborhood. They were known to be involved in violent actions, and were connected to Students for a Democratic Society and other aggressive groups. They had an agreement with promoter Bill Graham that Tuesday nights were "community" nights. The MC5 agreed to come and perform for the "community" the week before our big NYC premier. It was the best way to stay cool with the street people and our political comrades. We did the gig, and everything was fine. The following week was to be the official show.

We went up to Boston to play a gig at the Boston Tea Party. The Motherfuckers came up with us, and we let them have a few minutes of our set time for a speech. One of their people had been arrested and they needed to raise bail money. Unfortunately, they harangued the rock & roll crowd with a call to violent revolutionary action. They told the kids to burn the place down and to "fight American imperialism here at home, and off the pig!" There may even have been some violence out in the crowd because of their speech.

This didn't exactly endear us to the promoter, the ironically named Don Law. In fact, he declared that he would never book the MC5 again. This effectively cut us out of playing any venues he or his friends controlled. We played well, but the gig was strange because the other band, an art-performance act from New York called the Velvet Underground, was on another planet from all the drama surrounding us. They avoided us and our people completely.

Not that I blame them, considering how deranged and aggressive we all must have seemed. When the Velvets took the stage, their singer, Lou Reed, demanded that anyone who came to see the MC5 leave the club or they weren't going to play. And they waited until all our fans departed.

At a couple points in my performance that night, I made the mistake of leaping from the top of my Marshall speaker cabinets as high in the air as I could, then landing on my knees. I had been doing these kinds of acrobatic moves for a while now, and really enjoyed the physicality of it. Playing shows was an athletic event for me. It made for an exciting performance, and no one else in American rock was doing this kind of extreme stuff. The trouble was that the stage at the Tea Party was concrete, not the usual wood construction. Concrete does not have any give in it, and my knees absorbed all the impact of the landing. They swelled up like grapefruits. A sacrifice to the gods of performance.

When we returned to New York for the second Fillmore show, we walked into an even bigger political shitstorm. The Motherfuckers were jacking Graham for more free tickets for "the community." They demanded that I side with them and refuse to play unless Graham submitted. Graham, a Holocaust survivor, was not a guy who submitted to extortion from neighborhood thugs. Sinclair tried to mediate and got a number of tickets allocated for the locals, but this wasn't enough.

The Motherfuckers were demonstrating out in front of the theater when Graham confronted them. Someone hit Graham in the face with a chain, breaking his nose. Graham was certain it was Rob Tyner who assaulted him. I guess all white boys with Afros look alike. It wasn't Rob, but Graham thought it was, and that was all that mattered.

Backstage I heard about what was happening out front with the Motherfuckers, but tried to stay focused on our show. I was excited to be playing a sold-out house in New York City. We'd heard that Jimi Hendrix was in the audience, so I was pretty pumped up.

The Fillmore was the first place I ever played that had a brand-new technology called monitors. This was a whole new level of performance; I could actually hear what everyone was playing and I could hear Tyner's singing clear as a bell, right up front. It was glorious, and I was really looking forward to playing. I needed to show them what I could do.

The people responded to us with great rock & roll energy. Our show was pretty finely tuned by now, and given a chance, we could generate real excitement. Tyner, who never hesitated to express himself, said a few words on the controversy surrounding our appearance. "We didn't come to New York for politics . . . we came for rock & roll!" He was staking out his position. The crowd responded with a huge cheer, but the Motherfuckers took this as a slap in the face. They were hanging out all over the stage, standing in the wings. With Tyner's provocation, they started acting up.

Dudes started moving in on me as I was playing and dancing. I brushed them back a couple of times with spins, leaps, and general disregard for anyone in my vicinity. After all, this was my stage. Our crew picked up on the battle lines being drawn and joined in with some heavy body checks. It made for live-in-the-moment rock drama. We finished the set and when the curtain came down, all hell broke loose onstage. The Motherfuckers bum-rushed the stage and started trashing our equipment. I watched as knives slashed through the fire curtain, while mayhem exploded out front. Cymbals were crashing, amps were knocked over, and there was a lot of yelling and cursing.

It was time to leave the theater. I went out the stage door to see a limousine waiting. Normally this would have been a nice gesture by Elektra, I guess.

What no one realized was that the limo symbolized everything the Motherfuckers deplored. It was the perfect symbol of class war, parked at the curb, waiting for the "revolutionary" MC5. They should have sent a Volkswagen van or maybe an armored personnel carrier. For the hardline revolutionaries, this was the embodiment of poor people vs. moneyed elites. Street people vs. show business posers. We were cast as part of the pig culture!

I was blindsided when I walked out onto the sidewalk. The Motherfucker women were screaming, crying, and cursing, "We trusted you! You sold us out! You sold out the revolution!" Young men were kicking the limo's doors in. We had given out hundreds of free 45 rpm singles of our song "Kick Out the Jams" as special gifts for the fans, and the Motherfuckers were smashing them against the tailfins of the limo. It was surreal. My mind was racing; what the hell's going on here? These people have got it all wrong. We're not the enemy. Why have they turned against us? I attempted to talk to them, to reason with them. The rest of the band came out of the theater, paused for a minute to read the situation, got into the limo, and pulled away. Probably on their way to Max's for steaks and drinks.

I knew I couldn't leave. This had the potential to undo everything I had worked so hard for. That was what I felt in that moment. I was left in the street with the mob, trying to explain that the MC5 really was who we said we were. That we hadn't sold out the revolution.

I stood in the middle of East Sixth Street with the Motherfuckers shouting out political and ideological questions. Screaming out all the Marxist polemical arguments at the top of their lungs, along with the violent rhetoric we all used. The neighborhood nutcases, the speed freaks and junkies, bought into this and were adding the heavy vibes. The Motherfucker women were wailing. I saw the glint of a knife blade reflected in the streetlights. People were getting punched. I couldn't run, but it was becoming clear that I couldn't stay either.

If this idea that we were just a revolutionary hype took hold, we would be finished as a credible band. It wouldn't matter that I was part of a generation that was committed to justice and change in America. That the MC5 could be a really loud voice for all that was wrong in our country simply wouldn't matter, so there was nothing for me to do but stand there, confront, and argue.

Finally, two of the Motherfucker leaders worked their way through the mob and wrapped themselves around me to protect me. One stood at my front and one at my back, their arms around me like a sandwich. They said to start walking out with them. They stayed on me until we were a couple of blocks away from the Fillmore, and the mob had not followed any further. "You'll be all right now," they said, and turned back. I got a cab back to my hotel.

This was a prime example of the failure of the sixties militant mindset. They attacked their own comrades. We were on the same side, but they turned their revolutionary zeal against us. We weren't the people perpetrating the war in Vietnam. We weren't denying African Americans their rights or polluting the air and water. We weren't corrupt politicians in Washington, DC. We were a band that supported the same causes they did, because they were our causes, too. The Motherfuckers were fragmenting the mass youth movement better than the police or FBI ever could have.

Being criticized for not being revolutionary enough was a serious, ongoing problem for me through the era of the MC5. At 20 years old, I just couldn't understand it. I didn't have a sophisticated enough grasp on the history of revolutionary struggle yet. Much of what was happening in America was still a mystery to me. I was completely unprepared for the pushback against the MC5's stance.

Not that we weren't often disapproved of. I was once criticized in a local newspaper for my onstage antics. My super-tight stage trousers ripped open at the crotch during a show. Since revolutionaries don't wear underwear, my penis was exposed for a moment or two. The parental outrage was quick to surface. The local paper ran a letter from an irate parent saying that I had exposed my "personal self." John Sinclair answered with a witty response: "Wayne Kramer didn't expose his 'personal self.' He exposed his genitals. His 'personal self' is exposed all the time."

I could understand why politicians were outraged, and wanted to "do something to stop the MC5." They couldn't allow a rock band to go around telling young people that sex was good for them. That smoking reefer was a good thing. That running away from home and finding out what your possibilities might be was a good thing. That our own government was lying to us about Vietnam, and the war was a bad thing. That civil rights for Americans of color still were not realized. That racism was a bad thing. That police departments in every city in the country lied, murdered, and railroaded citizens into jail as a matter of course, with justice never entering the equation.

I expected the government to criticize us for these things. As the language of revolution became the language of violence, I expected blowback from the establishment. But what troubled me deeply was the criticism we got from other revolutionaries. Often the cynicism showed up in the underground press.

Following the Fillmore concert, I did a radio interview in New York. The guy asking the questions was a Students for a Democratic Society member, and he cut me to ribbons. Revolutionaries like this interviewer accused the MC5 of not only spouting revolutionary hype, but of co-opting the language of radical social change for fame and profit—as if some Madison Avenue ad agency said, "Hey, guys! I just came up with a great marketing scheme. Let's create a band, and we'll say they're 'revolutionary' and 'antiestablishment'! The kids will eat it up, and we'll all get rich!" If I was going to invent a band to sell to the youth of the sixties, it would be a nonthreatening, peace and love, hippy, trippy, cuddly band like the Monkees. And not, the revolution-spouting, Sun Ra–inspired, bra-burning, obscene-talking, reefer-smoking, gun-toting MC5.

We were in it with both feet. In fact, we put our career as a band on the line for the principle of revolution as we understood it, and we didn't end up so well. We were firebombed, harassed, beaten, arrested, jailed, and ultimately kicked out of the music business for our politics.

I struggled with the language of revolutionary violence almost as soon as I took it up. I owned guns, having bought them with the full intention of using them "if necessary." This intention was born of frustration and young male hormones, admiration for the Black Panther Party, and TV and movies. It was macho posturing at its worse: being one step badder than the next guy. But it was also a deadly mistake. In the real world, guns shoot real bullets, and real people get shot and killed.

CHAPTER 13

BACK IN
THE USA

In February 1969, the MC5's debut album was released. Recorded live at the Grande Ballroom in Detroit the previous Halloween, it sold an amazing 20,000 copies in the Detroit area alone. The single "Kick Out the Jams" climbed to #2 on Detroit radio.

J. L. Hudson department store refused to sell the record. The store pulled the album after learning about the obscenities in the lyrics and liner notes, and returned all our records to Elektra. I had been to Hudson's a thousand times in my life; it was a Detroit institution. I spent hours and hours there as a boy admiring the electric guitars in the music department, so when they refused to carry the MC5's records, I took it as a personal affront.

My friend Ken Kelley at the underground newspaper the *Ann Arbor Argus* was struggling with his bills. John Sinclair suggested we help him out with an ad buy that would also address our frustration with Hudson's. "Fuck Hudson's if they won't sell you the record, kick the door down," read the ad. We added the Elektra logo, and sent them the bill. Which they paid, since our contract said we had "complete artistic control" of all ad copy and publicity materials. In response, Hudson's removed *all* Elektra titles from its stores. Needless to say, Elektra was not happy.

In March of '69, we went on a self-financed West Coast promo tour, playing a few shows up and down the coast. One was in San Bernardino with Janis Joplin and her new band. After the gig, she flirted with me, saying how much she loved my "manly thighs," and invited me back to her hotel to get high with her. Since I wasn't yet into heroin, I declined her offer. Growing up in Detroit hearing Aretha Franklin, Martha Reeves, Tammi Terrell, Mary Wells, and dozens of other incredible soul singers, I wasn't exactly enthralled with her singing, either.

The People's Park was a highly charged local issue in Berkeley, and we jumped into the middle of it. Residents, students, and activists wanted to turn a UC-owned empty lot into a green park. When the university refused, peaceful protestors were tear-gassed, shot, and arrested. We played a benefit concert for the Black Panther Party in Oakland, and the next day we did a free concert in the park.

John Sinclair was friendly with Tim Leary, who attended the concert and invited us back to his home in the Berkeley Hills. Sinclair and Leary showed up an hour later than us because the cops had pulled them over and Leary had dumped his stash of LSD into a gallon jug of wine they were bringing to the gathering. I had a couple of glasses of the wine, which Leary assured us wouldn't be too strong.

Mildly stoned, I sat on his deck and listened to music as the sun set into the Pacific. The rest of the band wanted to go carousing, but I wanted to stay and have the total LSD experience with the guru of acid. Leary generously offered me some more, which I took happily. After a while, everyone in the band left except Dennis Thompson and me. After the sun went down, we found ourselves sitting in Leary's living room with his mother-in-law as the acid kicked in. Tim and his lovely wife, Rosemary, came out and announced that they were going to bed. "You guys make yourselves at home. See you in the morning." Whoa . . . I was now tripping in Timothy Leary's living room with his mother-in-law and Dennis, watching the fireplace flicker.

After who knows how long, Dennis and I decided to try to drive back to our hotel. That was a thrilling trip down the canyon roads, hallucinating our asses off. We missed a hairpin turn and drove into a guy's front yard. Somehow, we managed to make it back, none the worse for the wear.

The next night in San Francisco wasn't so good. Most of the band and I were in a rental station wagon on the freeway with a number of groupies, drinking and getting high, when one of the girls gave the finger to a passing San Francisco police car. They pulled us over, and it turned out they were part of the Tactical Mobile Squad. When Fred Smith got sarcastic, one cop punched him in the stomach and threatened to throw him off the overpass. They took us all to the county jail, where we spent the next week on charges of overloading a motor vehicle, open alcohol, contributing to the delinquency of a minor, possession of dangerous drugs, and resisting arrest.

As I was emptying my pockets getting booked into the jail, I set a large chunk of hashish on the counter in front of the desk sergeant. I nonchalantly retrieved it and swallowed it; the policeman didn't even see what I did. They put my stuff in a manila envelope and told me to sit down.

After a few minutes, the cops brought in a poor soul, a drunken Englishman. He had been beaten so badly that his head and face were a red mass of blood and gore, and his voice was distorted with pain. The big cop that brought him in began to stomp him again right there in the booking area. The other cops started yelling for him to stop, and after a few more kicks to the guy's head, he quit. The unfortunate bloke was beaten to a pulp.

By the time I was taken upstairs to the cells, thanks to the hash, I was nice and stoned for my first night in the San Francisco County Jail. I had an in-depth talk with a couple of older brothers about Ike Turner. The fellows there held him in great esteem. They marveled at his clothes, his cars, and his women. They told me he carried a matchbox full of black pepper that he'd blow in your eyes if you messed with him.

After we'd spent a week or so in jail, Sinclair engaged Terence "K. O." Hallinan to represent us. When I got to court, I found out K. O. had recently had a violent confrontation with the same officer who'd arrested us. Most of the charges against me and the guys were dropped, and I pled guilty to "open alcohol in a vehicle." A film crew was following us around, making a movie they called *Half a Can of Falstaff.*

Happy to be free, we flew down to Los Angeles and started recording our second LP at Elektra's beautiful Los Angeles studios, again with Bruce Botnick supervising. This was our first time working in a state-of-the-art recording studio where we didn't have to watch the clock. Bruce was the perfect producer for us. He allowed us to try things and experiment with arrangements until we were happy. By now, Bruce understood the band, and was glad to help us get the guitar sounds we needed. For the first time, volume wasn't a problem. Henry "The Sunflower" Vestine from Canned Heat dropped in to listen and brought some weed. He loved what he was hearing, especially the blues.

We recorded versions of "Teenage Lust," "The Human Being Lawnmower," "Call Me Animal," and a free-improv blues song. These were the best quality, most creative recording sessions we had ever done, and it left me filled with confidence for the future. I just knew these recordings would blow our critics out of the water and guarantee that our following would grow exponentially. This was going to work.

The next day, Bruce was in a massive funk. His friend Jim Morrison was arrested in Miami for getting too wild onstage. The Doors, whose label was also Elektra, joined the MC5 as another band that pushed their behavior too far for the authorities.

I met a beautiful, red-haired young woman who was a complete freak and would have sex with one of us—or all of us—at the same time. A photo of us taken by Emil in the hotel bed with her ended up being published in the *Berkeley Barb*, which didn't go over too well with our wives and girlfriends back in Detroit. We were scheduled to fly to Florida for an appearance at the Fort Lauderdale Pop Festival when our agent in Detroit informed us that the state of Florida had issued a warrant for our arrests because of the "obscene photo" in the *Barb*. We decided that flying back to Detroit was the smarter move.

Things got heated with Elektra. There were two rating services that reported to all the national radio stations, the Gavin Report and the Drake Report. These newsletters picked the next hits for the stations, and both enthusiastically chose the MC5's single "Kick Out the Jams" as a monster hit—only to retract those picks the following week when Elektra rushed out the album. We had recorded a version of the song with "brothers and sisters" inserted into the intro instead of "motherfucker" for the radio single. We weren't stupid, we knew a song with "motherfucker" would never get played on the air. The rating services received reports of outraged parents hearing the obscenity-laden album version and calling radio stations to complain. There were even reports of record store clerks being arrested for "selling obscene materials." Their advice to the radio stations was to kill our record.

Our original marketing plan with the label was to wait until the single had peaked on all the charts and was dropping off, before releasing the LP. We reasoned that once the single was a bona fide hit, the impact of the album's revolutionary content would blast us past any restrictions and propel us into international recognition with optimal effect.

But that was not what happened. Elektra saw the single zooming up the U.S. charts that first week, and ignored our plan and rushed the LP release. When the rating services killed the record, Elektra called an emergency meeting. Jac Holzman and Danny Fields flew out to Ann Arbor, and John Sinclair and I met them at White Panther headquarters to sort it all out. Jac and Danny made the case that they were losing sales, and implored us to allow them to release a "clean" version of the album without the "motherfucker" and without John's liner notes. We vehemently objected, countering that that would make us complete sellouts, caving in to business interests over our art and message. Since our contract gave us final approval, we would not permit it. They seemed to acquiesce to our wishes, but returned to New York and did it anyway. Clearly their priority was selling records not our artistic vision. Danny backed our position, but was slapped in the face by Elektra art director Bill Harvey and then summarily fired for his trouble. As were we.

For a band with a #2 single in Detroit, one of America's larger radio markets as well as charting in New York, Chicago, and other major and secondary markets, and an album at #30 in the *Billboard* charts, we were in a good position to find a new home. We had prime stories in the *New York Times* and *Newsweek,* along with most of the underground press. We were on the cover of *Rolling Stone* with a five-page spread before we'd even released our first LP. We were the hot band of the moment.

Danny went to Atlantic Records and found immediate interest. Atlantic knew there was a larger potential market share in the new hard-rock movement than they had enjoyed as an R&B specialty label, and they saw the MC5 as the leaders of this new rock revolution. Not that they completely understood us. They commissioned Jon Landau to write them a report on the band's strengths and weaknesses to confirm their investment. Landau studied the band, and his report was insightful and knowledgeable. He recommended they sign the MC5.

We were given $50,000 upon signing—the largest cash advance ever paid to a new band at the time. Since we were in debt up to our eyeballs, the band members only received $1,000 each. I walked around for a few days with my chest puffed out proclaiming, "Don't mess with me, I'm a thousand-aire." The rest of the money went to our bills and a down payment on our band house in Hamburg, Michigan. Living together with all of John's people and the White Panthers in the house on Hill Street in Ann Arbor had become impractical. We needed our own space to live and work in.

We had met an accountant who attempted to bring our business affairs in order. He suggested that based on his economic predictions, we could each buy a car. My choice was a gorgeous 1963 Jaguar XKE 2+2 coupe. It had an aluminum 6-cylinder engine with a 10-to-1 compression ratio, dual-overhead cams, tri-power carbs, and 265 cu. at 260 hp. It was plum opalescent in color, and it was as beautiful a work of automobile engineering as the world has produced. I loved that car. It was the only real material thing I had ever got from my work in music. I had to borrow the down payment from my mother, and she co-signed my loan.

We continued working on our second LP, now for Atlantic Records. Pressure was building because Sinclair's reefer case was coming up for sentencing, and no one had a clue what might happen. He'd skated past it all for so long that I thought maybe he would find a loophole and beat this thing. He was facing a mandatory nine-and-a-half to ten years for his third conviction of possession of marijuana. That was the law.

On top of the legal pressure, we had to gear up for the next record. It was make-it-or-break-it time. John had been in discussions with all the stakeholders in our sphere, and he concluded that bringing in Landau to produce the album was the best move we could make. Danny was close with Jon, and after reading his ten-page report and talking with him at length, I liked him, too. I was impressed with his understanding of how rock worked from the inside out, and I appreciated his analysis of the MC5's strengths and weaknesses. He realized that the MC5 was the only group out there to really connect directly with the audience's concerns. We didn't pretend to be blues masters, and we weren't poseurs. We were the real thing, and our roots were deep in the rock & roll traditions of Little Richard and Chuck Berry where they needed to be, to create music that would resonate with young people. He also saw the deficiencies that we needed to address. He saw it all. We all agreed Landau was the man for the job.

The storm was threatening. John's lawyers felt the sentencing might not go our way. The reality of John being sent to state prison for a decade was almost too much to consider, but it became clear to me that it must be considered and considered seriously. I had never faced a crisis like this before. Everything I had worked to build was in danger of fracturing in a way I'd never anticipated. Landau and I talked and talked.

I decided, and the band agreed, that we would commit a percentage of the band's earnings to John's legal defense and his family, however they decided to allocate the money. This would be an ongoing commitment, with no end date. I knew that the MC5 would still have to pay for management from the balance of our earnings, but it was the right thing to do. I loved John, and wanted to do whatever I could to help. We needed to talk about the possibility. We needed to have a plan.

When we had the meeting, John reacted badly. We all sat around smoking reefer as usual, but finally we got around to the subject at hand and he reacted to our proposal with outrage and defensiveness. He acted as if we were cutting him out and tossing him to the wolves. I was flabbergasted. I was trying to help him, but he rejected our commitment out of hand, saying he was "never in it for the money; he was in it for the music." It was as if he was blaming his bust on me and the band, and then punishing us for trying to help. I was confused, and didn't know what else to do. We were trying to come up with a realistic plan for honoring our commitment to our friend and mentor, while taking into consideration our own possible future without him. Figures and percentages were thrown around without any resolution and he walked out of the meeting feeling resentful.

GOING TO PRISON is stressful; I know that now. John was dealing with more serious issues than my rock band. He was looking at losing his freedom for a long, long time. He had two little children, a wife, friends, and followers who depended on his being there. He was understandably angry with a legal system that had viciously conspired against him. Ten years in prison for two joints was unfair and unjust to a degree that is almost incomprehensible. All he ever wanted to do was live his life, smoke grass, and create the best art he could. At John's sentencing hearing in Detroit's Recorder's Court the anger and frustration exploded:

THE COURT: Do you have anything to say before the court imposes sentence?

DEFENDANT: I haven't had a chance to say anything so far, and I'd like to say a few things for the record. The Court is aware that these charges have been fabricated against me by the Detroit Narcotics Squad . . . I had no opportunity to construct a defense. But I know what was going on all along, and it was a conspiracy by these people, to frame me on this case, and to bring me right here . . . And everyone who is taking part of this is guilty of violating the United States Constitution and violating my rights . . . And to take me and put me in a pigsty like the Wayne County Jail for the weekend is a cruel and unusual punishment, to sleep on the floor, to have no sheets, no blankets, pig swill to eat . . . but you can get away with this and you can continue—I don't know what sentence you are going to give me, it's going to be ridiculous whatever it is. And I am going to continue to fight it. And the people are going to continue to fight it, because this isn't justice. There is nothing just about this, there is nothing just about these courts, nothing just about these vultures over here.

THE COURT: One more word out of the crowd and I will clear the courtroom.

DEFENDANT: Right. And that will continue in the tradition that's been established here.

On July 28, 1969, John Sinclair was sentenced to nine-and-a-half to ten years in prison, and remanded to the custody of the Michigan Department of Corrections. Our greatest fears were realized. After the judge sentenced John, he was physically removed from the courtroom to the outrage of all in the crowd.

John was furious, and his fury extended to me. His disappointment and frustration was intense, and he lashed out. I was close to him and caught some. I didn't create the conditions of his imprisonment and I didn't deserve his anger. I was angry at the system, too.

In one sense, John was made the scapegoat for his work with the MC5. For years there was an ongoing effort between police and prosecutors to "do something about Sinclair and the MC5." We could not be allowed to act the way we did at our shows: Telling kids to resist authority. Telling women to burn their bras. Inspiring young people to reject conformity; to smoke marijuana and have sex. This just could not be allowed to continue. Imprisoning our visionary leader and band manager was the most direct way they had to disrupt our efforts. John was crucified, not only for his own defiance, but for the MC5's, too.

A few days later, Fred Smith and I decided to meet with John's wife, Leni, to see if we could do anything to help her and her family. She met us out in front of the Hill Street house in Ann Arbor, where we had all lived together for a year or so before the MC5 moved into our own house in Hamburg.

We asked if she needed money, because we had brought some cash we'd gotten from our accountant for that purpose. She was adamant that they didn't need any money, and that they were all doing fine. We told her we were willing to play any benefit concerts necessary to raise additional funds for John's legal costs. She again said everything was under control, and we left feeling even more disconnected than before. We couldn't force her to accept our help, and she was clear that our help wasn't wanted.

IN THE FOLLOWING MONTHS, I tried to focus on preparing for the re-cording sessions for *Back in the USA*. We decided on the title be-cause it was a Chuck Berry favorite of ours; he wrote it after return-ing from serving 20 months in federal prison for violating the Mann Act. I appreciated him even more, knowing that. The recordings we'd made in Los Angeles with Bruce Botnick were the property of Elektra records, and they wouldn't allow us to use those masters. We did manage to regain the rights to the songs themselves, and to re-record them for the Atlantic album. Atlantic paid Elektra $10,000 for the rights against our future earnings.

We found a studio that fit our needs in East Detroit: GM Studios. The *G* and *M* stood for Guido Marasco, and the studio that he'd built was next to his auto body repair shop. Guido had done well in the body shop, and wanted to expand his empire into the recording studio business. The good news was that Guido's partner was a talented engineer, Jim Bruzzese. Jim was a former big band drummer with great technical skills in the studio. A knowledgeable musician, he was helpful on the music side of things, too. They only had a four-track machine, but they assured us that as soon as we paid the first studio bill, they were buying an eight-track recorder, and we'd be able to take advantage of the latest studio technology.

We rehearsed in the garage of the house in Hamburg. I refurbished it the same way I had the Artists Workshop space back in Detroit, and the Hill House in Ann Arbor. Landau would come out and listen and make suggestions. He and I would sit up in my bedroom and talk about music for hours on end. We talked about the MC5's problems and strong points. He was trying to get us to think for ourselves; to move past the groupthink that we were accustomed to. We talked through the band's challenges in great depth. There were issues that I'd never addressed because of our boundless camaraderie. There were a lot of unspoken rules to being a revolutionary. We went through a phase where watching television was discouraged; TV being part of pig culture. As musicians we enjoyed a wide latitude of acceptance and encouragement from each other, with no critical discussion. Ever. This was both good and bad. We would constantly tell each other what geniuses we were, and what bad motherfuckers we were on our instruments. Sinclair encouraged us, pumping us up in the liner notes for *Kick Out the Jams*: "The MC5 will bring you back to your senses . . . they are bad. Their whole lives are totally given to this music . . . The MC5 is the revolution, in all its applications . . . and what you have in your hands is a living testimonial to the absolute power and strength of these men."

Up to this point, hardly any disparaging words had ever been uttered to us. My ego was stroked and stroked into massive grandiosity.

Over the first couple of days in the studio recording *Back in the USA*, one of two major challenges we faced as a band was revealed. Michael was ill prepared for recording. He had never learned to play the bass within the traditional musical constructs of harmony, tempo, timing, and consistency. From the start, I had encouraged him to play whatever he felt. He had developed a style of playing that was almost completely without form. This can be a beautiful thing when the musician has done the work of study and rehearsal, and has performed thousands of hours onstage and in the studio. But that was not Michael's situation. His playing was completely idiosyncratic.

I'd actually never listened to his bass playing closely enough to hear that his timing was inconsistent, and his grasp of structure and technique was elusive at best. Michael was having trouble making the chord changes to elemental rock & roll songs like "Tutti Frutti" and "Back in the USA." Simple three-chord stuff. We had never had the time in the recording studio to take a close listen to everything, and now with so much at stake, we weren't grooving on what we were hearing.

In the MC5, the guitars carried the form and arrangement of the music. Fred and I had no trouble locking in together consistently night after night and playing the songs as written. We had been playing together for years by then, and we were very tight. Michael's playing developed within the safety net of our carrying the forms. If he missed a change or two, who cared? It made for erratic but sometimes inspired live performances. But in the naked light of the recording studio, it did matter. On top of that his playing was pushing and pulling Dennis off tempo.

Landau didn't have the constraints that we did. He was hired to produce a record, and he spoke up. We tried for a week, but between Michael's lack of musical discipline and the tempo problem, we decided to go back to the rehearsal room to find a solution.

We had to go out to Boston for three nights at the Ark, and while we were there we met again with Landau to discuss the work. Landau was very patient with us, and spent a lot of time building rapport with the band members. However, things finally blew up in a bar after one of the gigs when Dennis declared that he wasn't going to play any "fascist marching music." Landau stood his ground and told him he could play free jazz if he wanted to, but he had to play it correctly.

Landau forced me to see the reality of how the MC5 went about the business of creating music in light of the higher stakes that were now in play. He believed the band could be the greatest American hard-rock group of our time, but we needed to face our weaknesses and fix them.

We tried and tried, but the only way we could get the songs recorded properly was to deconstruct the process. This was a total change from the way we'd made music in the past. We always played live as a band—altogether. There are great advantages to this: the natural, overall feel of humans playing together. This is probably the most elusive and magical aspect of the recording process, and the hardest to achieve consistently.

Think of the Wrecking Crew in Los Angeles, or the Funk Brothers at Motown. These people played at the highest level of musicianship that the recording industry could produce. When they played together, the combined sounds from their great skills as musicians were irresistible. The magic was in the interaction of highly skilled players performing their parts with authority and inspiration. Many of the English bands were pretty good, too, but many of those records were augmented with top-line studio pros. Getting a bunch of stoned-out, maniac 20-year-olds to play at that level was asking a lot.

By recording the instruments one at a time, we were able to ensure the performances were on the money. To their credit, Dennis and Michael ultimately accepted this as a necessity.

I was driven to make a great record. It was paramount that this second MC5 record answer our detractors and prove to the world that we were a musical force to be reckoned with. I'd had misgivings about the first album, and had lobbied to re-record it to no avail. I knew we hadn't played as well as we could on that live record, but that was water under the bridge. Now it was time to show the world that we were a great band who could write terrific songs and play our asses off. Landau once said that he thought Fred and I should be referred to in the same way that Carlos Santana or Pete Townshend were. That we were every bit as good as our contemporaries, and better than most. I didn't disagree.

WE WERE INTRODUCED to a new technology for setting the tempo in the studio. Called a click track, it produced a clave-like click sound in your headphones on the quarter notes, and you could use it as a guide to stay on tempo. Dennis mastered the technique, and soon he was laying down the drum tracks with power and accuracy.

The bass playing was an insoluble problem. Landau suggested flying in Jerry Jemmott, one of the premier studio bassists of the day. But after long discussions, it was decided that we should keep everything in the band, and I would play the bass parts. Michael was disappointed.

I didn't mind playing the bass parts. I have always had a fondness for the bass, and I knew that the parts would be recorded correctly. I tried to just stick to the basic parts and not get too jazzy. But mostly, I wanted it to be correct.

The sessions proceeded through the summer with occasional road trips. We would pick up a case of beer and a fifth of Jack Daniels every night, and drink it on the ride home. By the time we finished, we had all gained fifteen pounds, but we were all pleased with the record. Tempos were solid, guitars were in tune and well played, melodies were correct, and the lyrics were first-rate. These songs were the best we had written yet.

But things were getting complicated for us. Since John's incarceration, we had no management. I tried to convince Landau to manage the MC5, but he was determined to be a record producer and I couldn't alter his decision. I also pushed Danny Fields to take over the MC5's management, but he, too, demurred. They both knew the band was unmanageable, and that the headaches involved wouldn't be worth it. Our problems with law enforcement didn't help, nor did our drinking and drugging.

I had written John in prison soon after his sentencing and tried to rebuild our broken relationship, but his response was not what I'd hoped. He was bitter and angry with me for "betraying him and the revolution."

John was now inhabiting a new world: a maximum-security state prison. This is a hard world, and he was looking at doing a lot of time. The militant rhetoric of the day was the language we all embraced, and John used it to fire on me and the MC5. His family and friends resented us. As far as they were concerned, we were rich rock stars without a care in the world. Life was not so rosy from my perspective.

He then began contacting the press from prison. He vilified the MC5 in interviews in the *Village Voice, Rolling Stone,* and *Creem* magazine. The animus he'd expressed at that last meeting at the MC5's Hamburg house ratcheted up to a new level.

JOHN DIDN'T DECIDE to be a marijuana martyr; circumstances thrust that upon him. The current laws were bad laws, and his sentence was—as the courts ultimately decided—"cruel and unusual" as well as unconstitutional. But why did he hold me and my band responsible? Or at the very least, use us as a surrogate enemy standing in for the state?

I have tried to understand what happened. Why did he reject me so fiercely? There had been tensions between us before this; we had differing perspectives on many issues, but nothing that would justify such an extreme overreaction.

In his letters to the press, he repeated his feeling that the MC5 had made a power grab for fame and wealth, and sold out both him and the revolution. His quote, "They wanted to be bigger than the Beatles, but I wanted them to be bigger than Chairman Mao," was brilliantly lacerating. John has always been a master communicator and genius with the poetry of language, and when he turned his immense skills against me, it hurt. The unity we'd shared, which was the basis of our strength, was shattered.

The MC5 played benefits and raised funds for his legal defense, but we could not keep up any regular payments. We were broke ourselves. The MC5 was left without a business structure to manage our financial affairs. We weren't touring while working on *Back in the USA*, and there was no money coming in. We had leased a band station wagon that was repossessed. We couldn't make the rent on our house. There was nothing to do but put my head down and move forward as best I could.

After long discussions with Fields and Landau on the subject of MC5 management, we finally settled on Dee Anthony as our manager. Not only did Danny and Jon highly recommend him, he was one of the most powerful men in the music business. Dee was the American service management for Chris Blackwell's Island Records artists. He handled Humble Pie, Stevie Winwood, Jethro Tull, Blind Faith, and a number of others. Along with Dee came Frank Barsalona at Premier Talent Agency, the dominant booking agency in rock at the time. I hoped these guys could work past the mistakes we'd made and rescue the MC5's career.

Dee came to Detroit to meet us while on tour with his new artist, Joe Cocker. Joe and the MC5 were riding the first wave of the enormous expansion of the record business into the new hippy culture. Joe was on the Mad Dogs & Englishmen tour, and Detroit was a big stop for touring acts. We met Dee and his attorney at a motel just up the street from Motown Records. We sat around the room and listened as Dee held court. He regaled us with tales of the old days when he managed Tony Bennett, and how they knew a great Italian lady in Chicago who would cook pasta for them and put it into mason jars so they could take it with them on the train, and how he and Tony would smoke reefer, get the munchies, and scarf pasta covered in marinara sauce all across the country.

After an hour or so of these thrilling tales of yesteryear, Joe Cocker showed up. We all greeted each other, and Dee kept yakking. Joe brought out a plastic baggie filled with green leafy stuff that I figured was reefer. Hooray! We rolled some joints and fired them up. Dee kept talking as we passed the joints around. I noticed that there was a funny smell to this weed, but in the excitement of meeting with our new big-time manager and a fellow musician, it was all cool.

Then things started getting weird. I was having trouble keeping my mind focused. Everybody's face started to look rubbery and distorted. The sound of Dee's voice became multi-harmonic. At one point he stopped midsentence, looked at his lawyer, and said, "What was I talking about?" The lawyer looked back and said, "I don't have the faintest idea." The room fell silent. Cocker's baggie wasn't marijuana; it was oregano laced with PCP, and we were all totally fucked up. When we smoked weed in the MC5, we smoked it all-out, balls to the wall. We never half-stepped about anything, especially getting high, and so we smoked way more of this shit than anyone in their right mind would have done. The room was underwater, and it was hard to navigate out the door.

Whoa, now I had to actually drive the car about 45 miles, all the way back to Ann Arbor. To this day, I'm not really sure how I did that.

Unfortunately, we quickly found out that Dee couldn't handle the MC5. It was a profound case of round pegs in square holes. He was truly old school, and me and my band were as antiestablishment and unruly as they came. We couldn't be good little entertainers even if we tried. We actually *were* unmanageable.

I once went to Dee for guidance on a complex professional problem I was facing: How should I respond to hardline leftist journalists' questions about our politics? In the past, Sinclair usually handled the more didactic interviews, but now he was out of the picture and I was left to handle it. Tyner was pretty good with the press, and Fred had his own way of responding, but I needed guidance on parsing our revolutionary ideals with the realities of a critical press. Dee's response was, "Never talk politics, and if they ask you about your money, tell them 'ooga-booga.'" But I needed something a little more nuanced. I wasn't asking for an analysis of Marxist economic class reductionism; a simple response to tough interview questions would have been fine. We were clearly on completely different planets. I mean, we were an overtly political band, and he told me not to talk about politics. Ooga-booga!

Tax time came, and our accountant said that we had no money. Fred and I paid our own way to New York to meet with Dee and Atlantic to try and find a solution. We needed another cash advance to pay our bills. The daily expense of running the band and our time off the road had reduced us to poverty. We were slipping under, and needed financial help to function. It wasn't like we were blowing our money on cocaine and nightclubbing; even the cars we bought had to have the loans underwritten by our parents, and now we couldn't make the payments.

When we called Dee's office, they told us he was in meetings all day and couldn't see us. We went over to his office and camped out in the waiting room, only to have him sneak out a back stairwell down to his apartment on the floor below.

We didn't have any money for a hotel, so we went back to the airport and slept there. We came back into the city the next day to meet with Atlantic. Ahmet Ertegun finally saw us, and I explained our economic crisis. He responded by telling me, "Wayne, in the music business we have a concept called sending good money after bad, and we're not going to advance any more cash to the MC5." Then his phone rang and he swiveled around in his chair. With his back to us, he began speaking on the phone in French. Fred and I stood there with our dicks in our hands.

Before we knew it, Dee had gone to the National Labor Relations Board and filed a motion to dissolve our management agreement and to collect all his expenses and commissions. So, there we were. No agent, no manager, no money, and a record label that had given up on us. Atlantic didn't understand the MC5 any better than they understood any of the other rock bands they signed. But the MC5 was far more trouble than all the others. Jerry Wexler was about to retire, and signing the MC5 had been his parting shot to the industry. Here you go boys, have fun with these crazy motherfuckers.

Back in the USA didn't do very well in the charts, only making it to #137 in *Billboard*. What I wanted to accomplish by making a perfect record didn't translate to sales. The scandal surrounding Sinclair's imprisonment and the subsequent controversy in the press severed us from our hard-core Detroit fan base. They didn't hate the record, but they didn't love it either. I overshot the mark, and the record suffered from a lack of high-energy exuberance that *Kick Out the Jams* had in abundance. It was too tight, too clean, too controlled, and it confused music fans that had dozens of newer bands to choose from.

As the recording and touring business grew exponentially through the 1970s, the MC5 was out of sync with the popular trends. This was the era of touring bands doing 20-minute drum solos and 15-minute blues guitar solos. The hits on the radio were "Bridge Over Troubled Water," "Joy to the World," "Maggie May," and "Take Me Home, Country Roads." Our new record had terse, pithy, smart-assed three-minute songs like "Teenage Lust," "The American Ruse," "The Human Being Lawnmower," and Chuck Berry and Little Richard covers—two artists as unfashionable as possible in 1970.

But *Back in the USA* caught on in England because Atlantic Records had an active promotional office in London. They even organized a record release press party that I was thrown out of for getting out of hand with my drunken British friends, Mick Farren and some London Hell's Angels. This record was exactly what the punks were looking for; it was sharp and to the point, with short songs and a sarcastic perspective. The record was a rejection of the grandiose, overindulgent, superstar rock culture of the sixties.

Decades later, I thought about why British punk musicians didn't embrace *Kick Out the Jams*. The main reason was that there was no promotion from Elektra in the United Kingdom at all. None. And being released in 1969, it preceded the UK punk movement by a few years. It was a little too early for them.

I once asked Nick Lowe if he had any material for a new album I was recording. He told me, "I stole everything from you, Wayne." That was flattering, but it may have also been a gracious way to not give me a song. The Clash and the Damned both told me that *Back in the USA* was hugely influential for them, as did many others.

In the midst of all this, the Federal Grand Jury in Detroit handed down indictments for White Panthers John Sinclair, Lawrence "Pun" Plamondon, and Jack Forrest for conspiracy to destroy government property—the bombing of the covert CIA recruiting office in Ann Arbor in the fall of 1968. John was already in state prison, and Pun and Jack had gone underground.

CHAPTER 14

HIGH TIME

In 1970, a jury found the Chicago Seven defendants not guilty of conspiring to incite a riot at the Chicago Democratic Convention disturbance we played at two years earlier. The MC5 was the only band to go to Chicago and perform for the demonstrators. Apollo 13 lifted off for an ill-fated attempt to go to the moon. Four students were killed and nine wounded at Kent State. And Jimi Hendrix and Janis Joplin both died at 27.

I was out on tour, and had just checked into my hotel when the Hendrix news hit the TV. I was stunned. Hendrix was a great artist with an unlimited future and the potential to be part of the bridge between free jazz and rock. His loss was, to me, as great as the premature deaths of John Coltrane and Albert Ayler. Just 16 days later I was back on the road listening to the radio when we heard about Joplin. Even though I had had the one experience with her back in California, the Hendrix death hit me much harder. We had opened for the Jimi Hendrix Experience in Detroit on his second U.S. tour, and we loved him. I admit I had been jealous; we were doing similar things with the guitar, but he did it better.

In the winter of 1971, the MC5 was booked for a series of shows at several venues in New England, along with Mitch Ryder & Detroit, Teegarden & Van Winkle with Bob Seger, and Brownsville Station. Michael and I were really abusing alcohol and opiates. On one of the gigs, Brownsville leader Cub Koda offered to take over for bass player Michael Davis, who was clearly too stoned to play. "I know the tunes; I can do it!" he hollered into my ear between songs.

Performing hammered doesn't give you the feeling that you did a good job that night, and it was happening more and more often. This led to a phase where my goal for the night wasn't to go out there and destroy the audience; light a fire under them and rock them like they've never been rocked before. The goal became just getting through the gig and getting loaded right after (and during). This was a major turn for the worse for me. All the ambition and work that went into establishing myself and the MC5 was somehow not important. Blotting out the daily pain of having everything fall apart around me became my mission. I used narcotics when I was home in Detroit, and often suffered withdrawal sickness when I ran out of money. Opiate withdrawal is miserable. It's comparable to the worst flu you could imagine. You're chilled while sweating. You're nauseous and can't eat. And along with diarrhea, you can't sleep. The good news is, it only lasts for three or four days. I've done it more times than I care to remember. It doesn't kill you as alcohol or barbiturate withdrawal can, but it's no picnic either. On tour, I mostly drank.

Recording the MC5's final major label album took place between fall of 1970 and spring of 1971. We started writing the material with the new understanding that each writer or writers would be given their own individual songwriting credits. We still didn't understand publishing, but we all agreed that if you wrote the song, you should be the acknowledged composer. We had operated on the one-for-all-and–all-for-one basis on the last two records, but those of us who were doing the writing began to resent band members who were not doing the work, but still getting equal credit. Everyone agreed that this would be fairer.

I worked on my songs, as did the others. As they came together, we had rehearsals to arrange and perfect the performances. These were good times for me in the MC5. Creating new material is always the most exciting and fulfilling thing that happens in bands.

We rehearsed in a very funky studio in Ypsilanti called Head Sound. Just east of Ann Arbor, it was a good middle location between those of us who still lived in Ann Arbor and the others in Detroit. We called it "Ypsi-tucky" because of its large southern population.

I had been reading William Burroughs's *Junky* and a few other books on the subject, and wanted to try heroin. I knew Dennis and Michael were both using, and I asked Michael to pick me up a bag next time he copped. He brought it to our next rehearsal. That night I was home alone. I put on a John Lee Hooker record, which seemed like the right music, and snorted some. When the record ended, I realized I'd never felt better. It wasn't as if bells and fireworks went off and a new world was revealed to me. I just thought this stuff was pretty damn good. In the beginning, I did it on the weekends as a party activity. Slowly I graduated to Wednesdays (the first Friday of the week), and ultimately to "I'm awake, let's get high."

The MC5's last two records had been so stressful that Fred and I decided we knew enough about the process now that we could produce the record ourselves. That was our plan. Atlantic Records didn't quite see it that way, and insisted on someone from the company co-producing it with us. We reluctantly agreed, and started meeting people they recommended.

The first fellow who came out dismayed me when he insisted on discussing his sexual perversions with his girlfriend. He brought Polaroid photos. Not that I have anything against perversions between consenting adults; it just wasn't what I was looking for in a record producer. There were a couple more nonstarters, and then Geoffrey Haslam showed up.

I liked Geoffrey immediately. He was a musician himself, having been in the English band The Undertakers. He was low-key and comfortable, gently guiding us with encouragement. We'd write a few more songs, and he would come out to attend rehearsals. Over the months, song by song, the record took shape.

In July 1970, we traveled to the United Kingdom for the first time to perform at the Phun City Festival in Worthing. The day before our departure, we performed outside to a huge crowd at Wayne State University, which was a triumphant live moment for us as a group. Leaving for the United Kingdom the following morning seemed like a dream come true.

Having come of age during the first wave of the British invasion, one of my goals was to play in England. I had great confidence in the MC5, and knew we had a stage performance that outclassed and outworked almost every band touring at the time. I was extremely excited driving down to the site in Worthing, southwest of London. When we pulled up to the gate, our driver lowered his window and said to the gatekeeper, in the most highbrow English accent, "Artists, artists." We cracked up and began calling ourselves "artists" in a mockery of the British tongue.

The site was actually a giant muddy field in the middle of no-where. William Burroughs was scheduled to read, and Free and other more political English bands were on the bill. Apparently, the organizers were so lax that no money was being collected at the gate, and payment was not likely. Free turned their limo around and went home without stepping in the mud. But I wanted to play, and play we did. We rocked hard. I pulled out every stage move in my arsenal; I jumped, I danced, I spun, and everyone in the band did the same. I wanted to show the British how it was done. We won everyone over, and the event was a great success from a performance perspective.

The other aspects didn't turn out so well. A TV crew was there filming, but there were technical problems and they didn't get the audio. Then when it was time to get paid, I ran down our liaison, Mick Farren, who was wearing a wizard's pointy hat. He informed me that, as I expected, this was now a free festival and there was no money. Normally this would have generated a strong-arm response, but I was so happy with our performance that I dropped it. Farren offered to help us book some gigs when we all got back to London in the coming days, and he did. It was the beginning of my lifelong friendship with Mick Farren.

The day after the festival, we started recording our new album.

Atlantic set up the sessions at Lansdowne Studios in Notting Hill Gate. We had rehearsed Fred's new tune, "Sister Anne," back in Ypsilanti, and were ready to record. It was going to be a complex process because Fred had distinct ideas about what he wanted to include in the recording. For example, a jazz trumpet solo over a Salvation Army street corner brass band, playing an original melody he had composed for the coda of the track. Fred was in his most creative period during this record. At Lansdowne, we were just concerned with getting the basic band track recorded properly.

Michael Davis didn't like the bass he had for the session. Chris Squire from Yes, who just happened to be in the control room listening, offered to run home and get one of his Rickenbacker basses. Chris was a genial cat, and his bass came in handy that day. We hired a local session pianist, Pete Kelly, because Fred wanted a Johnnie Johnson/Jerry Lee Lewis/Little Richard–style piano on the track. We got it recorded and did some overdubs in a day, and left the studio pumped up about how good it sounded. We were making a cool record, and our flagging confidence level shot way up.

BACK IN DETROIT, in January of 1971, the first hearing was held on the White Panther bombing case. In Judge Damon Keith's District Court for the Eastern District of Michigan, John Mitchell's Justice Department attorneys refused to produce the wiretap logs or warrant authorizing a tap on our phones, where they allegedly heard discussions about procuring the dynamite used in the bombing of the secret CIA office in Ann Arbor, Michigan. The government claimed that because their actions were a matter of "domestic security," they were not required to have a warrant. This untested legal premise basically holds that if the government decides to do something that's extra-legal in the name of domestic security, it's permissible because they declare it to be so. Judge Keith disagreed, and dismissed the charges.

THE MC5 RETURNED from Europe to Detroit, and we settled on Artie Fields Productions to finish recording *High Time*. The studio was located in the old Alhambra Theatre just north of downtown on Woodward Avenue. The facility was mainly an in-house studio for Artie's commercial production music. A lot of Detroit radio and TV commercial voiceovers and music was recorded there in the 1970s. "Whatcha See Is Whatcha Get" by the Dramatics, *America Eats Its Young* by Funkadelic, and *Pleasure* by the Ohio Players were all cut there, too. The good news about the studio was that it featured a state-of-the-art 16-track recording machine and board. The place was big enough that we wouldn't have any trouble playing as loud as we needed in order to make it sound like us.

The old concerns over Michael's bass playing needed addressing. The rest of us determined that if we were recording a song and each of us was sure where we were in the arrangement, and Michael missed a chord change, we would just keep on playing and complete the take. We now had the benefit of the new recording technique of "punching in." In other words, Michael could make mistakes and after the take, he could go back and punch in repairs. Voilà. That took a lot of pressure off all of us. With repairs, his bass playing turned out pretty good. Everybody else was in top form for the sessions.

I'd drive down to Detroit in my Jaguar, and we'd work all afternoon and into the night. We had enough excellent new material, and good ideas for how to go about recording it. We finally had enough experience to know how to be creative in the recording studio. We could now combine the raw energy of *Kick Out the Jams* with the studio chops of *Back in the USA*, and have it sound like the MC5 on record. The sessions went smoothly.

Which isn't to say there was no funky behavior going on. My drug use remained a problem, and added a layer of complexity to everything I tried to do. I had an on-again, off-again heroin habit.

Fred used on occasion, but his drug of choice was alcohol, as was Tyner's. Michael's heroin use was full-on, and he and his girlfriend were dealing to maintain their habits. They were small-time by professional drug dealer standards, but it gave them all they needed and a little more. Plus, I could cop from them without difficulty, which made my hustling a little easier.

Michael knew a connection right around the corner from the studio. Naturally I went with him a few times to cop. The spot was an afterhours joint in the basement of a private residence. The dope was sold in three-penny caps, which were small capsules of "mixed-jive" dope: heroin cut with quinine to improve the rush. It was only for shooting; if you snorted this stuff, the quinine would burn your nose. Since I had not yet graduated to injecting, I snorted it anyway and endured the discomfort until the drug kicked in.

We had a good idea for a crazed jungle drum intro to "Skunk (Sonically Speaking)," so we invited Bob Seger, Scott Morgan, and a handful of other local players in to help. We had all been friends for years, going back to the record hop era in Detroit. It was a big city but a small rock community, and everybody knew everybody. Our idea was that they would all wail on the drums and percussion instruments to raise holy hell. We wanted an uncontrolled, high-energy blast to lead into Fred's guitar intro. Trouble set in almost immediately, as the guys had no frame of reference for what we wanted them to do. They kept playing grooves and beats, so after a few takes, we thanked them for doing a great job and they left. We did it ourselves in one take. We were crazy, and had crazy ideas to match.

I came into the studio late one session as the guys were recording Tyner's vocal on "Over and Over." They were pushing him to sing it full-voice, but the song was written in the key of A, which made for a great open-stringed guitar sound but was almost impossible to sing the melody in. It was way too high. Finally, Tyner muscled it up and cut the vocal, and came in the control room to listen. His judgment was that he sounded like "rough trade from Venus." We cracked up, and that expression entered our lexicon forever. He did nail that vocal, though.

When we set up to record the horn section of "Skunk," we brought in our friend, trumpeter Charles Moore. Charles had written horn arrangements for us in the past when we did special events with horns, and we all had been friends for years. He co-led the Contemporary Jazz Quintet with pianist Kenny Cox, and was as fierce an advocate for the new free music as we were. Charles brought tenor great Joe Henderson's equally talented younger brother Leon in on alto, Dan Bullock on trombone, and Rick Ferretti on trumpet.

Charles had written an excellent chart, and was out in the studio running the parts down with the cats. The engineer and I were alone in the control room. "Look, Wayne," he said conspiratorially, "I hear what you guys are going for, but these guys aren't cutting it. They're playing the wrong notes. I could bring in some union guys after the session to play this stuff right, in one take." This was amusing; another know-it-all technician.

The engineer was old school, and couldn't hear what Charles had written. The parts weren't traditional harmony; they were written to be dissonant. We wanted biting, extended chords, and that was exactly what we were getting from the musicians. Charles and the guys played brilliantly, and the recorded music is some of the best work we ever did as a band. The combination of hard, rhythmic guitar rock and complex, stretched-out horn section harmonics bridged the gap between rock and jazz, and brought a new music into play. This was what we were talking about: the new music.

I thanked the engineer for the suggestion and went back to work. The track came out marvelously, and it was that performance that pointed the direction for the future of the MC5.

In December of that year, the John Sinclair Freedom Rally was held at University of Michigan's Crisler Arena in Ann Arbor. I heard that the event was being planned, and tried to secure the MC5 a spot on the bill. It would be the right thing for us to play, but John's brother Dave didn't think so. He resented me from our falling-out with John, and wouldn't even meet with me or take my phone calls. Stevie Wonder, Bob Seger, Archie Shepp, Phil Ochs, and John Lennon and Yoko Ono headlined the musical side, with Bobby Seale,

Jerry Rubin, Allen Ginsberg, The Fugs' Ed Sanders, and others speaking. It was a cross section of the MC5's musical and political community, and the fact that we were locked out pissed me off. I tried as hard as I could to make it happen, but there was no reasoning with Dave Sinclair.

The day before the concert, the Michigan State Senate voted to remove marijuana from the state's penal code and reconsider all existing convictions. Three days after the concert, on December 13, 1971, John was freed from prison when the Michigan Supreme Court, on its own motion, ordered his release. Three months later, the court reversed his conviction after finding the state's marijuana statutes to be unconstitutional.

John was released from Jackson State Prison and had a joyful reunion with his wife and children that was carried live on local Detroit TV. He settled back into life in Ann Arbor with the former White Panthers, newly renamed the Rainbow People's Party. A month or so later, I stopped in to see him one night and he was happy to see me. He seemed to be his old self. He was genial, smoking a joint, and listening to jazz. It was nice to feel welcome in his company again. Our friendship had survived the stress and strain of his prison term, and I was happy about that. I had been frustrated with him and hurt, but I never resented his anger. It happened, and now it was past.

He told me about the federal government dropping the bombing charges against Pun, Jack, and him after the Justice Department refused to disclose the wiretap logs, and admitted that they had no warrant for wiretapping our phone. We were both relieved to have that behind us. Unfortunately, the Justice Department soon appealed the decision, which meant there would be more trials ahead.

CHAPTER 15

WHITE PANTHER JUSTICE

We knew we were being wiretapped back in 1968. I heard the clicking and buzzing on our phones all the time. It was part and parcel of the constant harassment we were getting from law enforcement. Police cars would park in front of our house in the middle of the night and shine their spotlights in our windows and crank their sirens up, then drive away.

This harassment was a result of J. Edgar Hoover and John Mitchell's Operation COINTELPRO, a secret FBI program to disrupt and subdue domestic dissent. They targeted organizations that stood in opposition to government actions and policies: the civil rights movement, the Anti-Vietnam War movement, the Black Panther Party, the Weather Underground, and every other group that opposed the powers that be, including us. They used dirty tricks. The FBI developed and distributed disinformation that fomented deadly rivalries between Black Panther Party members and others. They spread rumors of Dr. Martin Luther King's infidelities, along with those of many other prominent civil rights leaders.

They set agents provocateur on us. A guy showed up at our house in 1968, with an implausible story about wanting to "join up." I told him we weren't recruiting. Another time it was a woman.

I was paranoid as hell and suspicious of strangers. The acid didn't help.

When the Mitchell Justice Department appealed Judge Keith's ruling, the case was sent up to the Sixth Circuit Court of Appeals, which agreed with Judge Keith's conclusion. The government then appealed this decision to the U.S. Supreme Court: *United States vs. U.S. District Court*, 407 U.S. 297 (1972).

The White Panthers' attorney at the Supreme Court was the legendary civil rights and labor lawyer Arthur Kinoy. Kinoy was cofounder, with William Kunstler, of the Center for Constitutional Rights in New York and was a professor of constitutional law at Rutgers. In the fifties, Kinoy represented people being investigated by the House Un-American Activities Committee, and was once bodily removed from a congressional hearing after strongly disagreeing with a senator.

Kinoy's defense rested on the Constitution's Fourth Amendment, which provides "The right of the people to be secure in their persons, houses, papers, and effects, against unreasonable searches and seizures, shall not be violated, and no Warrants shall issue, but upon probable cause, supported by Oath or affirmation, and particularly describing the place to be searched, and the persons or things to be seized."

IN FEBRUARY OF 1972, in front of the Supreme Court of the United States, the government again argued that they didn't need to produce a warrant, as this was a matter of national security. As an illustration of this faulty legal reasoning, Kinoy contended that "for example, a sitting president could wiretap his political rival's offices, and call it 'national security.'" Later that evening after court, Kinoy reflected that perhaps he "went too far" with that example—never once suspecting what would happen later that year just up the street.

On Saturday, June 17, 1972, at the Watergate office of the Democratic Party, five burglars were arrested while removing surveillance equipment surreptitiously installed in that office. Two days later, on Monday, June 19, the Court handed down their verdict in favor of the White Panthers. The decision would be the new law of the land, and those unwarranted wiretaps would be illegal.

Our White Panther illegal wiretapping case was the spark that led directly to the resignation of Richard M. Nixon and prison terms for most of his gang. Rather than reveal the scope and details of their illegal operations, the government decided to withdraw cases grounded in illegal wiretaps against the Black Panther Party, the Weathermen, and various antiwar, civil rights, and other organizations across the country that were caught up in Operation COINTELPRO.

Since we were a small group of poets and revolutionaries and a rock & roll band, the government believed we'd be the easiest to railroad, thereby setting a precedent to crush all domestic dissent. After all, we weren't the Beatles or the Rolling Stones with millions of fans, or the antiwar or civil rights movements with the grassroots support of the nation. But we did have the U.S. Constitution, which provided protections from the overreach of a policeman, a prosecutor, or a president, and demonstrated that we are a nation of laws, not men. And for that one bright and shining moment, justice prevailed.

CHAPTER 16

LAST LEGS

We had burned so many promoters by being late that the MC5 could not tour enough to survive. Our drinking and drugging, combined with no management, resulted in us arriving late for concerts so often that word was, don't book them. When you're an active drug user, securing your drugs is a top priority. Leaving town in time to make the gig was secondary. Too many times we would pull into the parking lot just as the kids were leaving. "Hey man, what's happening here?" we'd ask. "The fucking MC5 was supposed to play, but they didn't show up." It was embarrassing and discouraging when it happened again and again and again.

The Phun City gig in England had sparked interest in the band in Europe. I met an agent who was willing to book a tour, and the dates started coming in.

We met Ronan O'Rahilly in London. Ronan had founded Radio Caroline, a pirate radio station, by outfitting a ship with radio transmitting gear and broadcasting unrestricted pop music to England from international waters. He was something of a legend, and he loved the MC5. It was Ronan's film crew that had shot the Phun City show. Ronan had a great partner in "Big Jim" Houlihan. I adored this guy. He was a hard-drinking, fun-loving giant of a fellow who had once sparred with Muhammad Ali. We became the dynamic duo of Bayswater, drinking and carousing all over London.

When we flew over to England to begin the next tour, Michael missed the flight. He was making more money dealing than the tour was paying, and he showed up a few days later. We had already played a couple of shows with a fill-in bassist.

Steev Moorhouse and Fred Smith had been pen pals for years, and when it turned out he was a working bass player and was available, we drafted him into the band.

Michael's playing and getting too high on the gig had been an ongoing irritation for Fred and me. I decided we needed to force Michael to shape up or leave the band. We had the meeting in my hotel room, where I asked Michael to convince us why he should remain in the band. He offered no arguments in his favor, and returned to Detroit.

I held out hope that with Ronan, we could resurrect the MC5. Steev was a solid player and would have been a fine replacement, but he had his own band and wanted to stick with them. We were in Germany when he had to leave our tour. I saw an ad on a bulletin board for an English bass player looking for work. I called Derek Hughes and he sounded competent, so he played bass for the rest of the tour.

Back in London, Ronan had us working on a musical score for his indie film *Gold*. The film was awful, but I didn't care because I liked the challenge of writing music for film. It was just the four of us, Fred, Dennis, Rob, and me. I played bass and piano on the session, and we came up with some of the most progressive music we'd ever made. We had also recorded some music for the score of the Living Theater's production of *Paradise Now* earlier in the year in New York City. I liked the process.

Ronan also got us booked on the first London Rock and Roll revival at Wembley Stadium. The lineup was stellar: Bill Haley & His Comets, Bo Diddley, Jerry Lee Lewis, Little Richard, and Chuck Berry, along with contemporary British acts like Screaming Lord Sutch, The Houseshakers, Joe Brown, Heinz Burt (with Wilko Johnson on guitar), Billy Fury, Roy Wood's Wizzard, Gary Glitter, and others.

We had been working all week with Ronan's friend Michael Joseph. Michael was an acting teacher who pioneered a new training technique using psychodrama. His goal was to teach us how to conjure up our emotions when we needed them in performance. We had been rethinking everything, trying to jump-start our career in Europe. I had decided that my long hair had lost its value as a statement, so I cut it all off. We were trying out various new ideas about how we looked onstage, and Fred was ready to debut his "Sonic Smith" superhero suit.

On gig day, I painted my skin with gold stage makeup and wore a black suit and sunglasses. Tyner bouffed his Afro out bigger than normal and filled it with glitter. Derek and Dennis looked relatively normal except for some face paint. Fred had transformed into "Sonic Smith." When we ran out onstage, there was a collective groan from the 60,000 Teddy Boys filling Wembley. We started rocking, and it wasn't going too badly when Tyner made the most strategic blunder in the annals of rock history. A beer can came flying in from the crowd, and he picked it up and threw it back. That simple act galvanized every one of those rockabilly fans. It was us versus them, and there was way more of them. Beer cans literally rained down on us.

If we had gone onstage in our street clothes, black leather jackets, Levis, and boots, they might have loved us. We were certainly rocking hard enough, but once they decided we were "rough trade from Venus," it was all over.

I HAD DEVELOPED FRIENDSHIPS in Ladbroke Grove through Mick Farren. I had a girlfriend there, and became friendly with members of the London Hells Angels. I cultivated a drug operation with one who had access to large quantities of Mandrax, the English equivalent of Quaalude. I had friends over from Detroit, and between us we did some business. Dennis had made a heroin connection, and he and I started copping. Later we discovered Gerrard Street in Chinatown, where you would seek out the best-dressed Asian man hanging out in a doorway and he'd usually provide what you needed.

The drug use was covert, but the bad behavior persisted. Ronan rented us a band house out in Dollis Hill. After a night's drinking, Fred and Dennis developed the habit of helping themselves to bottles of milk from people's milk boxes. On the third night returning from the pub, they were arrested. This was a serious offense in Britain. The judge admonished them that they were taking food from babies' mouths. That people in England had suffered through the great wars, and respected each other's property. They got off with a fine.

Ronan convinced a European label to sign us. The deal was agreed in principle, but they wanted to see us perform live before making the final decision. We were booked to play a festival in Belgium, and that was where we'd show them what we could do. We had already popped the champagne and lit the cigars.

As the evening wore on, the schedule ran later and later. Since the MC5 was one of the headliners, our showtime was pushed back further and further. My involvement in the Mandrax business meant I had plenty of these little pills with me, and Tyner and I took a couple early on in the evening. As time went on, we took more, and then more. When we finally hit the stage at around 7:00 AM, we were so fucked up we could hardly function. I couldn't feel my fingers on the guitar strings. Tyner was dancing clumsily all over the stage, and went to jump from the stage to a riser about five feet out. He misjudged the distance and fell down between them. We were unbelievably terrible, and the label deal disappeared.

Back in Detroit, the search for a permanent bassist was on. I was friendly with a good player named Ray Craig and he would have been a good fit, but Fred wanted to hold out for just the right guy. I was also friendly with Tony Newton, a first-call Motown session and road player, and asked him if he was interested. But he wanted to start his own group, The Eighth Day. He recommended his cousin, Charles Solomon.

Charles was, in my opinion, the perfect man for the MC5. In his midtwenties, he was a beautiful black man who dressed impeccably and could sing his ass off. He played bass in the James Jamerson style, but with rock power. For me, having a black man in the MC5 was a confirmation of everything we stood for as a band. And, as young Americans fighting the racist power structure, it would send a powerful message to the world that we were unified Detroiters.

Rob and Dennis were all for him, and I had never heard Dennis play as well as he did with Charles. But Fred rejected him, saying that he didn't think Charles had enough experience to be in a band of our stature. Rob and Dennis acquiesced to Fred's decision, and for me that was the straw that broke the camel's back.

After that, I couldn't mount the necessary enthusiasm to go into battle again for this band. I had made new friends in the musician community in Detroit, and there were other people I could see myself playing with, with whom I could enjoy the work and have fun playing music again. I wanted to play funk and free jazz and do cover tunes, and just be a musician.

Now I didn't care who played bass in the MC5. Derek Hughes did the next European tour, and I drank and drugged my way across the continent. I found a copy of Hunter S. Thompson's *Fear and Loathing in Las Vegas* in a train station, and it became the guidebook for my consumption of everything I could get my hands on.

In the fall of 1972, one last tour of Europe was booked; our sixth or seventh trip. Six weeks in length. Good gigs: two weeks in Italy, TV in Scandinavia. Finally, we would be paid decent money. It was at this point that Rob Tyner decided to finally quit the group. I agreed with him because I knew he wasn't happy being in the MC5. I was content to let him go. After all, if the guy doesn't want to be in the band, why force him to stay? I knew we could hire another singer; maybe it would even improve the band.

I reasoned that if we did this tour, we would all have some cash to tide us over till we figured out what to do next. When Dennis heard that Tyner quit, he decided that he needed to stay home and detox. I suggested that he continue using for the tour and then do what he had to do after, but he had made his decision. He had also been busted embezzling from the band, and just had no heart left for it.

Fred went over to Rob's house to persuade him to do the tour, and naturally it degenerated into a fistfight. I made an attempt the following night to reason with Rob, but he was ready to go to war with me with a golf club. He had made up his mind, and that was that. I got the message.

Rob had been quitting the MC5 every year for the last few years. In the beginning, we would hold these marathon fish-bowling sessions with him where he would attempt to convince us why he should leave, and we would quadruple-team him to stay. After the second go-round of this, I said I wouldn't do it anymore. These brainwashing sessions were ugly. We would just tear him apart. True, I had been critical of him over the years for not living up to my impossible standards of what a lead singer should be, but Rob was a mercurial artist. Sometimes he would follow his feelings onstage and say or do the exact wrong thing, and I would jump on him for it. He was a tremendously talented man in an untenable situation, and he wanted out.

Life in the MC5 had ceased to be a rewarding experience for him a long time ago. Rob had a family, and other things he wanted to do. So, when he quit again this time, I had no objection except that he should honor his final touring commitments. He did not. "The center cannot hold."

Fred and I went alone to Europe for the tour, and tried to salvage what we could of our professional reputations. We would have been better off staying in Detroit. We met Ritchie Dharma, the drummer Ronan had hired, in the dressing room of the first gig.

"You any good?" I asked him.

"You'll find out," he said.

He was, but we weren't.

The tour was a disaster. Dates canceled one after the other. The two weeks of Italian dates canceled. Everybody was angry and disappointed in us. And onstage, we sucked. There were no rehearsals, so we had to come up with material that we could play that everybody might already know. Singing MC5 songs was almost completely out of the question. Neither Fred nor I had ever attempted to sing these songs, and had no idea how to go about it. We didn't actually even know the lyrics to some of them. The material we played was simple three- or four-chord vamps with extended solos. We just tried as best we could to play for the contracted amount of time, to ensure we'd get paid. The performances had almost nothing to do with the MC5. We were a terrible representation of our former powerful stage show. Fred and I would have long talks in our hotel room, in which we tried to envision a future band with new players. We put on a brave face, but it was over. Hope is a great breakfast, but a lousy dinner.

THERE I WAS back in Detroit, a complete failure at 24. I had gone from truly unbelievable highs to pathetic and inconceivable lows in just four short years.

Tyner had quit, Thompson had quit, Davis was long gone, and there was nothing left to build on. I didn't know any of this consciously. I believed I had everything under control. I was on top of it. Right on. But I was reeling from uncontrolled anxiety and fear. I was disconnected from who I was, and I didn't know what would become of me. I sought shelter in any powder or potion that would slow things down and kill the pain for a little while. There were plenty to choose from, and I jumped into it with both feet.

An offer came in to play New Year's Eve 1972 at the Grande Ballroom. We all agreed to do it, including Rob and Michael. I was beyond broke, and my dope habit was in full effect. The offer was for $500. Short as it was, I needed the money. We started out at the Grande making $125 a night, and had soared to a high of almost ten thousand at our peak. Now we were playing for 500 bucks. On New Year's Eve.

There was no contact with each other before the gig. At the appointed time, we took the stage and tried to be the MC5. It wasn't working. The tempos were all over the map. I had no idea what Michael was playing. Rob was doing the best he could to front this mess, and Fred and I just looked at each other in dismay. My memories of the night are all in black and white. Near the end of the set, I was overcome with sadness and went over to Fred. "I can't take it anymore. I have to leave."

He nodded in understanding, and I walked off the stage.

PART 2

Falling into ruin was a bit like falling in love: Both
descents stripped you bare and left you as you were
at your core. And both endings are equally painful.

–J. R. WARD, *Lover Unbound*

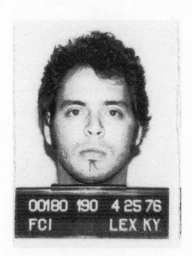

CHAPTER 17

SMALL-TIME DETROIT CRIMINAL

After the MC5 broke up at the end of 1972, I was desperate.

My girlfriend Eve and I rented a cute little house in Ann Arbor. It was across the street from the University of Michigan Stadium, and on Sundays during college football season, the entire neighborhood would literally rumble with the tumult. It was like a minor earthquake every time the team scored. Eve furnished the house with nice pieces she got from her family. We had great oriental rugs, antique tables and chairs, frilly lace curtains, nice dishes and silverware. She really tried to make a home for us, but I was still touring most of the time. When I was home, I was an active drug addict, so our life was anything but nice and normal.

At this point, I was out on tour and there was no money coming in. Eve couldn't pay the rent and moved out of our house. She stayed with one of her sisters until I returned. We began floating to various friends' places, finally moving in with one of my roadies and his housemates in a working-class neighborhood of East Detroit. Our house was called the Night Gallery because of the degree of debauchery that occurred there. During the day, it was a yard statue business, but at night, stoned-out, it looked pretty creepy, and we liked it that way. The landlord had a little shed in the back where he poured the molds and did transactions with his customers. The place was surrounded by birdbaths and religious statues of Jesus and Mary, all that ornate crap that some people think makes their yard look good.

One of my new roommates was a drug dealer, so there was a lot of traffic in and out. The big drug during this period was Quaalude. One of the roomies was connected to some mob guys who had a pharmacist with a gambling habit, and when he got in too deep, he paid off in thousands of these then-new and unregulated pills. People loved them, especially women. They were great for getting laid. There was a lot of that happening at that house; lots of single women coming through. It was a nonstop party house.

Eve had finally decided that being the girlfriend of a touring, drug-addicted, criminal musician wasn't exactly what she had in mind. She decided to move to New York to pursue an acting career. I agreed that it would be a good thing to do. We loved each other, but it was a first-love kind of relationship, and it had started to slip away as life grew more complicated. My addictions didn't help. I was on the road so much that it didn't really matter where I lived when I was in Detroit.

I couldn't make the payments on my Jaguar XKE because I was blowing all my cash on drugs. My bank officer refinanced the loan three times for me, but it was no use.

Some of the guys that hung out at the Night Gallery were professional auto repo men, and they told me my car came up on their collection lists. Since they were my friends, we stashed the car in one of their grandmother's garages.

As Eve and I were separating, I told her to sell the car and keep the money. She could use it to pay for her move to New York and pay her rent for a while, so she could get a job and get established in Gotham. Selling that car was one of my few regrets.

After the MC5 ended, I needed a new place to live. My mother owned a house on the west side near Plymouth Road and the

Southfield Freeway. At this point, I was basically homeless, and moved in with her and some other people she lived with. My mother liked having a lot of people around the house.

When Mable started making plans to move to Florida, I offered to take over the house payments so I could have a place to live and she could keep the investment. The house was pretty rundown and had some major plumbing problems, but it was solid and comfortable. The neighborhood was holding steady, and it wasn't an unpleasant place to land until I figured out what in the hell I was doing. My plan was to rent out some of the bedrooms to my musician friends to cover the mortgage and keep a roof over my head. I would be the proprietor of the itinerant musicians' boarding home. She agreed, and before long she packed up and moved to St. Augustine, Florida. She liked the St. Augustine area because it was where the Florida School for the Deaf and Blind was, and she wanted the best possible education for my little sister Peggy.

I was fishing around, looking for a band to join. I tried to talk Bob Seger into letting me join up with him. We had been friends for years, but he wasn't convinced. He said, "Sure Wayne, we'd have a cool band. We both write and sing, and you're a great guitar player. But I know the day will come when you'll leave the band, and then I'll have to go back and play those same clubs without you, and that will be a drag." It was a generous and graceful way not to hire me.

I had started playing with Melvin Davis and Tim Shafe and a few other people, but times were tough in 1973 in Detroit for working-class musicians. I had known Mel for years, and I had met Tim when we both were in an ill-fated band with Mitch Ryder.

I would book the occasional week or two in a bar for us, but nothing beyond what you could call survival wages. I really enjoyed playing with Mel and Tim. After almost a decade of playing music in a highly idiosyncratic way with the MC5, it was exciting to perform with new players. Tim and Mel were a beautifully strong rhythm section. They were first-rate musicians, and for a guitarist to play with a rhythm section that knows its business, it doesn't get any better. Melvin's drumming style was total soul with a touch of jazz.

Handsome and 6'5", he'd come up in the gritty Detroit R&B scene as a singer, songwriter, producer, and session drummer. He recorded for Fortune Records, and played sessions at Motown and for all the other indie R&B labels in Detroit in the late fifties and sixties. Mel is the drummer on the Capitols' smash hit "Cool Jerk." He worked with Smokey Robinson and the Miracles as a touring drummer and played drums on their hit "The Tears of a Clown." He knew all the Motown people, and was well respected by everyone.

Mel is well educated, well mannered, and interested in philosophy, politics, and spirituality. We would talk for hours, and we connected deeply. I loved him dearly, and still do.

Mel had also been a partner of the great Lyman Woodard in his jazz organ duos and trios with guitarist Dennis Coffey. Lyman was a legend in our circle. He had studied with Oscar Peterson, and was a magnificent jazz musician. We all became friends in '67, and remained good friends until Lyman's death in 2009. Lyman and Mel would book a nightclub and play three nights a week for years at a time. They always had a steady gig. This was my idea of a professional musician.

Tim, on the other hand, was short and white with a ruddy complexion and a wonderful smile. He had big talent and an even bigger heart, and as a bassist he was a quick study and highly skilled. He was a force of nature; the room lit up when he walked in. He was always cutting up and brutally honest, with a hysterical self-deprecating sense of humor. He was also the first guy I ever met who identified himself as an alcoholic. He would say it like it was just a natural fact. He treated it like it was a medical condition, that he needed liquor every day just to survive. We had an obscene amount of fun together both onstage and off. We also got into a great deal of trouble.

Melvin and I gravitated toward each other and became partners. We had both been trying to escalate our careers over the last few years. We figured that together, we could run a label, produce groups, write music for them, and perform on the recordings. We tried to sell our idea to anyone who would listen to us. With his experience in the Detroit R&B recording business and his time at Motown, and mine in the MC5, we covered a wide cross-section of popular music. We were connected to many of the best players in Detroit, and we believed in what we were trying to do. We got session work together from time to time, and we wrote and recorded together on each other's demos.

We tried to meet people with money who might like to partner with us in the label business, but investors were impossible to find in Detroit in those days. No one was really interested in something they couldn't see, touch, and feel. It was too abstract for them.

Money was a critical problem because of my on-again, off-again heroin habit; on when I had money, and off when I didn't. I found that when you didn't work, you tended to attract other ne'er-do-wells who didn't work either. A group of small-time crooks and scam artists comprised my social circle. Everyone seemed to be hustling everyone else. There was a crossover into the music world, which presented some dangerous options for me. I had never been averse to fencing hot TVs. If a thief came to me with a stolen gun, I knew people who'd be happy to buy it. I also ran a little weed and pill business.

Dealing dope is problematic when you're an addict. You can't keep your hands out of your own stash. Sell three, take two; sell two, take three. It never worked out right. I would spend my days driving all over town meeting with different guys, trying to set up deals or scams. I enjoyed the fantasy gangster life. Check me out, I'm a player. I romanticized the underworld life of the outsider, the social rebels, the reprobates, thieves, hustlers, pimps, dope house rip-off guys, and drug dealers—never once realizing that I was on a trajectory straight into the gutter.

I knew a bass player from the east side. Once, back in 1971, when the MC5 was making a last-ditch effort to stay together and I was looking for a new bass player, I offered this guy the gig. Mark wasn't interested, and that should have told me something. He didn't even know what the MC5 was, and he was a working rock musician in Detroit.

Word on the street was, he was a thief. It was called B&E back then: breaking and entering. Mark was also a heroin user, so it all fit together. He and I had tried to start a group together and had been rehearsing in my living room. I was attempting to do something musical since it was the only real-world job skill I had.

One day I was complaining about being broke, and Mark said he knew a way I could make some easy money. I put him off, although a little voice in the back of my head said, "Maybe." After being broke for so long, I started to give it some consideration. I was sick of being poor, and I wondered if I really had the nerve to rob people's houses. Could I actually do it? I had been stealing all my life, but this was kicking it up to a whole new level.

I had my daily costs down to about two dollars. I could get a box of Kraft Mac and Cheese for 22 cents, and buy a quart of Pabst beer with the difference. The staples of life. Without thinking it through too deeply, eventually I agreed to join him.

I thought he would have a detailed plan, and that he researched the jobs and sorted out the details. What I actually knew about home burglary I got from the movies, but that was not how it went. We drove around moneyed neighborhoods and picked houses at random. It was by feel or intuition, but mostly by chance. We would park in the driveway and knock on the front door. If no one answered, we went around the back of the house and busted in the back door, or went into the garage if it was open. Then we'd use the homeowners' own tools to break into the garage door to the house. We would use whatever was available: shovels, hammers, and so on. *The Thomas Crown Affair* we were not.

Going into someone's home gave me a hollow, sinking feeling. It was terrifying, dreamlike, and surreal. The first order of business was to find the liquor cabinet and slam down a few swallows of whatever they had in the house. "Hey, don't get fucked up now," Mark would yell at me. Yeah, right. We would take a quick inventory. Color TVs were a priority; I knew I could sell them quickly, no questions asked. Mark would decide what was worth stealing, and we'd load up the car as fast as possible. Sometimes we'd hit a house that looked expensive from the street, but when we got inside it was empty except for minimal stuff: beds, a folding card table and chairs in the kitchen. It was like these folks had a big front going, but no money to furnish the house.

We worked odd nights in different neighborhoods; no real pattern. I began to see neighborhoods differently. Now I was looking at the houses as scores, instead of homes where real people lived. Reinforced by regular heroin use resulting from the profits, an odd and perverse moral disconnect set in. Our routine was steal, cop drugs, steal, cop drugs. We had regular dealers who were always happy to have us over because they would get first pick of whatever we'd stolen that night. I overdosed one night and came to with a friend giving me mouth-to-mouth resuscitation. I was so high my first response was to joke, "Billy, we have to stop meeting like this."

Once we hit a mansion out in Birmingham, where the old money was. When we went in, I didn't see any TVs and said fuck this, let's move on. Mark, being the more experienced thief, clocked the beautiful oriental rugs. "Hell no, jackpot!" We started moving furniture and rolling up the rugs. Some were huge, and they were top quality. Heavy, too. We humped them into his station wagon, sweating like pigs. I thought, *If I wanted to work this hard, I would have gotten a real job.*

The next day, we went into downtown Detroit, to a big established antique dealer. We saw the kinds of rugs we'd stolen on his showroom floor with hefty price tags. The dealer had us unload the rugs on his loading dock around the back of the building, and his workers put them on an elevator. We unrolled them upstairs on an empty floor. The dealer asked where we got them, and I said from my grandmother who'd just passed away. When we unrolled them, casters were still wrapped up in the rugs. Oops. It was an awkward moment, but it passed. He made us an offer that was offensively low compared to the prices I'd seen on the showroom floor. We haggled a little, but took the money.

I got bolder and more relaxed on these burglaries, even pausing to get a bite to eat out of people's refrigerators. I even started stealing their frozen steaks and liquor. I had an uncle who owned a bar on the west side, and he would buy the liquor, no questions asked. When my lowlife friends heard what I was doing, they praised me. I had a perverse sense of pride about my new source of income.

Life around my house grew increasingly bizarre. One day the living room would be filled with stolen TVs and antiques; empty the next. The following day, it would be filled with band gear for rehearsals. The flow of characters was peculiar, as well. The Watergate hearings were on TV that summer, and my more politically engaged friends would join me in watching them. We'd smoke reefer, snort coke, and shoot heroin as the parade of thieves, hustlers, go-go girls, junkies, and musicians came and went. All the time watching the liars and criminals in DC on TV.

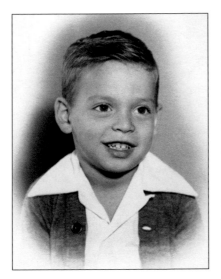

Me at age 4.

My beautiful strong-willed mother, Mable.

My sister Kathi and me outside our trailer on Harsens Island near where I started the big fire.

Here I am around the age of 7.

Drawing at my desk in our Elmer Street apartment.

My first electric guitar. A SilverTone Model 1420
Stratotone in Lincoln Park. Probably 1963. Note the
custom old-English script logo on the pickguard added
by yours truly.

Early MC5 publicity shot taken by Emil Bacilla inside the Grande Ballroom, 1967.

MC5 signs to Elektra Records in the dining room of 1510 Hill Street, Ann Arbor, Michigan, 1968. Jac Holzman, Danny Fields, John Sinclair, Sigrid Dobat, Fred "Sonic" Smith, Ron Asheton, Steve "The Hawk" Harnadek, Iggy Pop, Dave Alexander, Michael Davis, Scott Asheton, Chris Hovnanian, Ron Levine, Dennis "Machine Gun" Thompson, Becky Tyner, Rob Tyner, Wayne Kramer, John Adams, J. C. Crawford, Jimmy Silver, Emil Bacilla, Susan Silver, Barbara Holliday, Bill Harvey. *© Leni Sinclair*

A bad moon risin' at White Panther Headquarters in Ann Arbor, Michigan, 1969. Minister of Defense Pun Plamondon, Chairman John Sinclair, Minister of Culture in the Streets Wayne Kramer. *© Leni Sinclair*

MC5 at our original style peak.

© RaeAnne Rubinstein

A rare shot of the Grande dressing room.

© Allen Licari

Fred and me bringing it on a regular night at the Grande. © Allen Licari

Prepping for showtime, circa 1969.
© Mike Barich

Trying to explain the split with John Sinclair to Ben Fong-Torres for *Rolling Stone*. © *Charlie Auringer*

Derek Hughes, Rob Tyner, Dennis Thompson, Fred Smith, Wayne Kramer, Dollis Hill, London, 1971.

Radiation on a club date in Detroit 1974. This was the band I tried to fund via illegitimate capitalism. Melvin Davis on drums.

Me stylin' at FCI Lexington on the staff of the prison newspaper.

Red Rodney, my musical father. © *Frans Schellekens/Redferns*

My friend, saxophonist Jim Watts, visiting me at FCI Lexington.

Fresh out of prison with too much cash. With me is my girl, Sam.

Mick Jones and I meet for the first time backstage at the Clash's Detroit show at Masonic Auditorium in 1979. It was on this night that he and Joe Strummer gifted me a copy of their single "Jail Guitar Doors." © Robert Matheu

Johnny Thunders and me in the basement of the Second Chance in Ann Arbor, Michigan, 1979, not long after I was released from prison. We were Gang War. © *Robert Matheu*

The future had arrived in Was (Not Was). *Front row:* Dawn Silva, David Was, Don Was, Lynn Mabry, Ron Morris. *Back row:* Dave Mason, Carl "Butch" Small, Luis Resto, Wayne Kramer, David McMurray, Sweet Pea Atkinson. © *Robert Matheu*

On stage with Mick Farren at Dingwall's recording The Deviants album *Human Garbage*.
© Jeremy Bannister

Building a custom home in the Florida Keys.

Engineer Sally Browder, Epitaph Chief Brett Gurewitz, and me mixing *The Hard Stuff* at Devonshire Studios in Los Angeles in 1994.

An early incarnation of DKT/MC5, June 29, 2004, at The Echo in Los Angeles. *Front row:* Lisa Kekaula of The BellRays, Marshall Crenshaw, Michael Davis, Evan Dando, Dennis Thompson. *Back row:* Charles Moore, David Was, Mark Arm, Ralph "Buzzy" Jones, me. © *Robert Matheu*

Rehearsal for Road Recovery's fundraiser in 2009. Don Was, Iggy Pop, Tom Morello, Wayne Kramer. © *Tracy Ketcher*

Road Recovery Benefit on the night Jail Guitar Doors USA was conceived in NYC in 2009. *Front row:* Wayne Kramer, Boots Riley. *Back Row:* Eric Gardner, Gilby Clarke, Jerry Cantrell, Carl Restivo, Don Was, Tom Morello, Billy Bragg, Little Steven Van Zandt, Iggy Pop, Evan Seinfeld, Perry Farrell, Juliette Lewis, Etty Lau Farrell, Handsome Dick Manitoba. © *Tracy Ketcher*

Our class photo before entering Sing Sing Prison in Ossining, New York, April 29, 2009, with Road Recovery. *Front Row:* Gilby Clarke, Dave Gibbs, Tom Morello, Boots Riley, Jerry Cantrell, Jason Lemiere. *2nd Row:* Daniella Clarke, Vaughn Martinian, Handsome Dick Manitoba, Carl Restivo, Susan Silver, Don Was. *3rd Row:* Una Cote, Billy Bragg, Dr. Leslie Malin, Jack Bookbinder, Eric Gardner, Margaret Saadi Kramer, Scott Schumaker, Anthony Nater. *4th Row:* Etty Lau Farrell, Perry Farrell, Olga Marchese, Peter Jenner, Wayne Kramer, Scott Schumaker, Laurence Kern, Bobby Danelski, Kirsten Danelski, Anthony Nater. © *Tracy Ketcher*

Some of the men who participate in our Jail Guitar Doors program inside California Rehabilitation Center at Norco (2012). © *Drew Carolan*

Entering the maximum security Lancaster State Prison facility at Los Angeles County for a Jail Guitar Doors concert. © *Nicole Weingart*

Sharing a laugh with Charles Moore. © *Cali Dewitt*

Downright upright at the Grammy Museum in Los Angeles. Soon after, my album *Lexington* hits #6 on the jazz charts. © *Robert Matheu*

My dear friend and mentor in a principled life, Bob Timmins. *Photo courtesy of Denny Seiwell*

John, Wayne, and Pun together 50 moons later. © *Jenny Risher*

My wonderful wife Margaret Saadi Kramer. © *Gina Saadi*

My son, Francis Maron, and me. Fatherhood is the greatest. © *Margaret Saadi Kramer*

CHAPTER 18

MISFIRE

America was going through a major spasm. Along with most of my generation, I despised Nixon for his handling of the Vietnam War. He was responsible for the deaths of over 58,000 young Americans, and millions of Vietnamese. It was highly entertaining to see him and his gang getting busted for lying about wiretapping the Democrats, and then trying to cover it up. I enjoyed Watergate immensely.

One night after finishing a club gig at the Red Carpet Lounge on the east side, drummer Kenny Black, a tenant, and I were driving home at around 3:30 in the morning in his big-assed Cadillac Coupe de Ville. As was my style, I'd drunk heavily all night. I was in my rum phase, hitting that Ron Rico 151 pretty hard. As we were cruising across town, the police rolled up on us fast, lights flashing, siren screaming. We were smoking a joint, and I had two Quaaludes in my pocket that someone had given me at the club. Kenny ate the joint and I ate the ludes. The cops raced past us, pursuing someone else. I was way too drunk to have taken those pills. When we got home, I figured the best thing to do was to eat something. I started cooking some eggs. The phone rang, and I was having a conversation with a girl I knew, and then . . .

I came to on the floor with daylight in my eyes and a terrible, bitter odor making me gag. My head was pounding; I was nauseous and dizzy. I'd had a terrible dream about choking, and my head was lying in my own puke. The phone, which had one of those extra-long, curly cords, was circled around the room, hung up on a chair back with the receiver buzzing, dangling in the air. The stove burners were all on full blast, and a frying pan full of eggs had spilled. Egg was all over the stove and walls, and there was puke everywhere. It took a minute to figure out what had happened.

This was embarrassing and more than a little scary, plus a big mess to clean up. I knew that I'd been incredibly lucky; I'd dodged another bullet. This kind of behavior kills people every day; think Jimi Hendrix. Unlike Nietzsche, these things that didn't destroy me, didn't make me stronger. They diminished me. With each slip I had less dignity, less self-respect.

The drama was endless. My girlfriend Sam smashed her arm through a window banging on it when I stormed out in anger one drunken night. One of the fellows took her to the emergency room for 22 stitches.

Bass player Tim Shafe came in one day and said he had something he wanted me to try. He had some new cocaine that he called "popcorn."

"Great, let's snort some," I said.

He said, "No, I want you to try this." He pulled out a syringe, poured some coke into a spoon, added some water and drew it up through a piece of cotton into the syringe. Then he injected it into a big vein in his forearm. Almost immediately, he turned into a whirling dervish of enthusiasm. "Come on man, you'll see what I mean."

Up to this moment, I'd had a lifelong aversion to needles. My heroin habit involved snorting. I was a "tooter." But all it took to get over my fear of needles was one mainline injection of high-grade cocaine. I immediately sat down to work on a poster I was making for an upcoming gig. I was a scissoring-and-gluing maniac. I told Tim that I didn't think this shit was working on me. He laughed pretty hard at that. "Yeah, right." I asked him to sell me a piece and leave the syringe.

In the daily gloom that was my life, the home invasions were having a strange collateral effect. In the criminal underworld, burglary had a certain low-rent status. I rationalized my behavior with simple-minded logic: I wasn't stealing from people; I was liberating goods from insurance companies that were totally corrupt. No harm, no foul.

I justified everything I did in relation to how it turned out for me. From the time I was an eight-year-old thief on Michigan Avenue through my adult years, I could justify and rationalize anything for my own purposes. I never once looked inward to contemplate the implications of what I was doing; never thought about the possible consequences. I never considered the harm I was doing to people. This is known as magical thinking. Of course, I thought about what might happen if someone came home while I was robbing his or her house, but I didn't think about what I might do. The possibilities were too awful to contemplate. I was never armed, but Mark usually carried a pistol. I usually sold any guns that came my way, except for a rusty 20-gauge shotgun I kept in the house.

I was at a bar on the east side one night with my girlfriend, Sam, and we were drinking hard as usual. As the night wore on, I took some acid and then a lude, then snorted some coke with some guys. Sam and I got separated, and I went looking for her. I went out into the parking lot, where she was being helped, semiconscious, into a car by some guys I didn't know very well. One of my friends told me he knew them; the main guy was a coke dealer friend of his, and he was cool. It definitely didn't feel cool to me, but they were gone before I could do anything.

My car had a flat. I had no money, so I drove home on the flat tire, drunk, on ludes, high on acid, crashing from the cocaine. I was paranoid from the acid and raging with anger and fear of what might be happening to my girlfriend. When I got home, I loaded that shotgun.

I sat up the rest of the night, playing out worst-case scenarios in my mind. Swinging from fear to rage and back to fear again, getting more wired up with each passing hour.

Just after dawn, a car stopped in front of the house. Sam was in the front seat. I grabbed the gun and ran out into the street. She got out of the car and started walking up to the house. As the car pulled away, I aimed at the back of the driver's head through the rear window, and pulled the trigger.

Click! The shotgun didn't fire. There was dead silence in the gray-blue early morning light. The car turned the corner and disappeared.

I looked up at the sky. What the fuck did I just do? The stark realization that I'd pulled the trigger had let all of my anger out like a burst balloon. My head was spinning. This was how people ended up in prison for life: drunk, high, angry, driven over the edge of reason by a drug-fueled reaction to an insane situation. The driver wasn't the only one who dodged a bullet that morning.

Back in the house, Sam told me that the guy behind the wheel was just a nice kid she'd asked to drive her home after she walked out of the dope house. She was laughing at my near-lethal, macho stupidity, and showed me a $100 bill she'd palmed from the dealer while they were snorting coke.

I would have killed the wrong guy. That the gun didn't fire was unquestionably the most fortunate thing that ever happened to me.

The dealer came over later that day to retrieve his $100. I kept the shotgun close by during the awkward transaction: he was a music fan, he didn't mean any harm, they were just partying, blah, blah, and blah. "Fuck you, get out of my house."

CHAPTER 19

BUSTED

It was springtime 1974, and the weather turned pleasant again. Tim Shafe had returned to Detroit from New York, and Mel and I and a new organist were trying to get some work again. I was walking up to my front porch when I noticed a fleet of police cars coming down my street. A couple of marked cruisers and an unmarked detective unit, followed by another couple of black-and-whites. I thought to myself, *Someone's in serious trouble.*

They pulled up to my house and slowed to a stop. In the back seat of one of the unmarked cars was one of my tenants: a kid named Stuart. He was from the neighborhood, and had ingratiated himself into the flow at the house. He would show up from time to time with stolen goods, drugs, or guns, which I'd buy for resale. He needed a place to stay, and I rented him a room. I knew he was untrustworthy, but that was a case of the tosspot calling the kettle black.

He kept cracking on me to introduce him to Mark, so he could get in on the B&Es. I denied knowing anything about burglaries. I hadn't worked any robberies for a while because I was busy with my band again.

And now here was Stuart in the back seat of a police car in hand-cuffs, giving me the peace sign. The uniformed cops were coming up on me, guns drawn, and yelling at me to raise my hands and not move. A detective walked up and asked if I was Wayne Kramer. I mumbled, "Yeah," and he said in a reassuring voice, "Don't worry, son. You're not in trouble. We know *you're* not a bad guy. We're just trying to get some missing property back. Is this your house?"

My mind was racing; I couldn't figure out what to say or do. "Err, ah, well . . ."

"Can we just go in the house to talk and check for some property? If it's not there, we'll be on our way."

Before I knew what was happening, my house was overrun with cops. "We're looking for a set of large brass candelabras. You don't happen to have them, do you?"

The candelabras were in a corner of the living room; we were both looking right at them. Cops were running upstairs and down, going through the closets. They found all manner of loot. One cop said to another, "This motherfucker," referring to me, "is so dumb, he left the owner's identification sticker right here on the camera!" I couldn't have said it better.

I regained my senses and refused to talk to them without a lawyer, but the damage was done. I was in cuffs and on my way to the police station. The neighbors lined the curb as we drove away.

When I got to the Birmingham police headquarters, a detective stopped me as I was getting fingerprinted. He took a look at me and said, "I know who you are. I was on duty the night the call came in about a burglary. You and your buddy knocked on the door next to the house you robbed, and told the people you were looking for somebody but you had the wrong address. They said one of the guys had a weird beard." I had been wearing two small slivers of beard on both sides of my chin. I though it made me look rakish and distinctive.

A few nights earlier, Mark and Stuart had come out of a house they were robbing with their arms loaded with loot to meet an entire squad of cops, guns drawn, waiting for them. The police had been tracking our group for months, and took their time to set it up right.

Stuart turned over instantly, naming names. He made a deal to save his own ass, and brought the cops to my house. When I got into the holding cells, Mark was in the adjoining cell. He did a good job of acting shocked when he saw me. He was big-time dope sick; all he wanted to talk about was going to the hospital for his withdrawal sickness. I was sent to the Oakland County Jail for the next month because my bail was too high to post. While I was locked up, Stuart came back to my house and ripped off my guitars.

County jails, like city jails, are hard time. There's nothing to do, nowhere to go. You're on deadlock most of the time. You're stuck in a cell with the detritus of society: the entry-level losers, drunks, and fuck-ups. There were also a couple of hard-core convicts waiting to be shipped out to state prison. They were much easier to be around; at least you knew where you stood with them. I just kept quiet, read books, and waited. Some guys knew me from the MC5, so I had a little identity. Mostly, I just waited for some air. Finally, after a month or so, my bond was lowered and I got out.

When I called my mother to see if she could help me pay my lawyer's bills, she ripped me a new one. "How could you be so stupid? Don't you know better than to have stolen property in your own house?" she said, ever the pragmatist. She also said she wouldn't help me pay the lawyer. She was pretty disgusted with me, and I couldn't blame her.

The cops offered me a deal, but my lawyer said chances were pretty good that I wouldn't get any prison time. So, I declined the offer of part-time police work in exchange for reduced charges and other incentives.

I didn't see Mark again until the day of our sentencing. We both showed up in our best suits, and he had his wife and newborn baby with him. The judge gave me three years' probation and restitution. Because of Mark's deeper involvement and record, he got three years in state prison.

I met with my probation officer as instructed, and went on with my life. I didn't get the message; they give you more rope every time you go to criminal court. "We know you're not a bad guy, Wayne. Don't do it again." Every time I went to court, they gave me a little more rope. Eventually I'd get just enough rope to hang myself with. I had already bought my ticket; they were just waiting to punch it.

After the burglary bust, I needed to move. I found a commercial building for rent on Eight Mile Road near Van Dyke. It was a two-story brick structure with offices on the first floor and an apartment upstairs. It was a one-bedroom, but Mel said I should take it, as it would give us a base of operations and office/rehearsal space. I got the money together and moved in, but the madness from the previous house followed me to the new location. Several guys would come over every day, as if it was their job to show up midmorning and hang out all day and night. Drug dealers, thieves, hustlers, groupies, musicians—the riffraff of Detroit. My people, I guess.

I used to have target practice in the basement of the building. I carried an old tree stump down there, and fired pistols into it. Since Eight Mile is a very busy street, no one ever heard the gunfire.

I introduced a couple of rip-off artists to another bad actor who had some guns. They needed guns and a little cash to rob an out-of-state drug dealer. The rip-off guys came back with a lot of money, and everyone was happy. They did it again, but this time something went wrong and someone got shot. Now there was no money, no guns, and hell to pay. And I was in the middle of the mess. The guy who provided the guns and money was a hothead, and slashed the tires of the rip-off men, who responded by threatening to kill him. All of which culminated in a confrontation between my roommate—who was aligned with the guy who provided the guns—and Igor, a not-so-nice guy and known killer who was with the rip-off men.

Now one insane gangster was in my living room, holding the other one off with my shotgun. I was downstairs, waiting to hear gunfire when Igor came down and told me, "Don't be walking on the street next to that motherfucker. He's a dead man."

I wondered how in the hell I'd slipped down so far. I used to be surrounded by happy people who loved me. My big challenges were writing great songs and putting on a spectacular rock & roll show. Now, I was fearful a lot of the time, and my "friends" were a bunch of fucking cutthroats.

Sam and I had terrible drunken fights. There were fights with guys, too, fueled by booze, coke, or heroin. Black eyes and emergency room trips happened regularly. Glasses were broken against walls, doors kicked in, furniture broken in rampages. I was dope sick one day, too high the next. The amount of lying, stealing, and general criminal behavior was staggering.

I was at an all-time low.

CHAPTER 20

RADIATION

Dave Leone, a booking agent from the MC5 days, called up with a job offer. He was booking my old pal Ted Nugent, and they were trying to think of ways to draw crowds to his gigs. They came up with the idea of "guitar battles," like big-time wrestling. I agreed, and a series of events were booked. They would pay me well, and I was grateful for the work.

The night before the first show, we had a blowout party at my apartment for Tim Shafe's birthday. The drugs and booze flowed and flowed. A great deal of it flowed into my body, and when Ted's crew showed up first thing the following morning to collect me for the tour, I was in pretty bad shape. I slept in the back seat for the drive to Jackson, Michigan, where Ted lived.

When we arrived, I wasn't feeling much better, but I knew I'd have to pull it together and greet my host. I had known Ted for years; we went back to the midsixties and the old neighborhood music store Capitol Music in northwest Detroit. Ted had achieved some success with the hit single "Journey to the Center of the Mind" with the Amboy Dukes. He had left the group and was developing a solo career. These gigs were part of that effort.

I saw that Ted had a nice little spread. It started to dawn on me that, up to that point, Ted probably hadn't made much more money than I had in the MC5. In fact, the MC5 were a *much* bigger draw up until the end in '72. But Ted had carried on, and was doing pretty well. As I looked around, I realized that we were on *his* property; he *owned* it. He had a little lake with a boat in it. He had a barn and horses. When I went in the house to say hi to the missus and see his new baby, the house was full of stuff. *His* stuff: big color TVs, gun racks full of expensive hunting rifles, fur rugs, and appliances. He had a lot of material possessions to show for his work. And what did I have? A world-class hangover. We were both guitar players and bandleaders who'd started out at basically the same point, but our paths had diverged to such a degree that I was having trouble taking it in.

The guitar battle concerts were easy. I came out at the end of Ted's set and danced. Ted couldn't dance, so that was that. The fans had a great time, too. Back at the hotel, it was nonstop debauchery: young girls, impersonal sex, and lots of booze. Ted never drank or did drugs, but he kept up in the other departments. Even though we couldn't be farther apart politically, we're still friends today.

After the guitar battle tour, Mel and I couldn't get financing for our label. We were still playing dates around Detroit with Tim, and had added Bob Schultz on keyboard and vocals. Schultz is one of rock's unknown premier vocalists. He has a powerful, soulful style, and had been a local star for years going back to his time in Bob Seger's band. He had played on their fantastic local hit single "East Side Story." The band, which we'd named Radiation, had real potential. The combination of Melvin Davis and Bob Schultz's vocals would be unstoppable. The possibilities were exhilarating; we could have hit-songs-on-the-radio success.

Melvin was a world-class songwriter in the mold of the great Motown songwriting team of Holland–Dozier–Holland, but with his own take on the human condition. He was always working on a new song. Shafe was a brilliant bassist with solid instincts in song construction, and he was also a perfect collaborator. The bottom was funky and hard rocking. Bob Schultz wrote some, and I thought that if encouraged, he'd blossom as a writer. I brought my guitar playing, stagecraft, songwriting, and political consciousness. I was also beginning to collaborate long-distance with Mick Farren, who was sending me terrific new lyrics from England. We all liked and respected each other and got along together wonderfully. I knew that, between us, we could write and produce material that was commercially viable and artistically groundbreaking. The future was ours for the taking.

When I visited Leone's office to promote my new band, he choked out, "Wayne, you can't have a black guy in the band. The white girls will dig him, and it will cause a problem with the white guys in the club and there will be fights. Then the club owners won't book you. Can't you replace him?" I was stunned. I told him this was Detroit in 1974, not the Deep South in the '50s.

I was still angry when I told Melvin. He was patient with me, explaining this was how it was for black people in America. He wasn't upset in the least. He said I should relax. "This doesn't mean shit. We just keep on doing what we're doing." I was still idealistic and naïve about race in America. Mel wasn't going anywhere.

I believed interracial bands were going to be the future of pop music. I reasoned there were no differences between us that could stop us. Of course, we were different, but we were even more alike. Skin color just was not an issue that divided us. We were from the city of Detroit, in a time and place that allowed us to transcend the divisions that had kept people apart in America. We were the new breed of American musical artist.

I would do anything in my power to make this group succeed. The trouble was, we would need to shoot photos for publicity and needed gear to tour with. We needed a van, clothes, tape recorders, and demos to send out to labels. But studio time cost money, demos cost money, photos cost money, and there were countless other costs needed to launch the band. And I was impatient. I felt that if I didn't make something happen quickly, it would all fall apart.

I decided I would finance the band by dealing drugs.

I knew dealers around Detroit that were doing well, but I was seeing what I wanted to see. Most drug dealers were not wealthy;

most were subsistence-level dealers. I actually believed I was going to make a lot of money, and it was for a great cause. The truth was, anytime I scored a payday dealing drugs, the first thing I did was get loaded.

CHAPTER 21

NO
WITNESSES

The Motor City is literally a dark place for some five months of the year. When winter rolls in in November, the days get so short, it's like the sun only visits for an hour or so. It stays gray and dark until mid-April. Every day blends into the next, and when the snow comes, it gets dirty from the car exhaust and factory soot. Then it snows again, and the grime adds layers of black slush on top of the preceding layers until every corner has a huge black mound of frozen filth on it. It's depressing as hell.

By the midseventies, I had been on the fringe of the criminal underworld for years. Ten years prior, before the era of the hippy pot dealer, if you wanted to smoke reefer you had to know somebody. Some of these fellows were real Damon Runyon characters: Freddy the Waiter, Smooth Paul. Crime had an allure for me. I have always identified with and romanticized outsiders. It's rock & roll: being a rebel and all that. I read most of Donald Goines's black gangster novels, Burroughs's *Junky*, and dozens of other books about organized crime and lowlife dope fiends. I identified with them, and they became my new idols. The regular world had betrayed me, so I went to a new, harder, darker, sexier world where wrong was right. An upside-down world where stealing and pulling a successful scam was admired, and getting up and going to work was for chumps.

On top of all that, I was desperate. A dope habit requires cash every day. Selling my clothes, car, guitars, guns, and amps worked for a while, but eventually I ran out of things to sell.

Once you're in this world, certain kinds of opportunities open up. A guy comes into the city from some small town in the Midwest, and he's looking for some smack. Me and my partners thought nothing of collecting his money, copping the dope, keeping half, and replacing it with mannitol, a sugar made from cornstarch, and sending the boy on his way.

In the spring of 1974, an associate of mine known as "the Bug" brought a guy over who was looking for cocaine. His name was Barker. He said he worked for a mafia drug courier from New York, and asked if I knew where we could score ounces of blow for his boss. Cash was no problem. I made a few calls.

I met Barker and his boss "Tony" in a Ramada Inn bar in Ypsilanti. His boss certainly looked the part: big, Italian, all Jheri-curled. Tony was reluctant to hand over the cash without a sample of the blow, so I left, assuring them that all was kosher. I returned with a sample. Barker and Tony went into the bathroom for a taste, and a few minutes later, they came out satisfied. After a few more tense moments, Tony gave me the cash. I left again, and returned ten minutes later with an ounce of coke. Tony took the package and left. Barker and I drove back to Detroit.

On the way back to the city, I got Barker's story. He was fresh out of Terre Haute federal prison on a stolen car beef, and was trying to get reestablished. He said we should have taken a big piece of the coke for ourselves, that Tony wouldn't mind, but I told him I didn't know his guy and just wanted to do straight business. Like I'm all ethical and shit.

Our coke business with Tony grew steadily. Two-ounce deals became four-ounce deals, which became six. I started to feel like I was a real dope-slinging hoodlum. Driving around Detroit with my partners, going to meetings in restaurants, carrying guns. I still wanted to finance the band but the truth was I blew most of the profits from dealing on heroin.

One night in November, we had set up a fair-sized deal. We usually did the transactions at restaurants or bars, but this time we set up shop at the Shelby Hotel in downtown Detroit.

The Shelby had become the epicenter of a lot of cultural activity. It was run by a young entrepreneur whose dad was the owner, and there was a hip bar off the lobby where Lyman Woodard and his band had a steady gig. There was a concert room in the basement where bands could play. I had worked there a few times with Mel and Tim in Radiation.

To do this deal at the Shelby, Tim and I got rooms on the cuff from the owner's son. Our "security arrangements" were that we had the dope supplier in one room and the buyers in another room, and we were running product samples and money back and forth. We thought this was pretty safe for all concerned. I was getting ready to leave for the hotel when Barker called me and asked what room I was meeting Tony in tonight. Discussing this on the phone struck me as a bad idea, and I said I didn't know anything about what he was talking about. He pumped me a bit for more info, and then gave up. That deal went down according to plan, and I celebrated by getting smashed, as usual.

A few days later, I was at Leon's, a heroin dealer's house, on the west side. We were very high on a fresh shipment of high-grade heroin, and he casually mentioned that it was too bad about that one slipping through our fingers the other night at the Shelby.

I said, "What the fuck are you talking about?"

He laughed. That laugh struck me as odd.

"What's so funny?" I asked.

"Well, since I done let the cat outta the bag . . . When Barker called you for the room number, we were sitting over here with our pistols and a shotgun. Hell, Wayne, I thought you and Barker were tight and that you were in on this. Barker told me, 'There's gonna be a lot of cocaine in that hotel room and we're gonna take it all.'"

And then Leon casually added, "And Barker said, 'No witnesses.'"

I have no idea why he brought the subject up. I was stunned. He must have seen the look of shock on my face. "No witnesses" meant Leon and Barker were going to kill everyone in the room— Tim Shafe, the Bug, Tony, and me, too.

This kind of shit was happening all the time in Detroit. Drug related rip-off murders were common. I wasn't too worried about the police because I had read reports in the newspaper about how the Detroit police couldn't get large amounts of cash for major drug buys, and we were doing pretty big deals. Plus, the Bug rationalized that since he was with Barker when Barker shot and killed a guy in Florida, the police would trade a drug case for a murder case. In other words, in my mind, the Bug was our insurance policy.

My monkey needed cash, so common sense was out of the picture. I kept telling myself that it was gonna work out; I could pull this off.

I hadn't heard from Tony for a few months when he called and said he needed a big order filled. He wanted a kilo. I decided to step away from Barker & Co. and went down to Florida to arrange my own supply through contacts I'd made when I was on tour down there.

Back in '68, in the MC5, I'd done some scuba diving in south Florida with Tom, an ex-Marine who was in the drug business. Tom set up the deal with his connection, who was an older Italian, New York gangster living the good life in sunny Florida. He told us how the deal would go down. When I got back to Tom's house, I called Tony in Detroit. During that call, Tom decided to get on the phone to make security demands. There was a lot of yelling and arguing between Tony and Tom. Finally, he handed me back the phone.

"Wayne, I don't like your new friend," Tony said. "He's selling wolf tickets and I'm not buying. I'm pulling out of this deal." Financing for my band and drug habit had just sailed out the window. I was wiped out.

Once back in Detroit, Tim, the Bug, and I set up a new deal to sell Tony 11 ounces directly. Tim knew a guy that could supply it. We decided that, since we knew Tony and his partner Joe so well and trusted them, it would be cool to do this deal at my new apartment, an upper duplex near Seven Mile Road.

The night before the deal, I couldn't sleep. Everything told me this was all wrong. But I just kept thinking of what I was going to do with all the money I was about to make. I'd buy a big bag of that new China White that had junkies dropping dead from overdoses all over town. And maybe a new color TV and some band demos?

Just get through this one and then knock it off. One last big deal to set me up for a while, then I'd get straight.

The weather that day was awful. Dark gray skies, rain pouring down in torrents so heavy at times you couldn't see the street from the front windows. Tony and Joe showed up on time, and Joe asked if he could look around the apartment "just to be safe." No problem. I had my shotgun in the bedroom, but I said, "We're all cool here, right?"

Tim arrived with the sample, and Tony approved it. Tim went out to get the main package from our supplier who was waiting at a restaurant around the corner; 11 ounces of 98 percent pure Colombian cocaine. Tim returned, then Joe went down to his car to get the money. Joe returned with a briefcase. Tony and Joe, the two big Italians at my kitchen table, tried to open the briefcase, but it wouldn't open. They were getting frantic.

"No man, give it to me. I'll open it!"

"No man, I got it! I got it!"

They were struggling with each other and starting to raise their voices. Time started to slow down. Something was seriously wrong. I looked back down the stairs at my apartment's front door and saw that it had been left open. I rationalized this as they're being in a hurry to leave once we did the deal. I looked back at Tony and Joe grappling with the briefcase. I heard footsteps and men screaming. They were running up the stairs with guns drawn.

"Put your hands up! Hands up . . . hands up, motherfuckers! *No-body move!* You will be shot!"

A mob of bug-eyed white guys in windbreakers and bulletproof vests came pounding up. I turned back around, and Tony was standing in front of me holding a .45 automatic at my stomach. I looked down at the barrel opening, and thought, *Damn, that's going to make a huge hole.* My next thought was: *This is a rip-off, and we're all gonna die.*

The apartment was flooded with guys hollering, "Where are the guns?" I realized they were police, and immediately felt much better. I also noticed that my apartment stank to high heaven with bodily gasses. The agents were so stressed that they farted my place up. At that point, I didn't have any fear at all. After you've been busted a few times, you get to know the drill. But man, it smelled bad. I started to make a joke, but thought better of it.

They cuffed us and broke out DEA badges. Another lucky break. I was relieved to see those federal badges. I knew, no matter what happened, I wouldn't be going to Jacktown, America's largest walled penitentiary. At the time, Jackson State Prison had over 3,000 men locked up in medieval conditions. It was well known to be gladiator school.

Tony turned to my partner and said, "Tim, you're going to tell me where your connection is right now." Tim wasn't a big guy, but he could be as tough as he needed to be. He said, "Hell, no."

"No?" Tony said. "You're going to tell me right now, or else I'm going to take you into the bedroom and beat you so bad, you'll piss and shit blood for a month. But you won't have a mark on you tomorrow in court. I know how to do it, and I like it."

Tim faltered at this, but after a moment's consideration, he said, "I'm really sorry, but I can't tell you." Tony looked him in the eye and said, "All right, let's go to jail."

The agents had a good laugh, and carted us down to their van. On the way downtown to the federal building, Bob Dunn, the special agent in charge, pulled me aside. "Wayne, there won't be anything in the newspapers about this tomorrow, and you might want to keep this under wraps from your friends. There might come a point in time where you find yourself between a rock and a hard place. I might make a deal with you."

"Thanks, Bob."

I was released the next day on a personal recognizance bond. Obviously, the DEA was trying to get me to go to work for them.

I immediately went to see my friend and attorney Deday La-Rene. He confirmed what I already suspected: unless I went to work for the Feds, I was going to prison on this bust. I had already been on probation for the home invasion burglaries earlier in the year, so there was no way I was going to skate again.

That's the way they work it: You fuck up, and they slap you on the wrist. You fuck up again, and they slap you on the wrist again. This gets old after a few trips to court and eventually, if you keep coming back, they have to do something to you.

I went home and bawled. I never meant to ruin everything, but I had finally fucked off my life. Now I had to face the consequences. I cried big gulping sobs of self-pity. I'd thrown it all away: my career, music, friends, family, love, self-respect, everything. It was like I was walking underwater. Maybe I would wake up from this bad dream, and everything would be fine. But it wasn't a dream; it was a waking nightmare. At 25, I had flushed my fine young life right down the toilet. I was a user and a taker, and now I was going to have to pay the bill.

It took eight months for the indictments from the grand jury to come down. It arrived by regular mail. I was charged with 16 counts of possession with intent to deliver, conspiracy to deliver, possession and sale of cocaine.

The blanks in Barker's story got filled in, too. He was caught up in another stolen car ring, and had made a deal with the feds. He was working for them as a paid informer. They have spot on the wall at the federal building, and they nail your ass up there. You can get down anytime you want; all you have to do is put somebody else's ass up there instead of yours. Barker had been to prison and he didn't want to go back, so he went to work for the DEA. I found out that he was paid a thousand dollars for every ounce of cocaine I sold them. I also found out that Barker was a well-known dope house rip-off killer who would shoot first and party later. The DEA agents admired him. The agent who arrested me said, "Barker will shoot a nigger and walk down his street the next day."

Tim, the Bug, and I were all named in the indictments. Each of the 16 counts carried a 15-year maximum sentence; potentially a very long time in prison. The Bug left Detroit, and was never seen again. He was always a slippery dude and if he wanted to flee, that was his business. I didn't think it was too smart, but he didn't ask me. Tim and I were on our way to federal prison.

The DEA wanted to make a deal with me. Deday and I went down to the U.S. Attorney's office to see what they were offering. We met with Bob Dunn, the special agent in charge of my case, and Adam Christensen, the U.S. attorney. The deal was that if I testified in federal court against all the guys I got the coke from, then go to work for the Feds and find them three more people who would sell them at least one ounce of coke each, plus a minimum of 100 pounds of pot or 10,000 pills, they would recommend to the judge that I receive not more than a three-year sentence.

We were astonished. What the fuck kind of deal was that? I was going to risk getting killed, branded as an informer, and still get three years? I told them, "You guys don't understand. I *want* people to know who I am. I am a professional entertainer. I want to be recognized in public. Someday, hopefully, this will be behind me, and I want to be able to put the pieces back together." If I took their deal and went to work for them, I could kiss all that goodbye forever. If I wasn't murdered in the process.

It wasn't like I had an allegiance to any criminal code or honor among thieves, but I did know that snitches have a way of getting shot while walking down the street, and this possibility did not appeal to me. Many of the people I ran with in Detroit were serious people who would not take that kind of betrayal lightly. My allegiance was to my own well-being, and even if I had to go to prison, one day it would be over. Needless to say, I didn't take their deal.

I met with John Sinclair to get his advice on my legal situation and he was generous and empathetic. "All they're interested in is convictions, Wayne." I appreciated his perspective.

I called my mother when I knew how serious my case was, and that I would most assuredly go to prison. She told me, "Wayne, you know I would help you if I could, but I can't. Besides, you deserve to go to prison."

Even if someone had reached out to me, my omnipotence and grandiosity were so strong that I wouldn't have listened. I didn't make wise choices when I had the chance, and now I was all out of choices.

CHAPTER 22

JAILHOUSE BOUND

My sentencing hearing was filled with drama.

The week before my hearing, I had been on the road playing in, of all things, a Vegas-style show band. When I got back to Detroit, I desperately wanted to hold my girlfriend close and make love to her one last time. When I got there, she was stoned on heroin. It was like making love to a zombie. She was conscious but completely disconnected from any feelings of intimacy or tenderness. My heart was drained.

I showed up for court knowing that I was going down. I had known for the last eight months that I was going to prison. My worst fears were realized.

My lawyer had prepared me for seven years, maybe five if the judge was lenient. Not exactly great options. Sam came with me that morning, but she wasn't much support, as all she did was cry. The judge asked about the presentence report, and my attorney said that there were some discrepancies in it that we wanted to correct. The judge said he didn't care what was written in the report. This was good news for me, because I didn't look so good on paper, given my less-than-wonderful track record with law enforcement. Then the judge said, "I also don't care what's written in these letters of recommendation." I'd gathered testimonials from music journalists, friends, and even the head of the Catholic Archdiocese of Detroit, proclaiming what a good guy I was, and that maybe I could serve my sentence in an alternative way. Working with disabled children? Helping the poor? I was open to anything at this point.

"What I do care about is that Mr. Kramer had 11 ounces of pure cocaine in his possession in his apartment in the city of Detroit, and that he attempted to sell it to a federal agent. That makes Mr. Kramer a major narcotics trafficker. Mr. Kramer, I would have more respect for you if you had taken a gun and shot and killed a man rather than murdering the citizens of Detroit long and slow by selling them hard narcotics like heroin and cocaine."

"Hey," I whispered to my lawyer. "They didn't catch me selling heroin on this case."

"Shush," he whispered back.

After the judge's flawed moral reasoning, I figured I was going to get the maximum sentence. The judge then asked the clerk what kind of maximum sentence I had negotiated in my plea bargain. The clerk shuffled his papers and said it was a five-year max; then he said, "No, wait, that's a mistake. It was a three-year max."

Three years! Whoopee, I could do that standing on my head after being ready for seven. "Five or three?" the judge said. "Today's your lucky day, Mr. Kramer. I'll split the difference with you. Take four years."

Bang! went the gavel. The judge finished by admonishing me that the plea bargain was the best deal of my young life, because if I'd elected to go to trial, he would have given me 15 years.

My attorney asked the judge if I could have ten days to get my affairs in order. The judge said, "He's had eight months to get his affairs in order. He'll be in Milan federal prison at six o'clock tonight." At that moment, two U.S. marshals laid their hands on my arms, guided me out of the courtroom and up the elevator to the holding cells. Goodbye cruel world; federal prison, here I come.

The judge wasn't bullshitting me. By 6:00 PM, I was in the Federal Correctional Institution (FCI) in Milan, Michigan. Milan was fine with me. Just south of Detroit, it's an old prison built in the '30s. Since it was close to town, I figured I'd have visitors often and stay in the loop. Of course, I was terrified. I had been talking to everyone I knew that had been to prison about what to expect. I knew to keep my head down and my eyes open. Watch everybody and keep to yourself until you get to know some people.

I was celled up with an old-time jailbird named Goff. He was small and wiry, with greasy black hair and a knowing smile. He was so chill that he made me feel more relaxed. He was as comfortable being in this cellblock as a man in his own living room. He had been in the system a long time, and knew people there. He'd discovered a steel rod in the sink plug mechanism that could be sharpened to make a good weapon. Clearly, he was resourceful.

Goff started schooling me about life on the compound. I could see guys that were new like me, and who were going to have problems; guys who thought they were badasses. I could see that this kind of attitude could create serious difficulties for them, and it did. Almost immediately, a couple of fights broke out on the transition tier, and men were quickly sent to the hole.

Goff warned me about prison guards' attitudes. "However you want to play it, they're ready to one-up you. If you want to be hard, they'll be harder. If they don't want you to eat, you won't eat. You belong to them now."

One thing that didn't happen was the film and TV cliché of the new guy entering prison and a line of convicts assessing him like a delicious lunch. Never happened in any correctional facilities I went through and I never met anyone who had this happen.

I quickly decided that common sense would get me further than a tough-guy persona. There *were* tough guys around, real killers, but they weren't loudmouths. Everyone knew who they were, and they were usually quiet and minded their own business. I was furious about being in this place, but I knew enough to keep it to myself.

When you first get to prison, you get the worst job assignments on the compound. My new friend, Goff, and I got sent to the kitchen to clean the floor drain grease traps. This was a truly shitty job. The grease stunk to high heaven, and it stuck to the scoops we were using. The stench was so gross, I almost puked.

I wandered out into the mess hall and over to the windows. Through the prison perimeter fence, about 300 yards to the west, was U.S. Route 23. This highway is one of the main north–south federal expressways in southern Michigan, linking Ann Arbor with Toledo, Ohio, and points south. Many was the time I rode down that same freeway in the van with my brothers in the MC5, smoking joints and having a grand old time. I clearly remember proclaiming once, as we passed by on our way to rock & roll, girls, and glory, that I might do some stupid shit in my life, but I'd never do anything stupid enough to end up in that big ugly assed prison.

Now here I was, looking out at that same highway from inside this big ugly joint, wondering how it had happened. It was a real aha moment. I had waited all my life to fuck up this badly.

Those first weeks, my anxiety went through the roof. I couldn't sleep; I couldn't stop fixating on my girlfriend and a hundred other things happening back in Detroit. I told Goff, and he said, "You can't have your mind on the street, you gotta keep your mind in here." But that was easier said than done.

After a few weeks in Milan, I found the band room and started jamming with the musicians there. I still didn't know the prison routine or the rules. I was jamming away on the drums when a corrections officer came in looking for me. He said I needed to get back to the unit and pack my shit.

It was not my fate to stay and serve my sentence at FCI Milan. The Federal Bureau of Prisons had another plan for me. Because my case was drug-related, I qualified for a transfer to FCI Lexington. This had been my hope all along. I had heard about Lexington for years as the dope fiend/jazz musician jail where you could do easy time.

I was chained at the waist with handcuffs, and put in a van with a dozen other guys. We left Milan early in the morning, heading south. The trip was weird, to say the least. I had a lot of experience traveling in vans with a bunch of guys, but nothing like this crew.

They were a fine assortment of criminal persuasions. I was seated next to a big, long-haired fellow with granny glasses, and I mentioned that tomorrow was my twenty-seventh birthday. "Having a party?" he deadpanned.

We drove to Indianapolis, where we were booked into the county jail for the night. The Marion County Jail was a notorious facility with four-man cells along a walkway they called the Range. During the day, the cells were unlocked and people could move around, but they locked us in at night. I was in with two of my traveling companions, and it was obvious we were federal prisoners by our blue pajamas. Since I was wired up on my own adrenaline, sleeping was out of the question. I did sit-ups in my bunk, trying to tire myself out so I could sleep. Mostly, I just lay there waiting for morning.

The next day, we drove to the federal penitentiary in Terre Haute, Indiana, to drop off a couple of guys. There was a small, long-haired white guy who didn't talk during the whole trip. We had all loosened up and were making the best of a bad situation, but not this guy. When we arrived at Terre Haute, he started protesting that he couldn't go in there because he had enemies. The marshals were unmoved by his complaints, and they took him inside. In a while, they returned to the van and we resumed our trip. They told us the dude's story. Apparently, he was the getaway driver for a bank-robbery gang. He got scared and drove off without them, leaving his partners in the bank. That was who was waiting for him at Terre Haute. No wonder he didn't talk much on the trip. He had a lot on his mind.

By the end of the day, we arrived at FCI Lex. I was overwhelmed by the sheer size of it. Set back from Leestown Road on 1,050 acres in Fayette County, Kentucky, seven miles north of Lexington, it was a monstrosity of a facility. It looked to be five stories tall, and went on in the distance forever.

It had just started raining when we were walked through the gate and led across the compound to receiving and discharge. Out in the middle of a smaller inner yard, a highly muscled black man was naked and provoking two corrections officers to fight with him

in the now-pouring rain. The officers were circling him as reinforcements arrived and other COs ran in their direction. We were shut-
tled down into the basement to get processed, and didn't see what
happened up on the yard. Welcome to Lexington.

I had prepared myself for prison by getting fat. I drank beer and
ate pizza and ice cream until I ballooned up to 230 pounds. For me,
this was huge, from a rock & roll weight of 165. I figured it would
give me something to do: work out and get in shape.

I'd been warned by my criminal friends to stay out of the prison
drug trade, which I did. Don't mess with homosexuals, and don't
gamble. Just mind my own business, hang with my own crew, and
do my own time. I was fearful, as everyone is, of getting gang-raped,
but my friends assured me that probably wasn't in the cards for me,
and it wasn't. I guessed that there were probably more than a few
fellows just like me in there—regular, mainstream drug dealers—and
that was indeed the case.

I had a very hard time the first three months. I actually believed
that going to jail would be an easy way out of my terrible relationship with Sam. I thought going to prison was easier than breaking
up with her.

But when I got locked up, I became unexpectedly insecure. I
changed my mind, and tried everything I could to hold onto her. I
agonized over her, knowing in my heart that I was powerless; there
wasn't a damn thing I could do about anything. I so wanted her to
be someone she wasn't.

After a month or so in prison, I called her on the unit phone. You
have to call home collect. My ex-burglary partner, Mark, answered
the phone. He was a musician, too, and he had just been released
from state prison on the burglary case we had both been busted on.
I asked what he was doing in my apartment, answering my phone.

"I just stopped in to learn some bass parts off of your records,
Wayne," he said.

Right. Learn some bass parts. My girlfriend's parts were more
like it. "Get the fuck out of my house," I said.

After Mark was shot by the police in an armed robbery in East Detroit, I got the full story. Turns out that Sam was driving the get-away car; real Bonnie and Clyde stuff. Mark survived the shooting and went back to prison. Sam got probation, and became the recipient of love letters from two losers in the joint.

CHAPTER 23

THE WHITE BOY WITH THE WAH-WAH

FCI Lexington is a colossal brick and concrete institution built in the federal style. It's located in the rolling bluegrass country of north central Kentucky, an area of thoroughbred horse farms and big money. In summer, the weather is hot and humid, with absolutely stunning sunsets. Mild winters, and good farming country.

Originally designated the U.S. Narcotic Farm, Lexington, was opened on May 15, 1935. It was called an alternative institution within the federal prison system, which had, as a result of the Harrison Narcotics Tax Act, and to the dismay of prison wardens of the time, begun to be filled with a new class of prisoner: the drug addict.

Before the Harrison Act of 1914, drug use in America was unregulated, and a very small number of Americans used opiates regularly. Alcohol use was also popular for a segment of the population. For the religious right, both were tantamount to moral heresy, and could not be tolerated. The use of blatant racist and religious fears to push the Harrison Narcotics and Volstead acts through the U.S. Congress is a vivid and costly illustration of our country's occasionally less-than-ethical, misguided values. The Harrison Act was designed to regulate and control drug production and distribution, allowing doctors to prescribe them in their practice. Before Harrison a doctor could prescribe opiates to addicted patients, allowing them to live a normal life under their care. The cost was minimal and the impact on society was invisible. But in a cruel twist, the courts and police interpreted the act to mean that doctors could *not* prescribe to addicts, because addiction was not recognized as a disease. After the passage of Harrison, doctors were prosecuted relentlessly—turning a minor medical problem into a major national criminal-justice issue. Thus began the War on Drugs, the greatest failure of social policy in America's domestic history. Those attitudes, combined with the racist law-and-order politics of the last few decades, have evolved so destructively that, today, over two million Americans are under lock and key, with another seven million on parole or probation. And most are poor people of color, who use and sell no more drugs than whites do.

On the day I arrived at FCI Lex, I was sent to my assigned room in the Nu-Men Unit. It was recently vacated by a group of guys who were shipped out to the U.S. penitentiary in Atlanta for taking part in the gang sexual abuse of another inmate who had testified against them in court. Apparently, they had recorded the entire event, complete with a running narration, on a portable cassette machine.

I noticed that on one of the beds was a photo of a young white woman smiling for the camera. When the fellow who was to be my first cellie showed up, he explained that he'd left the photo out so I would know he was white.

He was a long-haired southern boy and genial enough. Not a raging intellect, but not dangerous either. It turned out he was state-raised, and coveted his new position working in the kitchen. He was happy as could be about it. He had arrived a few weeks before me, and he was finding his footing. We both liked to smoke weed, so we got high together and got along fine. I quickly discovered that any drug you wanted was available if you had money. Reefer in particular was abundant.

Some of the fellows on the compound were far crazier than he was, and this was an eye-opener for me. The place was full of loonies. Early on I mentioned to him that I was looking at doing my bit as a monastic experience of self-examination and study. Apparently, he repeated this to one of the guys on the yard, who woke me up from a midafternoon nap with a hypodermic syringe sticking out of his ear, saying, "Kramer, you need to take your penitentiary experience seriously." I thought this was very funny.

After I'd spent my first year in Lexington, I graduated to a single room. My new "house" was about five by twelve feet in size. With my arms completely outstretched, I could touch both walls. Since the facility was originally designed to be a hospital, there were also rooms for two, four, and even six to eight people, with their own toilets and showers.

I liked my single cell; it was my sanctuary, my cave. It was down at the end of the corridor on the third floor, and those of us who lived there had a good jump on the staff when they'd come snooping around. We had an early warning system of hoots, whistles, and assorted sounds that said, "Cops heading your way."

I used to practice the guitar in my cell every day after lunch because the unit was empty. One day, one of the gangsters was walking by. He stuck his head in and said, "Hey, you the white boy with the Wah-Wah. You cool."

CHAPTER 24

THE RED ARROW

Many of the greatest jazz artists of the forties, fifties, and sixties came through Lexington. In the dressing rooms off the stage in the auditorium, I found chord changes penciled on the walls. They were sophisticated substitutions, and I wondered who might have written them: Tadd Dameron? Lee Morgan? Gerry Mulligan? Word on the prison grapevine was that the legendary jazz trumpeter Red Rodney was coming to Lexington. Some of the older brothers were hard-core jazz fans, and they were excited he was coming in. I hadn't heard of Red before, but I got up to speed pretty quick. He had played with Jimmy Dorsey, Georgie Auld, Claude Thornhill, Gene Krupa, Benny Goodman, Woody Herman, and many others. The jazzbos on the yard schooled me that back in the forties, Red replaced Miles Davis in the Charlie Parker Quintet, and was regarded as one of the most formidable trumpeters in jazz.

When he walked into the entry of Nu-Men Unit, he didn't look like I'd imagined. I expected a tall, ultra-hip black man, but this guy was short, and he sure didn't look hip. He was slightly portly and he was also very white, almost pink, with a shock of bright red hair. "Danish Jew," he told me later. I approached him straight away. I told him that I was a musician, and we had a band here and maybe we could do some playing together. He was cool to the suggestion; he gave me a once-over and said, "Maybe. We'll see." I resented his attitude because I was being as sincere and respectful as I could be. Yet, it was understandable in the prison environment, where often nobody is who they say they are and trust takes time. Still, I thought he was a snob.

One day, Red showed up at my door with a trumpet under his arm and a jazz fake book in his hands. He asked, "Can you read these chords?"

"I think so," I said. I was surprised that he came to see me.

"Okay then. Let's play this one." Red handed me the book, pointed out the song, and counted off, "One . . . two . . . one, two, three, and . . ."

I struggled to keep up. The changes came fast and furious. At some points in the chart, there were four chords to the bar, and this was not at a relaxed tempo. Red played the melody, and when we finished, he said, "Good. You can play." It was a trying moment in my musical life, but I passed. Only years later did I realize that getting the stamp of approval from a musician of Red's caliber was a real accomplishment.

After I passed my audition, Red opened up to me. It was as if I was all right now, and we were on a level playing field. We began walking the yard and talking together a lot. He delighted me with tales of New York and the jazz world in the forties and fifties; being on the road with Charlie Parker and his early professional work with the big bands. He was a walking compendium of American musical and cultural history, and I grew to love him immensely.

At one point, he decided that my music education needed to be upgraded, and I was his willing student. Red had taken a Berklee College of Music correspondence course when he was in Lexington decades before, and he still had the books and coursework. We convinced the warden that this would be a good thing for the inmates. He agreed, gave us a classroom, and let us mimeograph the lessons and distribute them to our classmates. It was my first exposure to the numerical scale system and to harmony, and a lot of homework was involved. I was learning by writing out scales and harmonizing melodies. The classroom theory was applied when we picked up our instruments and played. I forgot I was in prison when we played and studied music.

My relationship with Red blossomed over the many months we were together. We spent long hours telling each other stories of our days in music and other adventures. We talked about our good and bad behavior; how we were similar and how we were different.

Red told me about touring the South with Charlie Parker, playing the Chitlin' Circuit joints, and how Parker had nicknamed him Chood and forced him to sing a blues song each night. "And I ain't no singer," he laughed.

A lot of the stories Red told me came to the big screen in Clint Eastwood's film *Bird*. Red worked as a consultant on the movie, and recorded much of the score.

He was exactly the kind of fellow I venerated. He was hipper than hip, cooler than cool. He was smarter than everybody and skilled as hell, and, unfortunately, back in prison again in his fifties. That made me think.

Red always had a great attitude. He was never depressed and, believe me, prison life has a way of getting you down from time to time. A bad letter from home, a setback from the parole board, loss of good behavior credits, or any of a hundred other dramas can throw you in the dumps real quick.

Red would say with a huge smile on his face, "Wayne, I like doing business with established institutions." He'd wave his hand around like he was the mayor of Lexington, its resident tour guide and host. In Red, I got to see what it really meant to be an opiate-addicted musician over a lifetime. How complicated and troublesome it all was, and how, once hooked, he had no choice but to ride it to the bitter end. I expressed my sincere desire to straighten up, but when he asked if my girl back home was using, and I said yes, he said I didn't have a chance. "Might work if it was the other way around. But you going out to a dope fiend woman . . . forget it."

Once, when I was getting short (nearing a release date) and had gone home on a five-day furlough, he asked me if I'd gotten high while I was home. I said, "Hell, yes." He said, "I ought to beat the shit out of you." Here was 53-year-old little Red Rodney looking up at me, with his fist balled up, furious. I loved him for that. He cared enough to get angry at me.

We played in our jazz group at any opportunity that presented itself. We did a regular Sunday concert schedule during the summer months on the small yard. We played special events like Fourth of July, and even produced and filmed a mock TV talk show, written by and starring inmates and staff. On a couple of occasions, we got to join some local musicians on supervised concerts in public parks in the town of Lexington. This was set up by one of the area musicians, a tenor player who worked for the post office. He'd been coming out to the prison to play for years, and had a good relationship with the warden. These were really fun gigs. We played jazz standards, and learning to comp through changes really helped my playing.

One of the park concerts was in the heart of the black community, and everybody was excited about us coming out to perform. They all knew it was Red Rodney on trumpet. The local drummer had asked for me in particular as "the white boy who could play blues like B.B. King."

We also played as the backing band for Unity, a vocal group from one of the other housing units who paid us for our work in heroin. After a lifetime of shooting up, Red had no veins left. He asked me if I could help him inject his shot. I wasn't prepared for digging in his arms with a dull, nasty, jailhouse syringe. Instead, we snorted the dope. It wasn't much to speak of anyway.

Once Red and I became close, he told me of his journey to Lexington this time. He had started his sentence at FCI Sandstone, Minnesota, while he was still on crutches. "Why were you on crutches?" I asked. He dropped his trousers to show me two large round pink scars, one on each thigh: bullet wounds. "Look what they did to me," he said.

He was sent to Sandstone because the prison is out in the middle of the boonies in Minnesota up near the Canadian border, and he was considered a flight risk. A flight risk . . . on crutches. The snow is so deep in the winter, you'd die of exposure if you attempted an escape. After a year up there healing from his wounds, he was transferred down to Lexington.

Red was married to a Danish woman who was the well-respected director of the Danish library system. He had lived in Denmark, and played in the Danish National Jazz Orchestra, as well as occasionally touring Europe with Dexter Gordon in their quintet. Red's habit was maintained through a government methadone prescription that arrived at his house by mail. Life was good.

In the early 1970s, George Wein, the New York jazz pianist and promoter, hired Red and Dexter for a tour of America with his Newport Jazz All Stars.

Red had an old friend who was a jazz fan and high-level mafia drug supplier. He sold Red two kilos of raw morphine base for $800. This was for Red and the other guys in the band who used, so they wouldn't have to go through the hassle of trying to score on the road, or not find drugs and get sick.

Red was no smuggler, though, and just packed the dope in his suitcase. The dogs discovered it at Kennedy Airport, and the DEA broke down his hotel room door just as he was doing his first shot in New York.

When he got to court, his attorney, Edward Bennett Williams, used Red's lifelong history as a narcotics-addicted jazz musician to convince the judge that the two kilos were for his personal use, and that he was not a dealer. The judge showed compassion, and sentenced Red to three years in federal prison.

Red had been to prison numerous times before in his life, and was scared of going back again. He fled home to Denmark instead.

Every year for the next few years, the United States would demand that the Danes extradite Red. Since he had dual citizenship, he was legally a Danish citizen, and the Danes refused. In Denmark, narcotics addiction was not a criminal offense, so he was not in violation of their laws.

One afternoon, Red was home alone. His doorbell rang, and two big Americans informed him that they were from the U.S. embassy; that there was a new ruling that would release him from his criminal sentence in the States. All he needed to do was sign this form, and it would be all over. Red told them he would have to get his glasses, and turned back into the house. Smelling a setup, he ran out the back door and was confronted by another American with a 9mm pistol pointed straight at him. He fired twice, hitting Red in both legs. They threw him into a van and drove him to an American Air Force base, where he was put on a military jet with tourniquets on his legs, flown back to New York, and arrested at Kennedy Airport. He waited nine hours before he saw a doctor in the prison ward of Bellevue Hospital. The entire ward was filled with guys who had been shot, beaten, and kidnapped by DEA agents all over the world.

When he went back to court for having fled from custody, the judge gave him an additional six months. Williams informed the court that the U.S. government had shot and kidnapped a Danish citizen—while living in Denmark—in violation of international law. The police in Denmark didn't even carry guns, and what the United States had done was indefensible. Red sued for ten million dollars.

A year or so later, Red stopped me on the yard to tell me that the warden just offered him an immediate release if he dropped his lawsuit. He asked me what to do. "Call your lawyer," was my response. He told me later that Williams informed him that his was not a personal injury law firm, they were a political law firm, and Red was going to stay in prison until they settled the suit.

Six months later, I was released on parole, and Red followed me into freedom some months after that.

I would run into him around Manhattan, and we tried to stay in touch. After I hadn't spoken to him in a year or so, I called him one day to see how he was doing. He was doing pretty well. He'd just bought a boat, a house in Florida, and a house in New Jersey. He told me he'd settled with the government for three million in cash.

No more jingle sessions for Chood. From now on, he would only play jazz when and where and with whom he wanted. He and his long-time partner, Ira Sullivan, were playing together, and he was having a ball.

Red died at his home in Boynton Beach, Florida, from lung cancer at age 66 on May 27, 1994. There will be no more like him.

The last year of my bit with Red was a gift. He was my mentor, and a father figure for me. We were both there because of major league bad behavior as adults and, as a result, any life truths that Red passed my way were subtle and hard-won.

But in music, he was unquestionably my true master, and I his humble acolyte. Those particular lines of demarcation were written in stone. Not in his demeanor or how he treated me, but in the clear recognition of his utter mastery of his instrument, and of jazz as the highest achievement in musical art. He was a giant in music, and I was well fed by the crumbs from his table.

CHAPTER 25

DAY-TO-DAY LIFE AND DEATH

Day-to-day life in prison is institutional life. Everything revolves around a routine. And, at Lexington, a job. All inmates were required to work. I started out as a janitor in the administration office of the prison hospital. It was a mindless task: empty the trash cans, vacuum the carpets in the offices, mop and polish the hallway floors. I could get everything done in an hour, and then I had the rest of the day to do what I pleased.

The trouble was, what was there to do? I hated hanging out on the yard with no activities to apply myself to. When you're not busy, time slows down. The minutes can be hours, and the hours can be days.

I didn't have much trouble with the guards at Lexington, except for one. We called him the Scarlet Esophagus. This guy would pull me over every time he saw me walking across the compound with my guitar. He would order me to open the case, then he'd take my guitar out, play a chord or two, and remind me he was a "gee-tar player," too. He was a pain in the ass, and I avoided him as much as possible.

Because the prison band gear was in such bad shape, I had my roadie bring an amp down. There were a couple of old Kustom

roll-and-pleat amps that didn't work very well, and I figured bringing one of my amps in was a good solution. When my amp, a nice
Fender Super Reverb 4x10 silver face arrived, it was put into a storage locker in the receiving and discharge (R&D) room. I had to get
it cleared by the lieutenant on duty, so I went up to his office and
presented my case.

"The institution gear is in bad shape, sir, and I had one of my
amps brought in for the band. I figure if my time here is going to
rehabilitate me, I should be able to improve my job skills for my
return to the street."

"What did you do on the street?" he asked.

"I'm a professional musician."

"Too bad you weren't a gunsmith," he said.

"I'm happy to sign a waiver of responsibility so the institution
will not be responsible for it, and . . ." I continued.

"Too bad you weren't a diamond cutter," he interrupted.

"Lieutenant, I'm not a gunsmith and I'm not a diamond cutter.
I'm a guitar player."

He responded with, "I'm not approving it."

My roadie came back down from Detroit to take the amp back.
But when I went to R&D to get it, there was no amp in the storage
locker. It had been under lock and key, and inmates didn't have
keys. My guess is that the "gee-tar playing" CO helped himself to
it. A footnote: after I was released, I threatened to sue the Bureau
of Prisons for the theft of my property. After a long series of ex-
changes, they settled with me by sending me a check for a new amp.

AT FCI Lex I had time to think about how I got there, and became willing to take a look at what I might do to make sure I never came back
to this place. I got into the available programs, and took advantage
of everything they offered to improve myself. I joined inmate book
study groups. I participated in Rational Behavior Training, Transac-
tional Analysis, Positive Mental Attitude, and group therapy, among

other therapies. I was selected to participate in a three-day Pacific Foundation Self-Image Seminar that was helpful in understanding how we program ourselves unconsciously to succeed or fail.

Courtesy of the Pell Grant program, I took college courses through the University of Kentucky. I took classes in media and poetry. The media course was where I first heard of a new project by Malcolm X's biographer, Alex Haley. Our professor brought in a black-and-white videotape of Haley giving a talk about his roots. Little did I know that all of America and the world would soon be talking about Haley's book and its accompanying TV special, *Roots*. But most importantly, I studied jazz and music theory with Red.

In the two prisons that I served time in during the midseventies, there wasn't a gang culture—except for the Mafiosi, who were very low-key. Most of the guys were young, black, white, and brown drug dealers from big cities east of the Mississippi: Detroit, Chicago, New York, Cleveland, Miami. Many were Vietnam vets who came home from the war with colossal drug habits and knowledge of weapons and tactics. They were bank robbers and dope dealers and dope house rip-off men. There were garden-variety mail thieves, organized crime types, swindlers, embezzlers, and a bunch of good-old-boy southern crime crews who stole everything in sight. Cars, trucks, tractors, trailers, mobile homes, combines, harvesters—you name it, they'd steal it. We didn't have many of the maniac-kill-your-whole-family types or the 7-Eleven shoot-the-clerk, armed robbery fools. We also didn't have many profoundly mentally ill people. These were the Carter years, before Reagan gutted our national mental health system.

There were killers to be sure, but the guys I knew would just tell you to your face: Don't fuck with me or I'll cut your head off. Fair enough.

We were allowed to wear some personal clothing items from home, like sweat suits, sweaters, jeans, etcetera. I was fine with the government-issued clothes. They were U.S. Army pants, shirts, and jackets available in fashion-forward khaki or subtler, earth-toned olive drab. I preferred the khaki, and had a guy in the laundry who would press all my clothes: 25 cents an item. He would deliver them once a week, on hangers.

I FELL IN with a small crew of dope dealers from around the East Coast. We all liked to smoke weed, and we would meet at night in someone's room and get high and play cards. In my first months, I learned that I needed to be busy every day to fight off anxiety and hold onto what little sanity I had. Depression was a regular state of mind. Through a friend I knew from Ann Arbor, I got a job as staff artist on the prison newspaper.

When I started in the *Flak* office, there was an understanding among the inmate staff that we would do absolutely as little as possible. We barely got the newspaper out once a month; quarterly was more like it. Our attitude was that we were in prison, and we were slave labor for the man. It was our criminal duty to avoid accomplishing anything of value. We were committed slackers.

This all came to an abrupt end with the arrival of a 6'5", 350-pound, cigar-chomping Jewish gangster-swindler named Nathan Cohen. Nate had just arrived from Terre Haute with a folder full of articles and a few short stories he had written. He asked if he could join our staff. I read his stuff and he was clearly a talented writer. No problem, Nate. The more the merrier. I mentioned it to our staff sponsor, and they got him assigned to the *Flak* office in a few days.

Nathan had big plans, and he knew how to implement them. He was a major-league operator from the East Coast establishment, and a contemporary of Spiro Agnew and Marvin Mandel, major criminals in their own right. He had been convicted of stealing a couple of million dollars by selling triplicate mortgages on the same properties in three different states. He was a top-shelf con man; not the pretend players that prisons are full of, but a true criminal mastermind.

The first thing he did was make up a new production schedule for a weekly newspaper and a monthly magazine. We were shocked into action. He organized the office and handed out work assignments. It was clear who was running things now.

I didn't like this at all. I resented his taking over what was a cushy, no-work gig. He picked up on my bad vibes right away and came at me. I was ready for a fight, fully prepared to defend the criminal code of defiance to never doing anything that could be considered cooperating with the man.

I was ready to tell him where to take his newfound editor/publisher credits when he completely and totally disarmed me. He used the powerful tools of empathy, logic, and reason. He asked if he had offended me in any way. If he had, he'd never meant to, and he apologized on the spot. He said that if I didn't like him, couldn't we talk about it so he could try to understand better, so we could get along together? He let all the air out of my sails with reasonableness and consideration for my feelings. I was dumbfounded into silence. I had never been won over so effectively in my life. He was using his formidable skills of persuasion and identification that I couldn't put up a defense against, and it was humbling.

He went on to explain that by being responsible and getting the newspaper and magazine out on time, we would build up our credibility with the prison administration so we could gain benefits for ourselves. That this was how you got power.

I was a Detroiter raised with a respect for labor. That's how I accomplished everything good that I ever did in my young life, by putting in the work. But I'd lost the plot in my criminal misadventures.

He went on to explain that this was how you got real money in the world, by being responsible. I had become confused, and for the last few years looked at life as a matter of "gettin' over," like I was trying to pull a fast one. I had come to believe that the goal was to get out of doing any real work.

Nathan Cohen was proposing a weighty concept, and it had the ring of truth: give them a quarter for their dime. And it was coming from a master swindler, a crooked lawyer who had made and blown more money than I'd ever dreamed of. I admitted Nate was right, and I went for it. We started cranking out the newspapers and magazines, along with special editions of inmate poetry.

We got the feds to buy us a camera, and we started publishing photos. In very little time, our office was a well-oiled machine. One side effect was that time sailed by. Nate took an interest in my work with Red in the prison band, and started working as our manager. He actually booked us gigs around the prison. "On Tuesday, you're playing a dinner for the Lexington Jaycees. Friday, it's a reception for the warden and some folks from Washington."

I did the pasteups and layout during the day. In the evenings I played basketball, and was the prison paddleball champ that first winter. I played some tennis the first summer I was there, too. In the second summer, I ran five miles a day, sometimes twice a day, and lifted weights, but I wasn't going for the big-muscled jailhouse look. I just wanted to get back to "date weight" so I could hit the streets lean and mean if I got an early parole.

Reading was a major activity for me. I would exchange books if someone found a good one. I read a lot of criminology textbooks and a fair number of psychology and therapeutic books. One book that really had an effect on me was *No Beast So Fierce*. This book was prized and passed around among our crew. The author, Edward Bunker, was unknown to me. I identified with his deep knowledge of life in prison and the criminal mindset. His characters were real and I loved the book. Reading was a good escape.

Except for a few times when some high-grade heroin came in and a couple of bouts with hooch, jailhouse whiskey made from fruit, sugar, yeast, and water, the time I was locked up was a vacation for my body. I believe it came at the perfect time to interrupt the serious damage I was doing to my internal organs. I ate well, mostly vegetables, slept regularly, exercised, and basically lived a healthy lifestyle for the time I was down.

I learned a lot from the men I did time with. As a dope dealer, I was an abject failure, but they taught me how to do it correctly. I was friendly with a middle-aged Italian from the East Coast who broke it down for me: "First Wayne, cop your own drugs. Get your own money together, and then go out and buy weight. You package it up yourself and then get guys to deal it for you. You advance them the product, and they pay you when it's sold. You always set the meeting place and time for getting your money and the re-up. If one of your people gets busted and there is the slightest chance they might talk to the police about you, you have to kill him."

I learned other things, too. I came to admire young black men who had pride and integrity to match their defiance and antisocial attitudes. I knew guys who would talk endlessly about getting over and winning and being number one, and yet seemed to be unaware they were living in a federal prison. I talked with my fellow prisoners for hours and hours on the issues of the day: politics, women, philosophy, music, literature, religion, history, science, and art. I knew young men who were state-raised, and who viewed time on the streets as a temporary interlude until they returned to their regular life in these institutions. And I knew long-term men who had served decades behind bars, and who had a resilience and stoicism that was beyond my understanding. I met people who understood power, and how to be judicious when necessary, and ruthless when the time called for it. And always humor. Sometimes you just have to laugh to keep from crying.

I had some interesting discussions with one neighbor, Shepp, who was a serious convict. He was a follower of Elijah Muhammad, and even asked me to join their group. I respectfully declined. Shepp and I had long talks about the history of various religious philosophies and politics. He lived two cells to my left.

Shepp murdered the bad-dude white boy who lived one cell to my right. Robert was a Vietnam vet, and a big-mouthed racist. Robert had advanced Shepp money to buy drugs while he was out on study release. When Shepp told him the money was gone and there was no dope for him, Robert went off. He thought he was going to intimidate Shepp by calling him out in front of everybody on the alley. I stood in the corridor with everyone else, listening to Robert berate Shepp, calling him all kinds of bigoted names, threatening to break his legs—and then when he got out of the hospital, he'd break them again. It was rough to hear, and we all knew this was very bad.

You couldn't disrespect someone like Shepp that way. It was a fatal misjudgment.

Lexington was a medium-security facility and we were not locked in at night so corrections officers could have access to us at any time. Shepp went into Robert's room in the middle of the night and stabbed him to death. Shepp ripped him off, plain and simple, and this was the endgame. It freaked everybody out.

I knew them both pretty well, and got along fine with both. Shepp had recounted to me other stabbings he had committed during earlier terms in other prisons, and I had no doubt he was serious and should be taken at his word. His credo was, "If you're not strong enough to hold it, don't mess with it." Because Shepp was bespectacled, tall, thin, and very soft-spoken, Robert thought he was weak. He wasn't weak; he was serious-minded and lived by a penitentiary code that was as severe as it was brutal. Shepp was arrested and taken to the county jail to begin his next journey through the criminal justice system. We had a few stabbings during my time at Lexington, but this was the first murder.

FCI LEXINGTON, KENTUCKY; FCI Fort Worth, Texas; and FCI Pleasanton, California; were designated medium-security facilities for federal offenders. They were also the most progressive correctional facilities in the system, and were known as "programming institutions"— meaning that numerous rehabilitation programs were available, and inmates were encouraged to take advantage of them. The goal was positive change and rehabilitation. All three prisons were co-correctional: men and women served their sentences in close proximity to each other. At Lexington, women were housed in separate units but shared parts of the compound during the day.

My time in the federal prison system was at the tail end of the era of rehabilitation in American corrections. When I arrived at Lexington in 1976, the population was around 600 inmates. There were day rooms where inmates could relax and play cards or shoot pool in their free time. When I left, the count was over 1,200, and the day rooms and corridors were filled with cubicles for inmates to sleep in. We were told that the new official aim was no longer rehabilitation, but accountability. As the War on Drugs geared up, America began warehousing humans.

Having women nearby didn't mitigate the fact that this was prison and I was serving four years. But I believe it made for a more civilized atmosphere. I also believe it serves the interest of society, in that men and women come from a world where both sexes are in contact with each other, and we return to that same world after we've paid our debt. There is no legal, social, or rehabilitative advantage in segregating men and women in corrections. Separating people serves to isolate inmates, harden attitudes, and reinforce antisocial behavior. It is also retributive, and carries a patriarchal callousness that is medieval.

In our system of justice, when we are convicted of breaking the social contract, we serve *time*. We lose our freedom for a duration of time. Time is our most valuable commodity, and it is finite; we cannot get back the time we lose. We are sent to prison *as* punishment, not *for* punishment.

PSYCHOLOGICALLY AND emotionally, being in prison changed me. I wasn't the bright-eyed, bushy-tailed idealist anymore. Rock & roll was not going to be my solution to everything. Emasculating pain is built into a prison term. You're not the master of your fate anymore; in fact, you're not in charge of much at all. It's their house, you just live in it. I was never safe, and it wore on me. It intensified my cynicism, hardening me.

BEFORE I GOT LOCKED UP, I had recorded a few demos with Melvin and Tim that I sent to Mick Farren in England. I was hoping he could find interest from a British record label. Nothing much came of it, but while I was in the gulag, he and some of the guys convinced Ted Carroll at Chiswick Records and Jake Riviera at Stiff to release the recordings as a seven-inch single to benefit me. They set up an interview with the British music newspaper *Melody Maker* from prison by transatlantic phone call, and with the publicity from the cover story, they sold 10,000 copies in a matter of days. I was a cause célèbre for a day or two in London, but that didn't help with the day-to-day dreariness of serving time. It was as if my old life as a recording artist existed in a different dimension. My real life was here in this prison.

CHAPTER 26
FREEDOM

The buildup to my release day was excruciating. I gave away all my worldly possessions. I had a nice collection of jailhouse accoutrements: shelves with books, a radio, a lamp, a fan, and a racquetball paddle. It was a veritable king's ransom acquired over the few years I was there. I had gotten word that the parole board was going to grant me an early release. My clean prison record and all the programs and classes I had participated in demonstrated that I had worked hard to change for the better and had earned parole. I was happy with this development.

As it turned out, one of the case managers, an old-time Bureau of Prisons hand, liked me and convinced the board that one of the charges on my record was irrelevant. I think it was the "open alcohol in a motor vehicle" from back in the MC5 days in San Francisco, or the "noise disturbance (loud band)" charge. The manager's intervention allowed me to qualify for an earlier release date.

The hardest times for me during my incarceration were the first three months and the last three months. In between, I was just living my life in the institution. "Jailing" is what we called it. My concerns were prison concerns, not street concerns. My life was in here, not out there. But when my time started getting short, I started getting anxious: "What's it going to be like? Am I going to be able to make a living? What about Sam?" I was facing an abyss. "Where will I live?

How will I survive? Will anyone remember me?" These thoughts chilled me to my bones.

I didn't sleep much the night before my release. I made the rounds at breakfast saying goodbye to my friends. At 9:00 AM, I walked out the front gate of FCI Lexington. My crime partner, Tim, was waiting at the gate. He was on study release, and he was going into town to attend college classes that day. We had grown further apart when I got an earlier parole date than he did. He blamed me for his getting into trouble in the first place.

This had always bugged me because I didn't force him to do what we did together. We had even discussed the fact that if we were busted dealing cocaine, we would both be going to prison. I felt bad that he blamed me, but there was nothing I could do about his attitude. I just hoped that one day, down the line, we could be friends again.

"Have a nice life," he said as I left. I wished him well, and took a cab to the bus station in town. I was numb. I couldn't feel my feet touching the ground. It was like I was dreaming. Floating along. An overload of emotion was flooding through me. It was all I could do just to keep moving forward.

I was 29 years old. I had served two-and-a-half years in federal prison, and was now facing 22 months on parole, as well as an additional three-year special parole term for drug offenders.

I had my release money: $200. I was supposed to buy a bus ticket to Detroit and check into the halfway house within 24 hours, but taking the bus was out of the question. My friend, saxophonist Jim Watts, met me at the bus station in his superfine, beautifully restored '57 Chevy coupe. We pulled out of the station and hit the freeway north. He had some superb reefer, and we got a nice buzz on for the five-hour drive back to the Motor City. Jim was anxious to talk about music and what I might want to do, but I was incapable of putting any thought into the subject. I was too overwhelmed.

He dropped me off at my girlfriend Sam's parents' house on the east side. She and one of her girlfriends were just heading out for work. She casually gave me a peck on the cheek and said that maybe we'd hang out later. She was high as a kite, laughing like a hyena with her pal about something I wasn't privy to. I thought, *Hang out later? What the fuck is going on here? I just got home from prison! I've been away for two-and-a-half years, and I get a peck on the cheek and "Maybe we'll hang out later?"*

I was dizzy with confusion. I was furious with her and her brassy pal who were shaking their asses and pouting like porno queens. I didn't get it. The sweet, gentle, loving, soulful reunion that I had dreamt of wasn't turning out as planned.

I had to check into the Federal Community Treatment Center (CTC), or halfway house, which was in a converted hotel downtown. They explained the rules to me: Curfew was 11:00 PM weeknights and 3:00 AM weekends. You must get a job. You must have a bank account, and show the on-duty officer your bankbook and balance every Friday. You must submit to random urine testing. No violence, no threats. You will not be granted weekend passes without a job and a $200 minimum bank balance.

A lot of guys from prisons all over the federal system were there. Some had just finished long bits: 10, 15, 20 years. Having been away for a long time, they were pretty tentative about everything.

My roommate was my friend and coworker from the prison newspaper. Big Darryl Gilbert was a 6'5" career criminal and lifelong drug addict. He had been in and out of prisons all his life, and he was comfortable with it all. He was a very cerebral brother, and a player in the Detroit dope underworld. He was already managing some dope holes out on Eight Mile Road, and he'd acquired a heroin habit while still in the halfway house. He used to shoot up between his toes every morning before he left for "work."

Darryl was a knowledgeable music fan and knew his jazz. We went shopping together one day and bought all manner of new pimp clothes for ourselves. We both got pink leopard-print nylon boxer shorts with matching wife-beater undershirts. We also both bought shoes with heels that were half-clear plastic. Pimps to the max. It was the culture of prison and the culture of the street that I embraced.

I bought a couple of pairs of high-waisted, double-knit Eleganza slacks that were flared with bell-bottoms. What did I know? I was completely out of sync with style trends on the street. I'd missed the coming of punk rock. When I went over to England later that year, some of the guys were asking me, "Is that what people are wearing in the States?" I wasn't with the tight black jeans, spiky hair yet. I still had my blow dry, bad-dude-white-boy-moustache, and polyester Nik Nik shirts.

I wandered the neighborhood around the CTC during my first few days free. It was in the Cass Corridor where I had lived in the early days of the MC5, so I knew the area well. I went into a local bar, The New Miami, ordered a glass of Lambrusco, and overheard the bartender tell his partner that he heard Wayne Kramer just got out of prison. I guess with my moustache and blow-dried hair they didn't think the dude at the end of the bar just might be the errant guitarist they were gossiping about. It was surreal.

I TRIED TO RECONNECT with Sam. I had been locked up for a fair amount of time, and had obsessed over her. Now I was back, and it was worse than I thought. I knew she was an addict. All the time I was locked up, I sweated her leaving me. I knew she was a wounded bird, and I knew she could not change. She loved dope. When you're convinced that you're not as good as others, narcotics are a great equalizer. When she was high, she was a different person: brassy, outgoing, and witty. Sober, she was introverted and painfully shy. I pined over her so much, and convinced myself I could fix everything when I got out. I thought that all she needed was a real man to love her, and I was that man. I wanted desperately to connect with her on an intimate level, not just through sex, but as a human being, a friend and confidante. I needed to be close to someone.

Make no mistake, the sex was important. I'd been locked up a long time, and I was a healthy young man. But it just wasn't happening. She was go-go dancing and making enough money to support her habit, and that was all she was capable of. Having just finished the most dreadful experience of my young life, I deeply wanted to be held and loved, and to give love in return. This should have been a joyous time. I'm free. I'm back. I'm home, baby! It's over! But it wasn't. It was awful.

She would sleep with me when it fit her schedule, but that wasn't too often because I had to get back to the CTC by curfew. I wanted to be with her, so I would end up in the car when she would drive over to the dope house to cop. Day-in, day-out, I was there watching her turn into the walking dead and then go off to rub guys' crotches for money.

I was so disoriented from prison that I didn't know what the hell I was doing most of the time. I was determined not to use dope again, but all I had going for me was willpower. I didn't know anyone that didn't get high on something every day. One day she told me, "Baby, I know you don't want to use right now, but if you change your mind, the shit's reeeaaal good." I had more orgasms in prison masturbating. She had a coterie of go-go girlfriends, some of whom were superfine and gave me that come hither look, but I didn't move on any of them because I was determined to establish a meaningful relationship with Sam.

I re-upped with John Sinclair, and now that I'd done a prison term, too, any bad blood between us was forgiven and forgotten. He had mentored me when I first caught my case and it was looking like I was heading to prison. I valued that. Now that I was out, we seemed to pick up where we left off before he went down.

John and I have never discussed what happened between us. We both have our own perspectives. It was extremely painful for both of us, and I don't think there is anything to be gained by revisiting that turbulent time again. I don't need John to come around to my version of history, and he doesn't need me to embrace his. I'd always loved John, and I was happy to have my old friend back. He was one of the few people in my life who understood what I was talking about.

A GUY CONTACTED ME at the CTC about a job. He led a band and had a regular booking at a local club. His idea was that I would be his band's special guest, and he would promote it and we'd all make a few bucks. This was just what I needed to get the restrictions lifted from the *federales*. I went to hear the band, and they were a decent club-rock group. They were very excited about the possibility of me working with them every weekend, so I agreed.

Now that I had a job, the curfew was dropped and I was able to live a little. It also got me weekend passes. As long as I didn't violate any rules and had clean urine, I was provisionally free.

The fellows in the band were nice cats and decent musicians. We played a variety of current rock and older material, some of the R&B standards I'd played in prison and a few MC5 tunes. It was fun to be playing in a club again in the free world. Musically, I had been playing and studying jazz with Red Rodney, and I missed playing with much higher caliber musicians. But there were fringe benefits to being in the free world that made up for that. I could drink a glass of wine, I could get laid. And within the rules of my parole, I could come and go as I pleased.

I was trying to readjust to life in the free world. It was not an easy time. I felt out of sync with everything. I punched out a few walls and went on crying jags out of sheer frustration. I had no male friends to confide in, and had nowhere to go with my anger, so I stuffed it down.

While I was at the CTC I got a telegram from my friends in England saying they were sending me a $5,000 royalty check from the benefit single. I was humbled and grateful that I would have a cash cushion to ease the transition from jail to the street. It was a hell of a lot more than most guys come home to, which is one reason a lot of people go back to prison so quickly—they come out with exactly what they went in with: nothing.

I thought it was pretty funny when the officer on duty asked to see my bank book, and flipped out when he saw a deposit for that much money. He asked where it came from, and I said, "It was easy. I copped a pound, stepped on it, put it on the street, and cashed out ... No, officer, just kidding. I'm actually a recording artist and this is a royalty payment for one of my records." He didn't seem to share my sense of humor. The police never do.

After I was released from the CTC, I rented a basement apartment on Chalmers Avenue on Detroit's near east side. I was frustrated, lonely, angry, disconnected, and no longer under the close control of the prison system. I also had a big pile of cash. So, after going with the girlfriend to cop again and again, finally, but predictably, I said, "Get me a couple, too." I was well and truly fucked again. The pain-killing properties of opiates were available, and I needed relief.

With the cash from England, I was able to score large amounts and stay high for weeks at a time. I hooked up with some dealers on the West Side, and burned through the money. I overdosed again and was revived by EMS workers. I still had to meet my parole officer once a month, but he was easygoing. I had to give urine samples, but if I had been using, I would just get a bottle of clean piss from a friend and empty it into the collection bottle in the bathroom stall.

Naturally, after the money ran out Sam began paying for most of our drugs. I would pay the rent and expenses from my gigs, but the club she worked in was closed on Sundays and that usually meant I got sick. Keeping it up week in and week out was a nightmare. There was no way to keep up with the relentless cost of two heroin habits. My friend Big Darryl told me he and his girlfriend had joined the methadone maintenance program at Herman Kiefer Hospital, so, after one too many nights of withdrawal sickness, Sam and I decided to join, too.

We fell into an easy routine. We'd get up around 10:00 AM, clean up, and head over to the clinic. Get our medication and go to breakfast. Usually, we would go into downtown Detroit where there were some inexpensive restaurants and we would wait for the methadone to kick in, read the paper, eat, and chat. The Detroit Institute of Arts was a regular spot of ours. We'd goof off the rest of the day, and if it was a working night, we would both go to our jobs and meet up afterward.

This was a realistic lifestyle for me. I wasn't ready to stop being high, but I couldn't afford the cost and risk of street drugs.

I found that I really liked the routine of the clinic. I think I missed the regularity of institution life. The prison takes care of you. It's your concrete mama. You follow the rules and all your needs are met—except for freedom. The methadone clinic was my new surrogate prison; it met my emotional needs. There were rules, and if I followed them, the clinic took care of me with the medication I needed. It was also very social. You would see the same people day in and day out, and we'd all bullshit and gossip about the everyday drama of the dope fiend life. Someone was always getting shot or overdosing; getting arrested or violating parole and going back to prison.

I began having complications with life in general, and relationships in particular. One day I was kicking it with a nurse, and she suggested I talk to one of the counselors. They have counselors here? That appealed to me immediately.

I stopped into Marv's office and sat down for a talk. This was a completely new concept to me. Here was an older guy, a brother, an ex-offender and ex-addict, who was qualified and available to talk with me about my problems.

He had done the same things that I had done. He'd been there— robbed, shot dope into his veins, gone to the penitentiary—and he was doing better now. He might have some much-needed wisdom that he could impart. I felt that I could talk to him, knowing that he understood me; that we understood each other.

The current issue was detoxing from methadone and the six weeks of lethargy that you go through to get straight after you come down slowly, gradually, from your maintenance dose. In my case, it was 40 milligrams a day. The clinic would lower my dose by 2.5 milligrams every few weeks. This way, the detox is hardly noticeable. Of course, you're nowhere near as high at 5 or 10 milligrams as you were at 30 or 40, but if you want off, this is how it's accomplished. It worked pretty well for me right down to zero, but by then I was just low-energy and I had trouble sleeping. Marv asked me, "Why don't you drink a beer and smoke a joint?" Sober it wasn't, but it was helpful in an enabling kind of way, and I really appreciated it. We had an enjoyable relationship for a few months until budget cutbacks and he got laid off.

PART 3

The point of modernity is to live a life without illusions,
while not becoming disillusioned.

–ANTONIO GRAMSCI

CHAPTER 27

WHEEL ME OUT

While I was in prison, a new music movement emerged: punk rock. I had read about it in music magazines while I was in Lexington. Some of these new punk bands cited the MC5 as a major influence. This troubled me because "punk" had a very different meaning in prison. I tore up the magazines and flushed them down the toilet. Under the circumstances, I didn't care to be associated with punk.

Just after I was released, I went to see the Clash play in Detroit, and they were very kind to me. I introduced myself to Mick Jones and Joe Strummer, who laughed and said they knew well who I was. They told me they had written a song about me—"Jail Guitar Doors"—and handed me a copy of the seven-inch. On it they had written in pen, "WK—#1 in the USA."

I had been playing jazz and R&B in Lexington, and the simple structure of punk rock was something of a letdown. It seemed to me that this new crop of players was reverting to old well-trodden guitar playing. To my ear, punk rock didn't sound musically revolutionary at all. I truly appreciated their gesture, but it took me a minute to come around to punk rock.

I had rented a basement apartment on the east side of Detroit, put a new band together, and was working with a new crop of players. My bass player Ron Cooke called up to ask if I was interested in coming to a Johnny Thunders and the Heartbreakers show at Bookie's Club. He said, "Johnny wants to meet you. He's begging for you to come and play with him." I had always heard that his former band, the New York Dolls, were MC5 fans, and I was flattered.

I was trying to reestablish myself on the music scene, and I thought this might help. Who knows, it might even be fun. They brought me up at the end of the set for the Contours' classic "Do You Love Me?" We rocked pretty well, the kids enjoyed it; after which, we retired to the dressing room.

Before we could talk, Johnny disappeared into a toilet stall and shot up. This was where I'd left off before prison. When he came out, he said that he wanted to start a new band with me. He had a booking in Chicago, and his plan was for us to start there. After a few days, we met at his house, snorted lots of cocaine, and played guitars all night long. We would call the band Gang War.

A week or so later, we booked a recording session at a small studio on Detroit's east side and worked all night, cutting a half-dozen tunes. Mostly covers like Fats Domino's "I'm Gonna Be a Wheel Someday," The Chantays' "Pipeline," and a few I recommended like James Brown's "I'll Go Crazy." We also recorded new versions of a couple of Johnny's tunes.

We started playing small towns around the Midwest. Sometimes, in a little club with almost no crowd, Johnny would brilliantly portray the rock & roll antihero. On nights like this, I felt like this scheme could work. Other times I had empirical evidence that it wouldn't. After waiting for him one too many times to cop before a show, I finally did what an addict does, and had him pick me up a couple of bags, too. I was off to the races again.

In the spring of 1980, I moved to New York City, and the Lower East Side was heroin heaven. The neighborhood below Fourteenth Street and east of Avenue A was an open-air drug market, 24–7; all you needed was cash. Johnny and I were frequent clients. There could be a large crowd of people aimlessly milling around the corner of Eighth Street and Avenue D. In the blink of an eye, they would coalesce into a perfectly orderly line on the sidewalk to buy their drugs and disappear. It was the Cairo bazaar of dope; Disneyland for drug addicts.

Every gig I played was a whirlwind of copping, getting to the venue, playing, getting paid, and copping again. The music was not much of a consideration; you just got through the gig for the real reason you were there, which was to get the money to buy more drugs with. I guess wealthy addict-musicians operate on another level, with dealers delivering their dope and plenty of cash to pay for it, but that was never my experience. It was always a hustle, and a hassle.

After a few months together, Johnny and I played a college bar in East Lansing and the place was packed. We had sold it out, and were well into a bonus on the door. Halfway through the set we played the Knack's "My Sharona," but with a Thunders' rewrite to "Ayatollah" for the chorus.

Ayatollah Ruhollah Khomeini was in the news, and this was Johnny's attempt to be "political." There were Iranian students in the audience, and they took issue with us ridiculing their hero and started throwing beer mugs at us. Big, heavy, glass, beer mugs. After a couple narrowly missed my head, I stopped the show and we walked off. A nasty scene started out on the dance floor between our fans and the Iranian students. The promoter was desperate to find a solution. I told him to remove the troublemakers and have the bouncers stand next to us onstage in a show of force. He agreed, and we came back onstage to a thundering cheer. It was a great moment of rock triumph.

Later, after we had been paid (including a healthy bonus), I was talking to some fans when Ron Cooke pulled me aside. "Wayne, you gotta do something. Johnny's stealing money from the manager's desk." This was news I didn't need.

I headed toward the dressing room when out strolls Johnny with quarters flowing from his pant legs, grinning like a six-year-old with his hand in the cookie jar. My girlfriend, Sam, came up and told me he just put a large roll of cash in her purse. I told her to go into the ladies' room and leave the cash on the counter.

I gathered everyone up and said, "Let's roll out as quickly and quietly as possible." I was sweating this because I was on parole. Any arrest would be a violation and send me back to prison—not to mention a new charge for robbery.

As we were getting into our cars in the parking lot, three police cruisers with lights flashing pulled in. The cops brought everyone back into the club to sort the mess out. I was furious with Thunders. In the confusion, as the cops were talking to the club owner, Johnny came over to me. "Wayne, what should I do?"

I told him he was going to go over to the club owner and tell him he was outta his mind on drugs and made a terrible mistake. And that you're so very sorry, and this is all your doing, and no one else had any part in any of this. I also said that if I had to go back to prison over this, I guaranteed him a major-league ass whipping.

Johnny did as I instructed. The police made all of us turn over all the money we had on us, including our wages from the gig, plus any personal money. What could we do? We were lucky they didn't arrest us. Bad news travels fast. Before noon the next day, every booking we had canceled. "Snatching defeat from the jaws of victory" became the band's motto.

Johnny and I played the odd gig here and there, and eventually we broke up over his wanting sole billing. In the end, he died on the floor of a guesthouse in New Orleans, having just been paid a large sum of money from a tour: a classic dope fiend ending.

Johnny lived longer than I ever thought he would. When he wanted something, he was capable of immense charm. He bought into the tortured romantic artist/junkie myth, and it killed him. Johnny was not an evil guy, but he was also just not the kind of guy who was going to get clean and join a gym.

What he was, was a man with an untreated and often fatal disorder: addiction.

WHEN I FIRST MOVED to New York, I landed in Long Island City, but quickly moved into the Lower East Side where all the action was. I found a one-bedroom, tenement-style apartment with the bathtub in the kitchen on the third floor of a five-story walk-up on East Tenth Street between First and Second avenues. Rent was $175 a month. The neighborhood was just transitioning from Wild West dope ghetto to punk-rock trendy. A judiciously applied hundred-dollar tip to the super got me in the building. I loved this place, and felt like I had finally arrived in a time and city where I could make things happen.

While I was making the transition to New York with Gang War, I had been trying to get a new solo single recorded in Detroit and met a guy willing to finance the project. He was awaiting sentencing on a drug conviction, and wanted to have a fling as an executive producer before he left. I recorded the tracks at a happening studio in Detroit: the Sound Suite. One of the other artists recording there was a local bassist, Don Fagenson. He had a new project he was developing, and wanted me to play on it.

He and his partner, David Weiss, had donned stage identities as "brothers" Don Was and David Was and had an idea for a new band: Was (Not Was). They were both Detroit-area natives, and much to my joy, were great MC5 fans. The band's influence had informed their new project with free jazz, soul, and avant-garde poetry, coupled with the then-emerging use of drum loops. I was happy to play guitar for them on the sessions. Their music was superb.

We recorded a 12-inch single for the dance clubs called "Wheel Me Out," and it was a hit. I was traveling back and forth from New York to Detroit with Gang War, and Don asked me if I knew any labels in New York that might be interested. I recommended Michael Zilkha's ZE Records. I had met with Zilkha recently, and he'd told me that he wasn't interested in releasing hit records. Instead, he wanted to release "different records, new and exciting, unorthodox records." This was a marriage made in heaven. Was (Not Was) signed with ZE, and we recorded a full album and assembled a band for a tour.

Gang War was not a full-time band at this point, and this new band featured some of the people who'd played on the sessions, and others who were new. I could do both. The Brides of Funkenstein, Dawn Silva and Lynn Mabry, were great. All the musicians were first-rate Detroit funkmasters, and we put together a knockout show. Vocalist Sweet Pea Atkinson was our secret weapon, bringing gritty Detroit soul vocals to the mix. I had great enthusiasm for hitting the road with this band. Was (Not Was) was fresh and exciting, and everyone played at the highest level of musicianship and professionalism. We were good. Real good.

The downside was that my narcotics use resumed with my new wages. My habit caused me the usual grief when we arrived in Los Angeles and I was broke, had no drugs, and had to kick on the road. What could have been a fun trip became a miserable slog for a few days.

The tour was a triumph but the hits didn't keep coming, and Don started taking on production work. He became one of the most successful producers in music with monster hits with the B-52's, Bonnie Raitt, Bob Dylan, the Rolling Stones, and dozens of others. Was (Not Was) stopped being a working band. My friendship with both of the Was bros. has survived and thrived. We still work together on occasion, and continue to share the same worldview.

CHAPTER 28

GOTHAM

By 1989, I had been in New York almost ten years, and wasn't any closer to being successful or happy—whatever that meant—than I was the day I drove up. The truth was, I wasn't really in New York ten years. I was in New York one year, that I did over again ten times.

I was getting studio work playing on different artists' records. I was represented by a small-time manager who had tried to manage Gang War. He was working on convincing a couple of record labels to take a chance on me, but my time with Thunders didn't enhance my salability. The drinking laws in New York changed from 19 to 21, and the bottom fell out of the club scene. Now the bridge-and-tunnel crowd that used to fill the New York clubs stayed home and drank in their local bars. Things got tight, and prospects were not encouraging.

The reality was, I was more interested in buying heroin on Avenue D. Getting high was my top priority; everything else was secondary. The dope was cheap, $10 a bag, and the quality was high and consistent. Sometimes I didn't even have to leave my building to score; I might run into someone who was holding in the hallway. No muss, no fuss. I could get high, hang out on the street, and have a perfectly enjoyable time. No career worries, no future, only feeling good right now.

My personal life was unimaginably muddled. Sam was coming and going. I was disengaged from any meaningful relationship, having occasional flings with different women in the city. A prison buddy visited me from Chicago and overdosed at a writer friend's apartment on one of the hottest days of the summer. EMS took him to St. Vincent's, where they revived him with a dose of naloxone.

My life was real and it was fun, it just wasn't real fun.

There I was shooting dope by candlelight because I hadn't paid the electric bill, with guys like Bobo Shaw and Mr. Steve, while complaining about those morons running the big record companies because they didn't have the good sense to sign a genius like me.

After the Johnny Thunders cockup, I saw no way to continue using street narcotics and again joined the methadone maintenance program, this time at Beth Israel hospital in Manhattan.

I was assigned a nice young Jewish woman as my case counselor. She was very helpful with filling out forms and dealing with the bureaucracy. The trouble was, she'd never gone to prison, shot dope, ripped people off, or any of the other less than admirable things I'd done, so there was a limit to how deep we could go.

One day, a tall, thin, aging white hipster named Stan stopped me in the hall and said, "You Kramer?" I said I was, and he said that he'd been looking at my file and saw I did time at FCI Milan. "Milan . . . man I did time up there back in the '50s, and all I remember was it was fucking cold out there." We shared a laugh about the Michigan weather. A few weeks later, a real problem surfaced and, instead of going to my counselor, I found Stan's office and we had a talk. He was perfect for me: ex-con, ex-junkie, older, hipper, and wiser. Stan helped me through my six-year treatment at the Beth Israel clinic. Stan was my man.

Methadone maintenance programs are a civilized and responsible alternative to illegal opiate abuse. They make sense from every perspective that matters. Change and recovery is a process; a lifelong, ongoing, living life process. Methadone can be a viable step in the early stages of that process. At least it was for me.

I still wasn't ready to quit getting high, but I was ready to quit the junkie life. I was sick of sticking needles in my veins. I was sick of being broke. I was sick of lying and stealing and hustling. I needed opiates, but now it was coming from a clinic and a doctor with responsibility for my care. In the context of the clinic, it was medication. The difference is not just semantic; it is also an attitude and a definition that changes the meaning of the activity.

The methadone maintenance program can serve as a bridge from one way of life to another. It allowed me to hold onto my money. I was able to consistently show up for work. My life became more manageable.

With my addiction more or less under control, I was able to form a new band and get back into music with both feet. I was able to hire superb players. Musicians have always held the MC5 in high esteem, and some of the best players in New York were happy to join up with me. Gigs were forthcoming for decent money, but it was feast or famine. I played up and down the East Coast. I got a royalty check and bought a '73 Cadillac Coupe de Ville from a guy in Detroit who couldn't afford to keep gas in it now that OPEC had raised oil prices through the roof. It was a great car for carrying musicians and equipment.

I was hanging out with a photographer, Marcia Resnick, and in my drug-fueled fog, decided to marry her. It was a disaster from the start, and the marriage was soon annulled. During the brief time I lived with Marcia in her loft on Canal Street, I had sublet my place on Tenth Street to a couple of prostitutes who then skipped town owing three months' back rent. I needed to move back into my apartment, and my "manager" said he needed a new place because his girlfriend kicked him out, so he suggested we move in together.

"Two swinging bachelors living in New York. This will be fun," he offered. Except the rent was three months behind, and to keep the lease, it had to be paid up completely. I was broke. He insisted the lease would have to be in his name if he was going to cover the back rent. I said he was trying to fuck me out of my apartment, but he assured me he wasn't. He just needed to protect his investment. He said we were bros, and he would never do that to me.

Two months later, he had the locks changed and put all my stuff in garbage bags in front of the building. Now I was homeless.

Tommy Flanders, a singer I was writing some music with, found me a room in an SRO hotel on Lexington Avenue. He lived there, too. It was nice, if you liked watching the rats scurry by your feet as you watched TV at night.

I got tired of being poor between gigs. Every actor, poet, and bass player I knew in New York had a day job. I had been a snob my whole life, thinking if you could play well enough, you wouldn't need a day job. Now, a day job was looking pretty good. I could hump books around a warehouse as good as the next guy. I answered an ad in the *Village Voice* for a lead guitarist. The bandleader was a roofer during the day, and hired guys on to help him. I told him we could talk further about me joining his band, but I needed the day job now. He hired me, and I started as his assistant.

After working as a roofer's helper, then a mason's attendant for a few months, I learned how to rig scaffolds on buildings, and did that for a while. I finally quit when I was partnered with a guy I didn't know and didn't trust while working from a hanging scaffold 28 stories up in Midtown.

I formed a partnership with a pal, and we found steady work repairing apartments for a slumlord in the South Bronx and Lower East Side. I was deep in my Charles Bukowski phase. My weight had ballooned back up to 200 pounds. I decided I needed to change. I joined the masters swim team at the Fourteenth Street YMHA, and started getting back into shape. I even took a job as lifeguard there, so I could get more hours in the pool. I found a new apartment on Thirteenth Street and Avenue A, and Sam and I moved in together again.

In the mornings, I'd often see the guy who ran a cabinet shop in the ground floor storefront of my building. My partner and I would be having a coffee getting ready for work, and I started chatting with him. We hit it off, and after seeing each other every morning for a few weeks, Francis "Frank" Mattiello offered me a job in his shop. I took it. Frank turned out to be a great teacher who brought me along in the trade of fine woodworking.

I really enjoyed the work, and found that I had an aptitude for building things. Maybe I got it from my father. I liked the engineering and attention to detail that fine-line work required, and Frank and I developed a lifelong friendship. I love him dearly, and my son Francis is his namesake.

My block improved over the last few years of the 1980s. The LES was gentrifying as more money moved into the neighborhood. We still had the occasional drama. One of the local gangsters murdered a rival in the building across the street, but generally the block was becoming safer.

I read that William Burroughs had written a screenplay based on the gangster Dutch Schultz, and I was intrigued. I found the transcript of the dying Prohibition-era gangster's deathbed statement. It read like a James Joyce poem or a Bob Dylan lyric. It was abstract, visionary, and filled with vivid imagery from his criminal life and times. I thought this was good subject matter for a song. I took some choice lines and put them into a rhyme scheme. I called the song "Who Shot You, Dutch?"

When I showed it to Mick Farren, he fell in love with the material and thought something bigger could be developed. "This is a musical," he said. I hadn't considered that possibility, but it sounded good to me, and we set about fleshing out the concept.

Mick's character was "Death," who was coming for Schultz, and he was the narrator of the musical. Mick wrote some dialogue and I started coming up with song ideas. We got a rough outline together and brought in singers, musicians, another writer, and a couple of actors. We had no underwriting to pay anyone and operated on the "artists for survival" basis, meaning, if money showed up they would share in it. And they did. We started rehearsing at Giorgio Gomelsky's studio in Chelsea. Giorgio had owned the Crawdaddy Club in London back in the sixties, managed the Yardbirds, and had given the Stones one of their first gigs.

The ground floor of Giorgio's building was a performance space he rented out to an S&M club called Paddles. Going to rehearsal often meant sidestepping their performances to get to the stairway up to the rehearsal space. Giorgio let us have the space on Sunday afternoons to try out the new show, which we called *The Last Words of Dutch Schultz.*

I would buy as much booze as I could afford, and take it to Giorgio's to sell at the performance. We never actually made any money on the bar because the performers would drink all the booze.

Little by little, we added new material, and the show started to take on a life of its own. We continued the Sunday performances for a few months, but I wanted to try to get some better bookings.

I got us a monthlong gig at the Pyramid Club on Avenue A, and then in June 1986 we moved into Tramps on East Fifteenth Street. Tramps became home base for the next year or so, and the show became an underground hit. We performed it at various other venues around New York and New Jersey, as well as a couple of university gigs. With 15 songs and 4 characters, it was a fun, funky, surreal show. Unfortunately, we never raised the million dollars necessary to go Off-Broadway, and by the end of the eighties, both Mick Farren and I left New York City and the project was suspended.

Lisa Lowell, a singer I knew, called one day and asked if I could recommend a guitarist for a gig she had coming up. "Tell me about the gig, and I'll tell you who I think could do it," I said. She said it was two weeks in a club in Key West, Florida. The money wasn't great, but it included round-trip airfare, free housing, free dinners, and half-price drinks. I took a look out the window at the Lower East Side on a brutally cold, gray January afternoon and said that, in fact, I'd be interested in this gig.

The band was a pickup crew made up of Lisa and her boyfriend Duke, a Texas blues guitarist. She had hired a cool professional bassist from New Jersey named Jeff, as well as Joanne Polana, one of the hippest drummers working in our scene. I had done a little work with Joanne around town, and I dug her playing. Plus, she was good people.

Bands like this can be either fun, or very unpleasant working experiences. This was a little of both. I got so hammered at the bar in Newark Airport that I left my bag with my new gig clothes and my two-week supply of methadone under my barstool. I didn't realize this until we arrived in the Keys, and that sobered me up. I had detoxed once before when I was fresh outta prison. This time, my methadone dose was already down to the minimum allotment of 5 milligrams, so I thought it couldn't be that bad to detox.

In fact, it wasn't that bad. I told myself that I'd made a decision for a new and better way of life. I was liberating myself from the addiction to methadone, and now I was some kind of hero. But I wasn't; I just exchanged the Beth Israel Methadone Maintenance Treatment Program for the Wayne Kramer Alcohol and Prescription Drug Program.

The job was at a club on Duval Street in Key West called Del Rio's. Jimmy Buffett later bought it and turned it into his flagship Margaritaville nightclub. Back then, Key West still had the feel of an openly gay/biker/hippy/fishing village, but this was at the end of that era. The luxury hotels and T-shirt shops were taking over. The club was just a funky tourist trap.

After a few nights there, I became friendly with the club's manager, Gloria, who was smart and cute. She seemed to take a shine to me. I was in a peculiar place in my emotional life just then. I had slept with various women around New York over the last few years, but there wasn't much substance to these encounters. Usually they centered around taking drugs first, then maybe sex after that. Sam and I were only occasional roommates by this point. I was emotionally numb.

I couldn't believe that Gloria might be interested in me. One night after the bar closed and we were alone in the dark, I made a pass at her and she didn't resist. After a few minutes of kissing, I started groping her like the rough-and-ready goon I was. She pulled back, hurt. She asked me why I was treating her like that when she knew I liked her. I was surprised. My experience was, when the door is open, you charge in. Here I was being called on it, and I didn't know how to answer except to tell her that there was something to be learned here. Apparently this impressed her. She told me later that she'd never known a man to admit he needed to learn something.

Soon after that, Gloria and I started a long-distance phone relationship. She proposed that I come back down to Key West for a visit, to see if there was life after New York. I went down to the Conch Republic in the Keys. We had a nice time, and I was intrigued by the possibilities.

CHAPTER 29

IN EXILE

In a matter of months, I wrapped up my life in NYC and moved to Key West. I figured I'd try it for a year and if it didn't work out, I could always come back. I had tried for decades to remake Sam into something she wasn't, and I finally abandoned ship, leaving her with the apartment on Thirteenth Street. I couldn't change her, any more than I could change myself.

A few years later, Frank Mattiello called to tell me that she was discovered dead in the bathroom of our apartment. Sam had died from cirrhosis. It's still hard to accept that she's gone. You're intimate with another person, you go through so much together, and it feels unreal that they're not in the world any longer. I don't think there is really any "closure" after a death. You just go on with your life, knowing that someone you once loved doesn't exist anymore. Never to be seen again, ever.

Life in Key West looked fabulous at the outset: a new town, a new relationship, and a fresh start. Some local musicians heard I was in town, and called me with an offer of work. I asked when the rehearsal was; in New York, everybody rehearsed a lot. You never knew when a producer, director, or record label type might walk into the club and want to sign you or use you for a project. But the fellows in Key West said they knew I could play and that I'd know all the tunes they were playing, so no rehearsal was needed.

I showed up at the first gig. I knew most of the tunes, and I could hear the chord changes of any songs I didn't know, so we were off and running. Key West was a pretty good place for a competent musician; you could have your happy hour gig or your sunset gig and a nightclub gig in any of dozens of spots up and down the Keys. Plus, there were banquet gigs at luxury hotels, and they paid a minimum $50 per hour per man, with a three-hour minimum. Sometimes you could do two a day. It was perfect if all you wanted was a steady gig on a tropical island. The downside was, that's all there was, and I was still ambitious.

In 1990, after being in Key West for a year, Gloria and I were married at sea on a little harbor cruise boat with a waiter officiating. He was also a notary public, so that made it legal. Mick Farren and a couple of other friends came down from New York, and my mother came from St. Augustine.

It was supposed to be a beautiful scenic Key West sunset. As it was, the seas were unusually rough, and the wind was blowing so hard it was difficult to stand up in the boat for the ceremony. Some of my friends were puking over the side. But we had a very nice reception party back on the island. All the local musicians came and everybody played, ate, and drank. There was a massive amount of cocaine. What does it say about the marriage when the groom is high on coke and spends part of his wedding night out in the street looking for more blow?

Life stumbled along. At one point, Gloria and I were talking about our problems. She presciently pointed out that my drinking and drug use were going to be our biggest problems. I didn't agree, but I didn't disagree, either.

I met some carpenters, and started working during the day doing commercial cabinetry and displays. I fell in with one local builder, and we got a couple of big jobs building custom homes. I actually quit playing gigs to build them.

I was intrigued by building something this comprehensive from the ground up. We did it all: framing, sheathing, decks, roofs, trim, kitchens, and baths. It was good, honest work, and we executed it with a high level of craftsmanship. Building these houses was very rewarding in a creative sense. I would drive away from the site at night, knowing I'd built something of quality that would last for a while. We'd build it right: plumb, level, and square, everything according to the architect's specs.

I liked the problem-solving aspect of building. It was like playing music and improvising a melody. I enjoyed using tools, too; that was like having a good amp or beautiful guitar. My mother had always told me to learn a trade to "fall back on" and now I had. But still, I drank and drank. It was a Key West tradition among carpenters and musicians and everybody else I knew. I lived in a drunken, coke-addled world.

At one point, Gloria told me she would leave me if I didn't do something about my drinking. I looked up Alcoholics Anonymous in the phone book and went over to a meeting. The meeting surprised me; I found the program nonjudgmental and sensible. I liked the talk about spirituality. It reminded me of the kind of talk we used to throw around in the MC5. Later that night, I read the twelve steps, and, while drinking beer and peppermint schnapps, declared to my wife that, if you actually did this stuff, it would change your life. Of course, I wasn't ready to do any of it. I read the AA pamphlets but I didn't go back to any more meetings. Just going to the one seemed to get her off my back for a while.

Even though building homes was satisfying, I missed the artist's life in the big city. I'd drink and call up my friends back in New York and annoy them with my drunken dialing. I felt like the world was passing me by.

MTV had become a major force in music by 1990, and Gloria questioned why I'd get so angry every time I saw rock band videos. I would rant and rage about these bands that had the look or moves of the MC5, but the MC5 could have eaten them for breakfast. The guitarists weren't as good as I was, and I resented the fact that they were getting all this attention, and I wasn't. I was sitting here drunk in Key West, building custom homes for rich motherfuckers. I resented the whole music business and everyone in it. In fact, once I got started, I resented the whole fucking world. I raged at everyone in my life that had ever stopped me from doing what I wanted to do. It was *all their fault*. They'd all fucked me over, and the only solution was to get hammered.

I wasn't any more capable of being a husband and a partner in Key West than I'd been in any other time or place. My marriage never had a chance. At the same time, I wanted Gloria to fix me. I thought she could, if she would just do what I told her to do. I wanted her to go to law school, then get into corporate law, and support me so I could return to being the artist I really was. I wanted to remake her, so she could remake me. But she couldn't fix me, any more than she could fix herself. I also believed that the solution to her problems was having a real man to love her, and I was that real man. But the last thing I was, was a real man. I was selfish, spoiled, resentful, immature, and had serious substance abuse problems.

Gloria had troubles of her own. She suffered from terrible migraines, endured three-day bouts of excruciating pain, and had to take various medications. On top of that, we continued to drink like fish.

In 1991, we agreed to leave the Keys. She wanted to go back to school, but she hated the idea of the big city. Nashville was the compromise. She was accepted into the graduate program at Vanderbilt. I knew I could carpenter there, and possibly do some music work, too.

CHAPTER 30

A DEAD MAN'S VEST

In the mid '80s, when I was living in New York, I got a phone call from my sister. Kathi said she'd found our father. "Huh? What? Really?" I was stunned. I hadn't thought about him in decades. Kathi has always been one to look for connections and history, way more than I did. She had just spoken to him, and he'd told her he would like to talk to me. This was unnerving; it made my stomach queasy. I thought it was all still too painful and better left alone.

But I took his number and said I would call him. I did, immediately. He answered the phone.

"Hello, is this Stan?" I asked.

"Yes, it is," he answered.

"It's Wayne. You might be my father."

And then, "Yes, I am."

He said he'd heard from Kathi that I was "some kind of musician," and said that I couldn't have gotten that from him. "All I know about music you could put on the head of a pin," he added. Our conversation was awkward, but not unpleasant. We tried to connect as best we could under the circumstances. Before we hung up, he told me he had terminal cancer.

He lived in West Elizabeth, Pennsylvania, with his wife, Annie, and they'd been there a long time. We agreed to talk again soon. This took a little while to absorb. I wasn't sure what I wanted from this. What was I looking for? What was the point? I knew there was no way to regain or reclaim what had been lost to time. There was no way to go back and build a father-son relationship, but the idea of learning who my father was appealed to me.

It was awkward and a bit strange, but I did call him occasionally over the next few years. It wasn't hard to talk to him; he was just a man on the other end of the phone that I had a genetic tie to. I didn't feel connected to him in an emotional way. I did want to learn as much as I could about who he was and what his life had been like.

He told me he'd quit drinking 20 years ago, and I asked how. He said he decided he would rather live a little longer than die a lot sooner. He didn't mention AA or any other mode of recovery. I told him I'd struggled with drinking, too, and he only said, "You can beat it."

I thought about his take on drinking. He was a real alcoholic for most of his adult life, but he had changed. I just wasn't ready to look inward at my own addiction yet, so I stayed in denial. I hadn't yet experienced enough pain.

By the fall of 1989, Stan was very ill. One night when I called, he couldn't stop coughing long enough to get on the phone. His wife, Annie, said to hold on a minute, that he wanted to talk to me. I told him I'd call him back later, that he didn't sound like he was feeling too good. He answered, gasping for breath, "Wayne, you win some and you lose some." Those were the last words he ever spoke to me.

He never complained about his cancer. I asked him if he thought it was from his smoking and drinking, and he said he was certain of it. I made travel plans to go see him on the weekend. His wife was asleep on the couch when I arrived at their home. It was a small bungalow on the banks of the Monongahela River. I could see Annie through the window in the front door, and I woke her up with my knocking. She welcomed me and broke the news that my father had died the night before, while I was en route. She told me his last words were, "Can't they do something about the pain?" It hurt me to hear that his doctors couldn't, or wouldn't, provide him with enough medicine to ease his pain in his final hours.

I had carried the idea from childhood that my father was a bastard, a no-good drunken bum. My mother encouraged this attitude. I was an angry little boy, and I grew up to be an angry young man. I carried the image of him as a desperado, on the run, friendless, wandering the back alleys of American cities, hiding out in flophouses on skid row. Now I was in his nice little house with his sweet, mourning wife.

I decided to stay for a day and attend the funeral. We met with the funeral director, who drove us out to the cemetery. We picked a nice spot on a grassy hill, overlooking the river.

When the time came, I decided to wear the vest from the suit he would be buried in. We went to the funeral home. My father's body was in an open coffin. He seemed smaller than I remembered, and he had a full head of black hair. That was annoying, as I was almost bald at that point. He looked like the Greek he was.

I figured this was what becomes of a guy who runs out on his family. He was dead and alone, with no friends. It was me, Annie, and her friend sitting quietly in the room, just the three of us.

Then people started to arrive. First a couple, then a few more, then more and more. Soon the room was filled beyond capacity. People spilled out into the hallway. Folks were weeping and telling me how much I resembled him, and how sorry they were to lose him. The town postmaster was weeping inconsolably. I was blown away. I had carried a myth in my head and heart throughout my entire life. It was obvious that he was a well-respected member of his community, much-loved and appreciated by so many. His friends on the Save the River Committee told me about his activism and all the good works he'd done.

I wasn't prepared for this, and it sent me reeling. His wife told me about his dissatisfaction with some young guys who'd installed their new kitchen cabinets. I would have made the same complaint about their shoddy workmanship. It was curious how much we were alike. I have talked all this over with my sister, and we both have had to revise our long-held feelings about our father. He wasn't a "bum" or a "rat." He was a wounded war veteran suffering from severe PTSD at a time when help was not forthcoming.

In later years, I discussed all of this with my mother and she, too, arrived at an understanding that there were forces at play that could not be fully understood at the time and that everyone made mistakes, but did the best they could. She was much harder on herself in the end than she was on him. Mable said she always loved him, and I believed her.

Annie and I met with the funeral director again the next day, and we went to the cemetery. We arrived at the nice spot on the hillside. It started to rain. We said our goodbyes, and then I left.

CHAPTER 31

NASHVILLE CATS

Gloria and I rented an apartment on the west side of Nashville. I hooked up with some guys who were building giant mall installations for special events, and went to work with them building all manner of bizarre displays. I was knocking back a pint of vodka like water on the drive home from work, and stealing prescription drugs from my wife. On weekends, I drank a fifth a day. I'd stay hammered and do nothing until returning to the shop on Monday morning.

I bought a little four-track cassette portastudio and started to record song ideas on the weekends before I got too drunk to function. Mick Farren had left New York for Los Angeles, and was writing some good new lyrics that he would fax me. At least I was writing and recording again. I joined the YMCA and resumed swimming regularly.

I became friendly with Henry Gross, a singer-songwriter whose big hit was "Shannon." I did a little pickup work with him on bass, and started to meet some of the other local players, which rekindled my sense of being part of a musician community.

After a year or so, Gloria decided to leave school. It was at that moment when the bottom of our marriage fell out, too. She had been complaining for years that she was too educated to be tending bar or managing restaurants, and now her schooling was over. I did a little production work with some local artists and sat in with a few groups I heard around town. I was trying to reconnect with the music scene, but it wasn't easy when I was falling-down drunk.

Something was compelling me to find out why I was such an alcoholic fuck-up. Why was I always the last one to leave the bar? Why couldn't I stand the way I felt and had to manipulate my feelings with alcohol and drugs as fast as possible? Why did I gravitate toward the worst group of lower companions in town, and not only enjoy their company but consider them friends? Why did I feel comfortable with the dregs of society, and ill at ease with regular people? I wanted to know what the hell was the matter with me. I had wondered about my behavior for years, and now I decided to talk about it with a qualified professional.

Charles, my first therapist, was a streetwise black man from Newark. He was working in Tennessee on his master's degree from Vanderbilt. At our first session, he asked for my story. I gave him the CliffsNotes version. He asked about the MC5; did we have any songs he might have heard? I said I doubted it, because we were banned from the radio before we broke into the big leagues.

Charles asked, "What was your most popular song?" I told him, "'Kick Out the Jams.'" He said, "Motherfuckers?" I was amazed. He laughed and explained that in the '60s, he had been the minister of defense for the Black Panther Party of Newark, and he knew all about me. Thus, we connected as brothers.

Charles asked me once if I would consider residential treatment for my drinking and drug use. My immediate response was to dismiss it out of hand. I thought that going through rehab on a hospital ward was for nutcases, and that wasn't me. Charles wouldn't address my substance abuse again. He said that if I wasn't willing to look at it honestly and didn't think I had a problem, he wouldn't force the issue. Instead, we worked on my reactions to the world, and why I couldn't honestly express my feelings. I was trying to get a read on what I was feeling, and he worked hard on getting me to express my bottled-up anger and resentment. Charles was a small island of sanity in the sea of madness that was my life. After almost a year, he rotated out and referred me to another therapist.

Phillip was burly and quiet-spoken. He wasn't an ex–con, or an ex-druggie/ex-alkie, but I liked him anyway. He had a quiet tough-ness, and I liked that. He was a natural-born counselor, and really knew how to cut through my bullshit and zero in on the point. We did a lot of work on my childhood.

The deeper we probed, the closer to the truth we got. I finally came to the insight that I was an abandoned child. That was my core psychological scar: I was a fatherless boy. I'd never had a man who loved me and modeled what being a man meant. How a man should act. How to love and be loved. How to be responsible to, and for, others. How to have integrity and self-respect. I had a massive hole in my development, and this was where it came from. This was the original source of my shame and anger, my core revealed.

I wasn't really sure what to do with this revelation. I thought that if I got to the source, I would be instantly relieved of my addictions and finally be at peace, but I didn't actually feel any different. The reality was, this revelation had no effect on my alcoholism or my drug use.

This may have been a core issue, but there were more immediate cognitive problems to deal with, like making sense of my everyday life. I was working a 40-hour week as a cabinetmaker, and drinking at least a pint of vodka daily, along with a six pack and as many pills as I could get my hands on. I was also philandering my way across Nashville and every other city I visited.

Then one night, Phillip suggested that maybe my problem was that I wasn't really a carpenter. Maybe I was a musician, a song-writer, and an artist. Maybe I was trying to pound a round peg into a square hole.

Working a day job back in New York had been necessary for my survival. But now, ten years later, it had gotten out of hand. I built beautiful woodwork for wealthy people, but I had another trade that I was eminently qualified for and had been practicing all my life. In that, I even had international professional equity.

I don't know why it took so long to get to this. I guess I had to strip off all the layers of denial in order to determine what was the truth and the lie of my life. I had been lying for so long that it took real effort to finally begin to see the difference. When I left Phillip's office that night, my mind was reeling. This would mean reinventing my life; a complete realignment of everything. But it felt good. A big change was coming, and I was ready for it.

Mick Farren was sending me more lyrics, which I crafted into songs with my little four-track recorder.

On September 18, 1991, my friend, the writer Ben Edmonds, called and told me Rob Tyner had just died in Detroit. I was struck numb with the news. Even though I knew that you couldn't out-argue him, out-smoke him, or out-drink him, still, I'd never thought about Rob or any of the MC5 guys dying, just like I'd never thought about my own death. The reality was so terrifying that I had to stuff it down emotionally. Rob would never walk the earth again. My old friend, partner, and mentor of my teen years was gone. It took me awhile to call his widow, Becky, to offer my condolences. I also offered an apology for how rough I'd been on Rob when we were younger.

Rob's death represented the death of the dream of my youth, which I'd held onto for decades. The dream went something like this: Someday it will all turn out right. I'll be recognized for my contribution to pop culture, politics, and music. Everything I'd tried to do and failed at would be made right, and I would be made whole. The MC5 would all be great friends again, and we'd rock this MTV generation into a new sonic dimension with the most advanced, hardest-rocking, most soulful music ever heard. We'd usher in a new movement of high-energy music, art, and politics that would break all the old restrictions and power us into the future.

Now Rob was dead and we would never be reunited. I thought about his wife and children, and how terrible this must be for them. It had been so long since we'd been in touch, 20 years in fact, that I didn't really know him or his family. When Ben told me that Rob had had a fatal heart attack in his car at 47 years old, it was the beginning of my facing finitude. This was the end of the beginning of my time on earth, the beginning of putting my past to rest, and the demarcation point of the next chapter.

We all suffer two deaths. The second is actual death, which happens to us all. But the first death—the death of my youth—meant coming to grips with unrealized plans. I had to accept my failures as well as the fact that the past was not going to return to be straightened out to my liking.

It was clear to me that my time was finite and if I was ever going to accomplish something further in music I'd better get to work. I constructed a plan. I knew Nashville was not the place for me. I needed to be in Los Angeles where there were options and possibilities.

I knew two guys in Nashville who were building a recording studio. Brad Jones and Robin Eaton were good people, and they were willing to help me. By this time, I had demoed up 12 songs with my four-track, but I knew they needed to be recorded properly to present to record company people in LA. Brad and Robin agreed that if I would help them build their studio, they'd compensate me by recording my new songs. I hired the best players.

Gloria dreaded moving to California. It didn't help that, on the day the guys were coming to load up our moving truck, the 1994 Northridge earthquake hit.

I decided to wait a few days until the water and electricity were back on before we moved. On the four-day drive to the West Coast, I watched as a steady stream of people in U-Haul trucks and vans headed back east.

I was ready to rejoin the world, and that meant going where my job skills as a musician were marketable. You had to take your pigs to market.

CHAPTER 32

WELCOME TO THE BEST COAST

In 1994, Bill Clinton was in the White House, Nelson Mandela was elected president of South Africa, O. J. Simpson was charged with murdering his wife and Ronald Goldman, and gasoline was $1.09 a gallon. And I left Nashville for Los Angeles.

On the drive out, we stopped at Gloria's parents' house, and they gifted us their '87 Buick Regal. It was a great car: big V8, two-door, gunmetal grey, only 60,000 miles, and they had maintained it perfectly. I loved that car and drove it for the next 12 years. I customized it and achieved true ghetto stardom by sporting rims that cost more than the car itself. It lasted longer than the marriage did.

Gloria and I moved into a residential hotel on Hollywood Boulevard. It was funky, but ok. It had a kitchenette, and the neighborhood wasn't bad. After getting settled in there, I set out to find an apartment. The fact that the quake had just hit and there was still debris being cleaned up made it a renters' market. It took about two days to find what I was looking for in West Hollywood: a clean, second-floor, two-bedroom apartment with parking. I picked the neighborhood because Mick Farren lived close by, and I could walk to the bank, grocery store, post office, and pharmacy. I was so excited to finally be back in a big city again, with real possibilities at my fingertips. I loved the police helicopters overhead, the noise and smog and traffic. I was back in the real world!

Once the phone was turned on, I started calling everybody I knew in town to set up meetings. I worked the Detroit homeboy network, and rattled everybody's cage for information on record labels, publishers, managers, and publicists. I called all my musician friends in town. With my funds decreasing daily, I felt pressure to find someone who wanted to make Wayne Kramer records. I went to meetings with artists and repertoire people. Some were very kind, and listened to my stuff; others, not so much. I was genuinely impressed that major label executives returned my calls, and that they were sincerely interested in meeting with me. At least I was getting a fair hearing. Not everybody wanted to hear from me, though; a few labels had never heard of me or the MC5. That was a reality check.

Now that I was in Los Angeles, I could increase my efforts to bring the MC5's old business affairs up to date. Former journalist and MC5 fan Danny Goldberg was now an attorney who had become the president of Atlantic Records. He guaranteed a resolution to our problems, and I felt good about that.

I was still getting drunk every night, and I had been taking sleeping medication for years. Gloria hated LA, and felt completely out of sync with it. She was deeply withdrawn, and rarely left the apartment.

One day I was returning from a meeting and was sitting in my car at the stoplight at Fountain and Genesee, when a massive 5.1 aftershock hit. The car was rocking back and forth like an amusement park ride; for a minute, I thought the transmission was coming apart, causing the shaking. It's funny what your mind will tell you when you have no frame of reference for what's going on.

People on the street were aghast, and everyone had stopped walking. After a couple of minutes, traffic resumed, and I pulled around the corner onto my street. All the neighbors were out, talking about what just happened. When I got up into our apartment, Gloria was in tears, nearly hysterical. This had pushed her over the edge.

Mick Farren's girlfriend was a prescription drug abuser, and it didn't take long for her to turn me on to the deal in West Hollywood. There is a large Russian community in the Fairfax District, and numerous Russian doctors in the area who, for cash, would be loosey-goosey with their prescription pads. After a while, I had about six doctors writing prescriptions for medications, usually opiates in any available form, such as codeine syrup or Vicodin.

Life was a merry-go-round of doctors' offices and pharmacies. I had to stagger them so I didn't overload any particular one too much, and it was expensive, to boot. Only on rare occasions did someone complain. Assuring them that the medicine was only for a particular ailment or pain usually did the trick.

Before leaving Nashville, I had gone to a hipster clothing store and saw an MC5 T-shirt. I noted the name of the manufacturer, and looked them up when I got to Los Angeles. I walked into their office on Vine, and surprised them with my request for an accounting for the use of the name and my image. They took it well, and after a few minutes' calculations, they cut me a check for a few hundred bucks.

They were smart young guys, and while I waited for them to do their math, we made pleasant conversation. They asked me what else I was doing in town, and I said I was looking for a record label that wanted to make records with me. They told me there was a label across the street that seemed to be doing well enough to afford a forklift in their warehouse. I was impressed; an indie label that sold enough records that they needed a forklift was the kind of label I needed to sign with. "Who are they?" I asked. The guys answered, "Epitaph Records."

I started asking around about Epitaph. I had a friend, Andy Somers, who booked shows for me back in New York. He had relocated to Los Angeles, and was enjoying success as an agent for the latest generation of punk rock bands. Knowledgeable about the LA scene, the music business, and all its players, he filled me in on

Epitaph. He took me around to gigs and exposed me to the exploding SoCal punk rock movement.

Epitaph was at the epicenter of it all, with four of the hottest bands: Bad Religion, Rancid, NOFX, and Pennywise.

We went to a giant indoor concert event at the USC Field House. I was floored; over 5,000 kids were there to see Pennywise headline a show with the Cadillac Tramps, Korn, and another Epitaph band, The Offspring. I was hip to Los Angeles street-conscious rappers N.W.A. (I thought they picked up where the MC5 left off), but I was completely unaware of these punk bands. Obviously, they were hugely popular here. I watched from a balcony up above the floor, as three or four slam circles would form when the bands tore into a new number. It was really peculiar to me. To my ears, the music they played sounded alike. Very fast tempos, maybe 150–160 beats per minute. They all played short songs with no discernable melodies or choruses. The music had an almost 12-tone avoidance of standard key structures.

I was mystified at this massive musical movement that I'd missed completely. Punk rock ruled in LA. The audience's near-indifference to whichever band was playing intrigued me. The event was really more about the kids in the mosh pit than the bands, and the night was more an athletic event and rite of passage than a musical concert.

I found out that Brett Gurewitz of Bad Religion had founded Epitaph. I called him up, and he was very open to talking to me. He made some oddly humorous remarks about getting David Coverdale of Whitesnake to join me in a new MC5. We agreed to meet, and I went over to see his forklift.

Epitaph was a bustling, impressive operation. Brett gave me the 50-cent tour. I played him the Nashville demos, and he responded by saying that he thought the songs were great, but he couldn't sell that sound to his customers. However, he offered to re-record the songs. He told me there were many talented musicians in town who would love to play with me on it. He also offered that, after it was all recorded, if I didn't like it, we'd just call it a day, and I wouldn't owe him anything for it. Which sounded good except for the fact that if we did like it, and he released it, I would be paying for it.

Needless to say, I wanted to sign with Brett and Epitaph. In the middle of all this, Brett asked me to do a session for the new Bad Religion record, *Stranger than Fiction*. Happy to be asked, I met him and the guys in a first-class studio out in the Valley. I liked the song they asked me to play on. I recorded my solo and brought my unorthodox, kinetic textural playing, which seemed to light up the control room. I always enjoy it when my fellow musicians appreciate what I play.

Then Brett and I went across the street to a restaurant to sort out my solo deal with Epitaph Records. It wasn't like we actually negotiated; it was more like we just figured out what would be fair from both sides. He put up his company and money, and I put up the music, agreed to tour, and to promote the records. If we did well, it would be good for both of us. Brett left the question of which musicians to use up to me.

Brett had a different perspective for how a record company should be run. Not like the old model where the artist works for the company in a state of perpetual indentured servitude, but a new way where the company works *for* the artist. It was record company as artist's advocate, and it included artist involvement in all aspects of the process. Epitaph was still a record company with a ledger sheet that required that advances, recording, and promotion costs be recouped from the artists' royalties, but it was a much better record company than I had ever dealt with.

One day, when I was in Brett's office, I noticed a big box of books in the corner. The books were Donald Passman's *All You Need to Know About the Music Business*. Brett had bought them to distribute to the bands on the label, so they could learn about business principles when he needed to discuss it with them. I knew this book well, and I was impressed that it mattered to him that his artists actually understood what they were agreeing to.

Gloria was pleased that I had secured a recording contract, because there would be a cash advance to cover our expenses for a while. She had delusional ideas about the music industry, and would say things like, "When the money comes . . ." As if one day you were struggling, and the next day, as if by magic, you were wealthy.

The sessions for the first Epitaph record got underway. They were fun, yet businesslike. I was sober for the sessions, believing that it was time to get serious about my work. I'd still get hammered by myself at night at home and took all the prescription opiates I could manage, but I was totally covert in my behavior. I had been given a gift with this contract and my newfound patron, and I was determined not to blow it. I had been around recording studios and musicians for the better part of my life, and I knew how to record and produce recording sessions. Now I was fortunate to have great engineers and to be in first-rate studios with talented musicians, so we rocked.

Successful recording sessions are a complex business. It's not the kind of work you can just walk into and do well. It takes a lot of hours in the studio to fully understand what's at stake, and how to go about achieving what you want. The technical side can be intimidating, but I didn't sweat it. What I didn't understand, my recording engineer Sally Browder did. I knew I had to be completely prepared, so the songs were all written and arranged beforehand. Mick Farren and I had a stockpile of material that was good to go. I had also rehearsed the players, so they were ready to go, too. After setting the lineup for each day's sessions and arranging the gear and the players' fees, we would meet around midday and set to work. I was content to sing the tunes. I'm not a great singer, but I can express myself and I enjoy singing immensely. Plus, the idea of finding a new vocalist to collaborate with was not something I'd even considered.

The goal is to capture joy. At least that's *my* goal. That elusive moment in time when the song and the players and the sounds all come together in imperfect beauty. In my experience, this will happen in the first couple of takes. After that, you start to become an imitation of yourself, and the life drains away from the performance. First takes can be the best, but often the second or third will be the one. Most seasoned players know this, so I didn't need to announce my intentions. Just get ready, hit "Record," and count off the tune. I used a number of the best LA punk rockers and a couple of older pros, and I was very satisfied with the result. I even had the Melvins on the record doing an MC5 song I'd written, "Poison." They were slamming. Brett loved what I did, and that guaranteed that Epitaph would get behind this record, which we decided would be called *The Hard Stuff.* The possibilities were very exciting.

There was a promotional campaign to execute, and I enjoyed the process. It was flattering to have day after day of photo shoots and interviews to set up the record's release. I wasn't Pollyanna-ish enough to think this was based on merit, but I can't say I didn't like being the center of attention.

In the music business, column inches and feature stories do not appear from worth or value; instead, flattering news coverage is usually bought and paid for. Not always in money; sometimes it's favors and perks. Epitaph hired a high-end publicity firm, and because I was emerging from years in exile, there was some extra excitement attached to the press meetings. I was certainly pleased about everything the label was making happen for me. It was a little intoxicating.

ON NOVEMBER 4, 1994, I got a call from Michael Davis. He told me that Fred Smith had just died in Detroit. My boyhood guitar partner in the MC5 was gone. We'd been through so much together since we were boys back in Lincoln Park. I went to Detroit for the funeral and mourned his loss along with his family, our surviving band mates, and friends. Fred and I had not been close in the years since I was released from prison, and it hurt to know I would never see him again. From time to time, both Fred and Rob return to me in my dreams.

CHAPTER 33

BACK ON THE BOARDS

An offer came in for me to perform at the Trans Musicales Festival in Rennes, France. This is a very cool event that features only new artists. You can only play it once. This would be my first gig with a new label and a new record in the modern age.

I needed a band, so I hired Jon Wahl from Claw Hammer on rhythm guitar, Randy Bradbury on bass, and Brock Avery on drums. Jon and Randy had played on my Epitaph recording sessions, and I found Brock through Johnny Angel, another musician friend I knew from my days in Boston as a member of the James Montgomery Blues Band. Johnny had relocated to LA years before; he knew the local scene, and he highly recommended Brock, who turned out to be a remarkable drummer and friend.

We rehearsed a set of songs from the new record, and flew to France. There was no way it could have been better, considering that we had never played onstage together, and I had very little idea of what would work and what wouldn't. We just played the songs as best we could, and it was a credible performance. What it wasn't, was a mind-blowing, stage-proven, barn-burning show—at least not yet.

My British road crew requested a wall of Marshall amps, and when I went out to plug in, they didn't work. Right at the very beginning of my set, the momentum slipped away. I think the wall of amps was considered gauche by the punkerati. Maybe I was over thinking it, but the Marshalls, a bit of '60s culture in this new age of hip hop and loops and samples, made me feel like even more of a dinosaur than I already did. I heard a recording of the gig the next day, and it was pretty ragged. The other bands were Steve Albini's Shellac and Soul Coughing, a new band from NYC that I liked very much.

The day before the performance, I did press meetings. I wasn't prepared for what was to come. I was comfortable with the one-on-one interviews I had been doing in LA, and thought this would be more of the same. When I was escorted into a small amphitheater, I was met by a couple dozen reporters and photographers in a state of frenzy, and it threw me for a loop. Here I sat in the center of a hurricane of journalists with flashbulbs going off in my face, as if I was the Rolling Stones in 1968. One fellow took charge of the situation and translated the questions from French to English for me, and then my answers back. Things calmed down, and I started to get a sense of what was going on. I had underestimated the MC5's legacy in Europe; having me there was a big deal to the European music press. The reporters asked me thoughtful and probing questions, and treated me with great respect. I responded candidly with good humor, and it was an amazing experience.

Later the next day, I was in the hotel elevator with the translator, and thanked him for his accurate, considered work. I mentioned that I had no idea the MC5 meant so much to all those journalists. He said, "Wayne, you don't understand. Your records are *our* music, too. They are part of *our* history." This was more than a compliment; it was humbling. In the '70s, when the MC5 toured Europe, we did well wherever we played. There was a rabid European fan base for American rock groups, and we probably did six or seven tours from one end of the continent to the other. It was a great time. But I had no idea the MC5's legacy had endured there.

Since I was released from prison, I had lost touch with what was happening musically in France and the rest of Europe. I had some writer friends that I communicated with from time to time, but the emerging European music scene was a mystery until now. Through Epitaph, I discovered that punk rock was thriving there.

A Euro tour was booked, and I reduced the band to just a trio. Brock Avery, Randy Bradbury, and I became a strong touring unit, and we worked it pretty hard for the next few years. They are both excellent musicians and good brothers. I was very lucky to have them along.

Now that I had returned to my real calling full time, I had some adjustments to make. I was not the ebullient, young, long-haired, flash-dancing, sex machine I was at 20. I was nearing 50, and the world looked a little different from this perspective. I didn't know how to present myself onstage anymore. I couldn't muster the gyrations and balls-to-the-wall theatrics of my youth. I couldn't dance with the uninhibited abandon of a young man on the make; to do so would have made me feel silly, and more irrelevant than I already felt.

Shaking my booty just didn't feel right, and I was at a complete loss as to what to do about it. Finally, I decided to take a Miles Davis stance and just grit on everybody. My musicians and the audience all got a scowling, mad-dog stare from brother Wayne. Often, I turned my back to the crowd and just played as fiercely as I could.

I did a one-time super-group tour of the States with members of Blondie, Guns N' Roses, The Smithereens, The Go-Go's, and others, and I overheard some of the guys I was playing with say they were concerned because I looked so angry onstage. I was having a great time, but I didn't know how to express it.

Luckily, I ran into Lisa Mende, an actress in Los Angeles. I confessed my dilemma to her, explaining that since I wasn't up onstage trolling for babes, I wasn't able to bump and grind like I used to. I was a married man and trying to stay married, and being raunchy felt phony, undignified, and inappropriate. Lisa explained that onstage we were playing a role, and whatever character was being portrayed wasn't who we were in real life. This was a revelation to me. I hadn't considered this perspective. In the MC5, I was as real and in the moment as possible. There was no separation between my personal identity, my desires, and my professional performance.

That wasn't where I found myself in 1995, but Lisa gave me permission to bump and grind, dance like a demon (if my body would allow it), and generally act a fool onstage if I wanted to. She instructed me to have fun performing, because that's what it was—a performance.

This was liberating. I love playing music for people, and I love entertaining them. I never met an audience I didn't love. Now, the newly liberated Wayne Kramer could go out and wiggle my guitar without being chained to my old ideas about who I was supposed to be. I could rock, and keep my dignity at the same time. As Rob Tyner so aptly put it, "Let me be who I am."

Touring was grueling. A bunch of blokes in a van driving across Europe and then the States in the middle of the winter is no holiday. Fortunately, we were all sober on the road, and professionalism and good camaraderie was a priority. We had fun, and we made good music.

No one got rich on these tours, but it was steady work and it helped my record sales to be out there hitting the boards every night, winning over new fans. I ran into a few MC5-era people, and it was usually nice to chat about the old days. I enjoyed playing night after night. When I play every night, my playing starts to get focused. I begin to lean into it more, and the music takes on a force that is very enjoyable. I can think about what I played the night before, and go a little further the next. This is one of the good aspects of touring. There aren't many others.

I never drank on these early tours. Never used opiates either; the work itself was enough for me. The travel and lack of sleep was brutal. I was running on pure willpower and ambition, and for a while, that was sufficient.

The Hard Stuff sold pretty well; Brett and I were seeing some success.

Back to Los Angeles to write and record a new record. *Dangerous Madness* was released in 1996, and another round of touring started. I've lost track of the number of European tours I did. Offers came in from Australia, and we went down there. Then Japan. It was all good.

I never cheated on my wife during these tours. I was 48 years old, and the idea of picking up groupies after gigs had no attraction for me. The reality was, I was emotionally numb, and sleeping with the damaged girls that made themselves available after gigs was, for me, unmanly and unseemly. It wasn't worth the emotional cost, not to mention the STDs. On these tours, I just had no sex drive.

Gloria hated my touring. Something exciting would happen out on the road, and I'd want to share it with her on the phone. Her response might be, "How much longer are you going to do this?"

I didn't know what else to do. I was a musician, and this was how I made a living. Plus, I liked what I did, and not many guys had the good fortune that I was enjoying. But she didn't make it easy for me. She liked me better when I was making cabinets and drinking myself unconscious every night back in Nashville. Somehow, I thought it would all work out, and one day she'd come around and appreciate what I did. We would finally be happy, someday, someway.

I still drank and used prescription narcotics when I was back in LA. I drank alone at home; getting loaded had stopped being a social activity decades ago. My wife went to sleep early due to her own medication, and I would walk down to the liquor store and buy another pint of Popov vodka. Slam it down mixed with Diet Dr Pepper, one or two pints a night. Plus whatever pills were around.

I reconnected with my old band mate, David Was. He had relocated to Los Angeles a decade earlier and was working as a writer and occasional jingle composer. We shared a love of avant-garde music and art. He was an intellectual, and I enjoyed his company. I asked David to come on board for my next Epitaph record as co-producer.

He had just learned how to slice and dice audio files using the then-new tool computer sequencers. He was able to take guitar parts

I had recorded or drum beats from the sessions, and decontextualize them to create new and exciting sounds. We wrote some songs together and had a good rapport.

The record was a change from the style that Epitaph was used to. Where the first two records were explorations of the guitar-driven, high-energy style that I had pioneered in the MC5 and brought up to date as a corollary to modern punk rock, this was going to be different. I wanted to explore some new things that departed from the punk aesthetic: slower tempos, horns, samples, and loops, deeper bass tones and aural collages. I wanted to dig into my love of experimental and free music. We brought in producer Jason Roberts to raise the octane level on a few tracks.

This was a problem for Epitaph. It seemed to me that their most popular bands had perfected a sound that fit the relatively narrow parameters of punk rock, and then they never deviated from that formula. The bands were doing great, and I couldn't argue with success, but I felt it would be better to follow my own instincts about the kind of music I was creating.

To their credit, Epitaph encouraged me to follow my muse. I played Brett some rough mixes, and he was visibly excited, shouting out "Artistic integrity!" as he pounded the dashboard of his car. If he really hated it, he did a great job of convincing me that he loved it. I think the musician in him liked what I was doing, but the label executive was troubled.

Guiding an artist's career is a full-time job. I had been self-managing my career since the mideighties, and sometimes it put me in a tough spot. I had to advocate for my own best business interests while maintaining the image of the creative artist.

In midwinter 1996, I was in a secondary market in the Midwest for another club tour. I was on the phone with a record plugger, trying to get reports on how many stations were playing my records. It was one of the most awkward conversations I'd ever had. The guy was a big fan, but he hadn't placed my record anywhere. I hung up, thinking, *What in the hell am I doing here? I'm playing another punk rock shithole tonight, and I'm trying to work my own records, and nothing is making any sense.*

I asked an old friend in New York, Bill Adler, to step in as manager. He agreed, at least on an unofficial basis. Bill is a very bright man, and he was a strong advocate for me. But some trouble seeped into my relationship with Brett.

I was starting to be a problem for Epitaph. First, I was older than the bands they were used to dealing with. I wasn't about to sleep in the same single hotel room with my band and road crew, or in a punk rock crash pad after the gig. And second, I wasn't making generic punk rock records. I was closing in on 50, and there was a culture clash. I appreciate punk rock, and I get the aesthetic completely. It's been said I *invented* it. I remained a punk *philosophically*, but I wasn't about to become a punk as in the latest cultural iteration. I hadn't been that since I was 20 years old. Epitaph told me that my new record, *Citizen Wayne*, didn't have anything on it that was radio friendly. There were "no singles" on the record, and we were arguing over the costs of my tours.

On top of this, my marriage was in trouble on every level. We were kind to each other, but there was a deep resentment building under the surface. I was carrying the full load, and there was no way that Gloria would be able to get a job. She hated Los Angeles, and she hated my work and my traveling and all my musician friends. I saw no way out.

I had been traveling all over the world meeting people, including, occasionally, fantastic women. I never slept with any of them. And I met a few who were substantial. These were beautiful, educated, single, ambitious women who were taking a bite out of life. Women who were actively involved in their lives and wanted to see where the future might take them. I was too fractured, too hollow, too unsure of myself to admit I was attracted to any of them.

My life may have looked okay on the outside, but inside, it was a fraud. I didn't like myself, let alone love myself, and I was utterly incapable of loving another person. I would just get high, alone in the hotel room or at home. It was easier to black it out and do it early, so I could keep up the front again the next day.

In 1995, I had met a journalist in Cleveland named Margaret Saadi at a promo event in a record store in Cleveland. She was an editor at a business magazine and wrote about the arts for Cleveland publications. She had a sparkle that was irresistible. We had done an interview, and she really liked my new record. I had just bought my first computer, and this new feature, email, was exciting. Epitaph was a high-tech company that had been computerized for years, and I wanted to get in sync with them. I thought this would be a more efficient way to work with the label.

I started corresponding with Margaret by email. I was scheduled to go to Detroit to do some promo for *Citizen Wayne*, and she suggested I have Epitaph fly me into Cleveland first, and she'd set up a press day for the record. She met me at the airport and whisked me off to the first stop at a local radio station.

Epitaph had been telling me they just didn't have the juice to get *Citizen Wayne* played on the radio, and that there were no singles on the record, blah, blah, blah. But here we were at a major Midwest FM station at morning drive time, and they were playing tracks off the record and raving about it.

I knew that one station didn't make a hit, but still, they liked the album. The rest of the day was a whirlwind of print interviews and photo shoots. We finished, and Margaret dropped me off at my hotel. She was fun to hang out with, and very professional. She picked me up in the morning and delivered me to the airport for my flight to Detroit. I wasn't looking, but there was no doubt she was an exceptional young woman. We started emailing, and she was very sharp, with a great sense of humor. We were becoming friends. Something was stirring.

Epitaph was facing major challenges. After the incredible successes of the Offspring and Rancid, serious forces were pulling the company apart. Something was definitely off kilter, and I often felt like I couldn't connect with Brett. Bill Adler had to scale back his work with me. At one point I had asked Margaret, if she moved to Los Angeles, would she consider being my assistant? She was incredulous. "Assistant? Are you joking? I have two college degrees and I'm running a company here. I'll run companies in Los Angeles, too." I quickly realized the depth of my misjudgment and apologized. Bill then suggested that Margaret take over as my manager.

We had decided to make a fourth record, a live one. We had been playing a months-long residency at a nice club, The Mint, on Tuesday nights. This seemed to be the right place and time. They had a built-in recording facility, so we had Jason Roberts come in to produce and engineer the sessions. The band had evolved at this point. Randy Bradbury had joined Pennywise, and Brock Avery had moved on to work with a number of other Epitaph bands. Bass was now Doug Lunn, and drums was Ric Parnell. They had been a working rhythm section in Los Angeles for a long time, and were world-class players. Ric is the drummer in the film *Spinal Tap* who is interviewed in the bathtub wearing a shower cap. We had toured the states and Europe, and played well together. Doug became one of my dearest friends. Doug was my bassist for the next 20 years until his death in 2016.

We sorted out a management agreement, and Margaret started putting my business affairs in order. We were both in relationships that had run out of time. I wasn't looking for someone new and neither was she, but we were attracted to each other.

CHAPTER 34

A FAREWELL
TO WHISKEY

On weekends in the midnineties, when I passed the corner of Fountain and Fairfax in LA, there would be a crowd of people hanging outside the church there. They were a motley crew (it might have actually been Mötley Crüe). Motorcycles, lots of ink, punk rock types. I wondered what the hell was going on there at 11:00 AM on a Sunday morning.

I knew better than to hire drinkers or druggies in my LA bands, and I had an all-sober crew. I tried to only hire sober guys or reliable, non-addict/alcoholic musicians. Brock told me it was a meeting called Artists Living in Sobriety, and that it was pretty cool and I should check it out.

The next weekend, I went over there to see what was going on. I went again the following weekend, and then a third time. I was taken with what I experienced in that room. Here was a whole group of men and women of different races but hip, young to middle-aged, all in incredibly good spirits. Apparently all sober. As they spoke, I learned that many had not had a drink or used drugs in years, and there were longstanding relationships between some of them. Many seemed to have great affection for each other, but not in a sexual or romantic way. I was attracted to their mutual respect.

There would be a speaker, and he or she would tell their tale of debauchery and misery, then they'd conclude with how they had a very different life today. I noticed that, even though they all told different stories, they all ended up with a degree of peace of mind that mystified me. They all seemed to have found a workable, practical answer for their dilemmas. What I heard was different from the things I heard in my day-to-day life.

These people were telling the truth about how they felt, and things they did that, at least in my experience, people never talked about. If you were in a prison cell with your crime partner you might get that intimately honest, or if you were in some other intense peak or valley of life with someone you trusted. They were talking about terrible experiences and being honest in a way I'd never heard before. There were also great spasms of laughter coming from the audience, and from me, too; especially when the speaker described something that I'd done myself.

I didn't know what it was or how they did it, but I was intrigued. Whatever these people were doing was working for them, and they didn't seem to be that different from me. Maybe it could work for me, too.

I walked over to the meeting every weekend for a month or two. I'd sit in the back, not engaging anyone, and certainly not volunteering to participate. I wasn't sober; I was an outsider looking in.

I also attended a private get-together with some sober men on Monday nights. I had been invited by a guy named Bob Timmins. It was held in a lawyer's office in Beverly Hills. There were a couple of musicians I knew from the old days in Detroit who had relocated to California decades earlier, stayed active in music, and had done quite well. The others ran the gamut from lawyers and business professionals to actors, writers, ex-cons, and general ne'er-do-wells. Often, I felt out of the loop, but sometimes guys would say things that made a lot of sense to me.

I continued to get high in secret. I would stop on the way home from the group, buy a pint of vodka, and drink it like water in the car before I got home. I lied and made up a number of years I had been sober: six. The amount of time without drugs or drinking seemed to be a big thing to them. They were a pretty open-minded and non-judgmental group of men. They would also talk about this spiritual thing, but I didn't really get what they meant. When I heard God mentioned, my mind closed to whatever anyone was saying. I knew that when I moved to Los Angeles that I would have one chance to make a good first impression, so I did all my drinking and drugging covertly. No one ever saw me loaded at a party or high in a club, but it was all a false front. I was attracted to this group of men because I desperately needed to be part of a community, a movement—something. I was alone, and I didn't like it or feel safe. I knew my track record, and I wasn't getting any better on my own power.

Margaret saw me struggling with my substance abuse issues and was hanging in there, hoping against hope that I might find a way out.

The famous people in the Monday night group didn't impress me, but I was fascinated with a few of the other guys who talked openly and honestly, revealing their vulnerability. I bullshitted when it was my turn to talk. Every now and then, I'd hear something that was profound, but I was still an outsider looking in.

I continued to attend the meetings, but I had a problem. I couldn't shake my feeling of disingenuousness about being there. After all, I was still getting loaded, and lying about it to them. I was a fake, a fraud, just as I was in most other areas of my life, but being around this group pushed it to a head. To make matters worse, I respected some of these men and what they were doing. I didn't get it, but obviously they had discovered something that helped them on a very deep level. They had found answers for the overwhelming problems life throws at you, and I felt creepy and voyeuristic being in the room with them. I determined that the only honorable thing to do was to be honest and, as gracefully as I could, step away.

I announced my decision to quit the group at the next meeting, and I was taken aback at the reactions. Everybody seemed to react in their own way: one guy was visibly upset, another was sarcastically dismissive, others were sympathetic, but many just continued talking about their own issues with a steadfastness that was impressive. I didn't ask for anyone to sympathize with me or be on my side, and I was sorry for upsetting people, but it seemed like the right thing to do.

Afterward, one of the musicians said, "You know what your trouble is? You want to be in control." I agreed with him. I didn't know any other way to be, and yet I deeply doubted that I could handle whatever came at me.

Bob Timmins and I met for lunch the following week. He knew me better than I knew myself, and was gentle and reassuring without being judgmental. I expressed my appreciation for his inviting me to the group, and asked what he thought my next move should be. I still wanted to get sober. "I think you should learn more about a principled life," he told me. Timmins didn't have an opinion about whether I was right or wrong, or whether the support group was or wasn't for me. He just thought these principles were a "good way to live your life." He was a man that had done the things I had done and worse, yet he'd made a remarkable, fundamental change, and now he was trying to help me. I started to think that if he could change, maybe I could, too.

Margaret and I worked hard together, and we traveled a lot on tour. She had her hands full trying to resuscitate my career. She was tenacious and determined, and after some heroic efforts on her part, things started to go our way. She sorted out a new publishing contract for me with Rondor Music, and we launched MuscleTone Records. It was nice to have an advocate in the business world that was devoted to moving my work forward.

Six weeks later, I went back on tour, and things went from bad to worse.

I got hold of some morphine, and I'd been using it regularly over the weeks before the tour was to begin at New York's Knitting Factory. After I completed the sound check and stepped down from the stage, I couldn't catch my breath. I turned to Margaret, and gasped, "I can't breathe." She and Frank Mattiello rushed me to St. Vincent's emergency room, where they gave me a breathing mask and medicine that opened my lungs. I stayed in bed at Frank's with pneumonia for nearly a week until we were able to travel back to LA. There, I laid low and recuperated. I had another European tour coming up. Blowing this American tour did not help my relationship with Epitaph, and I had run my health into the ground. I was getting sloppy.

Doug Lunn was not available for the next tour, but fortunately Bryan Beller was available on bass, but I made the critical mistake of hiring a drinker on drums.

We had embarked on another grueling European tour, this time without Margaret. I started asking my British tour manager to grab me a bottle of wine after the shows. Then after a while, I'd hit the minibar in the hotel rooms, too. My drummer was getting loaded on the gigs, and this further fueled my discontent. The only enjoyable thing for me on these tours was actually getting to play music for people, and now I couldn't even enjoy that. I would get angry with the drummer, so I'd get drunk, too. This was the convoluted logic of alcoholism: he did me wrong, so I'll take poison.

Finally, on the flight back to LA from London, I let it all hang out. I bought two boxes (the limit) of legal codeine at the Boots pharmacy at Heathrow Airport, and ate a box of them, which was not easy when I discovered they were fizzy Alka-Seltzer-like tablets.

Then, on the plane, I decided that I might as well drink with my hard-drinking drummer, since the work was done now and I could relax. He and I were the only two from the band on the plane. We dove into the vodka, and drank ourselves into oblivion. We started off talking and laughing, having a fine time. Then the conversation turned dark and bitter, and my sarcasm surfaced. I provoked him with my frustration and cynicism. It degenerated into a whirlwind of drunken, drugged madness. Finally, I covered my head with the blanket to drift off into unconsciousness.

I came to with a female flight attendant wagging her finger in my face, telling me she was having me arrested when we landed in the States. I was disoriented, in a fugue-like state, and it took a few seconds to remember where I was and what was happening. Her face was contorted with emotion. "What did you say?" I asked. She repeated that she was having me arrested when we landed, and that she'd been warning me for the last hour to lower my voice and to stop cursing. "Look how you've upset everyone on this plane!"

I looked around; there was a security zone of empty seats surrounding me, with other passengers looking on with serious concern. My reaction was to shift the blame to the drummer. "You're not talking about me. You're talking about him," I pointed. "He's an alcoholic!" She assured me, "No, mister, I'm talking about YOU."

The moment was suspended in time. Everything slowed down and stopped as the full weight of what was happening hit me. In that instant, I could see it all played out as if it was a movie. I would be arrested in New York. I would be taken into custody, and transported to Rikers. I would be back behind bars again with a terrible hangover. The news reports would say, "Another rock musician was arrested today on a flight from London. Guitarist Wayne Kramer was taken in handcuffs . . ."

My façade of sobriety in Los Angeles would be exposed for what it was—a ruse. All the lies I told in the press about my new, improved, redeemed character and my fine new career would be revealed. I would be the laughing stock of the guys at the Monday night meeting and the people at Epitaph. All the promoters I worked for, and the fans who believed in me, would see that I was a liar and a fake. I had exposed myself for what I truly was: an obnoxious, stoned-out drunk. Exactly the kind of person I would cross the street to avoid.

I was the kind of guy I couldn't stand to be around: a loud-mouthed, ego-tripping, drunken, rock & roll asshole. I saw clearly who I really was, and I was devastated.

I rode out the rest of the flight in sullen silence. There was a connection from New York to LA, and when we landed, the flight crew just let me off the plane and I went straight to the bar. I still had some codeine left, and I swallowed it along with many servings of red wine.

By the time I landed at LAX, I was crying my eyes out. Crushed emotionally, physically, and spiritually, I was incomprehensibly demoralized. Later, it occurred to me that this must be what they were talking about in the support group when they mentioned "hitting bottom." It wasn't an economic bottom or a physical bottom, although it could include those conditions. It was a psychic and emotional bottom. It was the realization that everything you tried just kept blowing up in your face.

But this was because of me, and *only me*. I created this circumstance. I was the architect of my own ruin. Maybe for the first time in my life, I caught a glimpse of the truth. I wept in the car on the ride home; big, wheezing sobs of emotion dripped out of me.

I was in a daze for the next couple of days, until I remembered Timmins's nonjudgmental invitation to join him in "a good way to live your life." I called him and asked if he could meet me for lunch. After we ordered, I told him what had happened on the plane, and that I was a sick man. I asked if he would help me. He said, "Yes, Wayne, I can help you. We don't shoot the wounded." I had never heard sweeter words. It was humorous, gentle, reassuring, and deeply compassionate. "I'll make some calls when I get back to my office," he said. Bob knew exactly what I was going through, and precisely what steps to take to get me the help I needed.

I still stopped for a pint of vodka on the way home from lunch. I had the most horrific dreams that night: violent, bloody nightmares featuring flesh-ripping, body-dismembering, stabbing, shooting, beating with clubs and fists. I'd never had dreams like that before. Two days later, Don Was put up his credit card to help get me in a local hospital's detox unit. It was the last day of my using life, and the first day of the rest of my life.

It was midyear 1999. I was 51 years old. I soon learned that having time away from drugs and alcohol doesn't mean you've necessarily changed—beyond not drinking or not using. I know now that sobriety is the general goal, but there's way more to it than that. If I didn't change the attitudes and feelings that drove me to drink, then I was not only not better; I was worse. Without the relief of being altered, my irritation was unrestrained. I needed to change how I experienced the world.

Now, I try to live well in the day I'm in. If I had to deal with events for months and years to come, I'd wig. I can usually handle today, and today's plenty. Any change that can be accomplished can only happen now, in the moment I'm in. Not yesterday, not tomorrow. Only now.

Life in the detox unit was pretty strange. I was medicated for the first few days, and for the first time, didn't enjoy it. I wanted to get on with the work of change; I wanted to get better, now. I have always been impatient; it's part of my problem.

I lined up at the nurses' station for nighttime meds and asked for my "dope." The nurses ignored me and took care of all the other patients, and everybody went off to bed. I realized that I had broken some kind of protocol, and finally asked a nurse to explain it to me.

"We made you wait because we don't distribute 'dope' here. This is a hospital, and this is medicine. You may find it helpful to think about the words you use, and how they reflect your attitude about your drug use," she said. I was taken aback by her statement. I had never considered that language can inform our feelings. I liked this recovery stuff.

I had trouble with my fellow detoxees' lack of commitment. I knew I was a long time coming here, and if I didn't change I was sunk. But I couldn't see the same gift of desperation in most of the others. They were looking for ways to get out of doing what was being asked of them. I asked a staff counselor about it. I told him I could see how he was committed because it was his job, and he had changed himself. But it wasn't my job, so how could I handle the idea that all these young people weren't hearing the message and were doomed to use again?

He pointed out that the best thing I could do for them, was to take my own life seriously. Just to do the best I could to change *me*. That improving my own life was the most important thing for me to focus on.

I left the hospital after a couple of weeks and moved into a sober living house. I knew that if I went back to my apartment and wife, my odds of staying sober would diminish exponentially. At least here, in a therapeutic community, I could find steady support. My roommates were mostly older guys like me. Of the five men in that house, only I and one other are still alive as of this writing.

There's a high attrition rate in the drug-and-alcohol crowd. I started attending regular support sessions, and even returned to the Monday night men's group I'd "retired" from. To their credit, not a single man busted my balls. There were no snide remarks, no sarcasm; just an honest welcome back. I felt lucky to have stumbled into that men's group. I have continued to participate in it, as well as another one I enjoy, and have developed deep and abiding friendships with a few of the men over the years.

In the midst of all this change, Gloria and I hit the end of our road together. Our differences were insurmountable. We tried counseling to no avail. It was over for us, and we both knew it. We decided to mediate our divorce, and it was done with a minimum of acrimony. There wasn't much to argue over. I was broker than broke. We had been living on what I could make as a touring musician, and that wasn't enough to meet expenses. I remained in sober living for the next 13 months.

I met a guy in rehab who, like me, had done a prison term. He was a filmmaker and we talked about music and film and the parallels between us. He was working on a new movie, *Animal Farm*, that he thought I could score. I went with him to meet the writer to discuss it. The writer turned out to be none other than Edward Bunker, the author of *No Beast So Fierce*. I was a huge fan and understood him to be one of the greatest prison writers of our time. Hell, one of our generation's greatest writers period. Getting to meet him and talk about scoring his movie was a trip. As it turned out, he didn't have any say in who the composer would be and I didn't get the job, but meeting him and connecting a line from Lexington to Hollywood was an unexpected gift.

I took the work of change seriously, and started to educate myself about alcoholism and addiction. I found a couple of people in the community who had deep knowledge of recovery and addiction. I spent time with them and asked a lot of questions. I needed to know something about the mental disorder I have. How does it show up in my life? How is it that I change my mind after swearing I won't use again, over and over for years? What is the mental and emotional mechanism that needs to change if I am to stay sober? Where did it come from? What are its psychological and experiential roots? How does my malady rob my life from me without my permission? Why do I say one thing and do another? Why is it that I mean well, but I just can't *do* well?

If I didn't change, then all the pain I'd caused and endured over my life would have to be repeated again and again. I would be hurt again and I would hurt others again. I learned that there were dual goals: attaining sobriety and maintaining freedom from my addictions. This was something of a challenge because in the recovery community in general, there wasn't a lot of discussion about the history of alcoholism and the evolution of treatments. I heard a lot of slogans, rhetoric, and a lot of drunkalogues that were entertaining but usually didn't reveal a lot of hard info on how change actually happens. I learned that it might be wise to select a mentor, someone who had been around awhile and understood how to best apply the available knowledge.

CHAPTER 35

NO EASY WAY OUT

I asked Bob Timmins, and he said he would be honored to mentor me. Honored? I was floored again. He demonstrated a degree of humility and compassion that I never knew existed. And he did it in a way that completely baffled me. Bob was a serious man and known to be "heavy does it," but with me he had grace, and he was warm and easy to talk to. If you had asked me at any point in my life up to that day if I would be able to ask another man something so intimate, I would have said you're crazy. The very idea that I would share my deepest innermost feelings and experiences with someone else would have been unthinkable. Especially completely sober.

As we got to know each other, Timmins revealed his past as a dreadfully damaged child. His mother had had a psychotic break and murdered a neighbor, and she was turning on him just when the police arrived. He went to a dark place, left home as a young boy, and later became a teenage LA street gang member, drug addict, alcoholic, Hell's Angel, armed robber, Aryan Brotherhood member, and San Quentin enforcer. I knew the kind of guy he used to be. I was around them in prison and back in Detroit when I was younger, but I could see that an almost unbelievable transformation had occurred. Here was a guy who just helped people. That's all he did. He helped alcoholics and addicts in court, in detox hospitals and rehabs. He helped families and professional people of all kinds. It occurred to me that if this guy could change, so could I.

Timmins was a man of few words, a true Buddhist, so to really learn what I needed on a granular level, I had to move out into wider circles in the recovery community in Los Angeles. If I heard someone talking and he or she sounded like they knew what they were talking about, I'd ask them to lunch and pick their brains. That was how I discovered the work of Dr. Harry Tiebout.

Dr. Tiebout was a New York psychiatrist in the '50s and '60s who had tried without success to treat alkies with Freudian psychiatry. He learned about the work of Bill Wilson, Dr. William Silkworth, and others, and started to study their ideas. He became an advocate of their efforts, Alcoholics Anonymous, and carried their message of this new treatment model to the American Medical Association and the American Psychiatric Association. Dr. Tiebout got both professional associations to recognize, for the first time, addiction and alcoholism as diagnosable mental disorders. He became one of the architects of this new program, and his contribution to my understanding of my problem has been invaluable.

Dr. Tiebout wrote that all addicts have "persisting elements of the infantile ego in the adult psyche." This was a game-changer for me. He also explained that I was subconsciously ruled by my "defiance, impatience, omnipotence and grandiosity." I had absolutely no trouble connecting these concepts to my behavior. He had described me perfectly. My problem is powered by my immature ego. My own sense of "self" is the fuel for the engine of my destruction. This is not to be confused with the childlike aspects of my personality, such as curiosity, silliness, the ability to play or be in wonder, but instead with my immaturity. I may look like a grown man on the outside, but inside, I have the emotional maturity of a bratty four-year-old.

When I experienced "deflation at depth" on that airplane, my ego's power was temporarily diminished. This opened the door for enough humility to be able to ask for help. To surrender. But this humility needed to be implemented in an ongoing way of life to keep my immature ego's recuperative power minimized.

I got a good look at the recuperative power of ego when I was getting a publicity push for one of my records with Epitaph. There was a newsstand down the street from my studio, and I would know that a magazine was coming out with a story on me. I would walk down and buy the magazine on the day it hit the stands, read the story about me, then get immediately disappointed because that was the only piece about me in it. It was stunning how insatiable my desire for recognition was.

The recuperative power of my ego was one explanation that helped me understand why people I knew would get sober for a while and their lives would get better, but then, after a year or two or ten, they'd decide to drink or use again. There are, of course, other reasons as well. Addiction is a complex and sometimes baffling disorder. Often, depression is at its root.

Timmins and I worked through the process. I was learning an ancient set of universal ethics and how to apply them in my life daily. Most people learn a fitting code of conduct early in life. I probably did, too; my mother was no social deviant or nihilist. She had straight-up, working-class values, and she did her best to pass them along to her son. *I* fucked it up. I'm the one who did things according to my plan, on my schedule, based on my pain, my fear, my anger, or my shame.

As soon as I left home at 17, I decided I would do what I wanted to do, whenever I wanted to do it. If I wanted to smoke weed first thing in the morning, that's what I did. If I wanted to drink beer for breakfast, I did. I did things according to my ambitions and desires. I did this to myself and lost my way. I got lost in the dust of the chase for what I thought was happiness.

The notion of self-honesty took some getting used to. I had one idea of the kind of guy I was, but when I honestly reviewed my behavior over my adult life, I wasn't the guy I thought I was. I had to stop lying to other people; but I also had to stop lying to myself.

These were hard pills to swallow, but swallow I did—point by point, event by event, and relationship by relationship. I had carried destructive resentments for decades. I hated the record company executives who'd sabotaged my ambitions, never once admitting that I'd put myself in those contracts. I *wanted* to be in business with them. I resented the MC5 and everyone connected with the group for not fulfilling my ambitions and expectations. I created the entire setup out of my own desires, and then ruined it with my addictions and immaturity. I hated the police and the government for their hypocrisy in locking me up, never conceding that I knowingly violated the law for my own gain. I always justified my crimes like I was some kind of Robin Hood.

Facing my fears and working through them was another task, as was my sexual harms over the years on tour and at home. I found myself talking about things that I swore I would take to my grave, only to have Timmins say, "Yeah, me too." I was astonished. All along I thought I was surely the most aberrant degenerate in town.

And Timmins wasn't the only one. As I grew more comfortable talking about my deep dark secrets, I found out that others had done the same kinds of things I did. I wasn't radioactive after all; just a garden-variety addict-alcoholic like thousands of others. What a relief that was. No better, but truly no worse. I'm never a perfect angel, and never a total beast. The goal became to be fully human: perfectly imperfect. The solution to my problems lay in engagement with others, not isolation from them.

There came a point where I had to begin cleaning up the messes I'd made over my years of addiction, and there were many. I had to learn what it meant to be an adult. To start acting like a grown-up. To be responsible to, and for, others. Sometimes a simple acknowledgment of harms done was all that was needed, and I made plenty of those. Usually people were so relieved to hear me admit my wrongs and finally have the hurt acknowledged that they were happy to forgive, but forgiveness wasn't the point. If it was offered, of course I accepted it gratefully. But the core intent was that I take responsibility for my actions. I had to own them. I did this methodically and comprehensively. If I could remember the incident, I made the effort to admit it, and this process helped heal me.

In the midst of all this, Tim Shafe called to say he had terminal cancer. I went down to Myrtle Beach to see him and we spent a few days together filling in the blanks and enjoying each other's company again. He died in November of 2002.

I was the de facto leader of the MC5. I started pulling the musicians together when we were kids, and I was the motivating force behind all the associations we developed throughout our brief but power-packed run. First in, last out. Generally, none of us paid much attention to our actual business interests, and this was a fatal flaw. I wanted to know the royalty rates and the publishing splits and fees promoters paid, but beyond that, I didn't have much interest in contracts or business. I wanted to destroy the power structure with the force of the electric guitar and be as high as possible in the process. I wanted to be famous and wealthy and have all the sex I could handle. I viewed meetings with accountants and lawyers as something to be endured, not the crucial pivot points in building a sustainable enterprise and future career.

After the band's final dissolution in 1972, and after I went to prison, the MC5's business interests could not have been in greater disarray. After I returned from prison, I wrote to all the record companies and music publishers to inquire if any monies had accrued on my behalf while I was "out of circulation." They universally ignored my requests, but I was persistent. Through sheer tenacity, I forced dialogues with all of them. Later, when I moved to New York City, I met an attorney who was a fellow heroin user. He offered to help me find any money sitting in record companies' or publishers' bank accounts with my name on it.

After some sleuthing, he found some; not a fortune, but a payday. I didn't know what had accrued, what my share was, and still didn't completely understand music publishing. He collected the check and released the money to me. I went on a tear. I was fresh out of prison, living in the Big Apple where heroin flowed out of the faucets, and I went wild. This was during the Gang War period. I ended up financing not only my habit, but my girlfriend's habit, too, and sometimes touring expenses for the band. I burned through the money in record time with nothing to show for it but a monkey on my back.

Every now and then, I would get a call that some company or other had a check for me. I would happily run across Manhattan to pick it up, cash it, and go party. As the years went by and I left New York, I kept writing letters to the various companies with requests for an accounting. They never volunteered a penny. They never gave me an accounting without me hassling them relentlessly. In fact, the only time I ever got a proper response was when I had lawyers call on my behalf.

Finally, I was fully in the system and started receiving regular publishing and artist royalty statements and checks. In all these transactions, I asked only for Wayne Kramer's money. On the odd occasion when I would hear from former band mates, I encouraged them to go get their money, and I shared whatever contact info I had with them. I knew they were receiving payments, too, but I didn't know who got how much, from what source, or when. My concern was only my own money.

So, during my recovery, there I was, figuring out just what money came from where. This was no small task, but if I really wanted to change—if I was going to be the man I wanted to be— then I had to step up and clean up the mess. The first thing to do was to talk to all involved. Even if I didn't *intend* to collect other people's money, I acknowledged that the result was harmful to them, and, that I was truly sorry. When someone is deprived of what's rightfully theirs, it harms them, and I took responsibility for that. Then I had to figure out how to make it right.

Margaret and our attorney, David Wykoff, developed a complex agreement between the surviving band members and estates, and the record labels, whereby I would forgo royalty payments until all accounts were even again. I agreed, and slept well that night.

In the ensuing years, there were countless business deals that Margaret and I developed, which wouldn't have occurred if we hadn't initiated and executed them, all of which have generated income for the MC5 members and their families. But I didn't consider any of that part of my amends. All additional monies generated were passed through to them.

Since the day I entered detox, I have not taken a penny that wasn't due me. Margaret and I have been completely transparent in all our business dealings, and we have never avoided an inquiry into our business practices. I'm not perfect. I still make mistakes, but I know what to do when I make one, and I do it. As my man Timmins told me, "It's a good way to live your life."

I HAD A THERAPIST through my divorce who recommended that I live alone for a while and figure out who I was. I had been in sober living for over a year when I rented a great apartment in West Hollywood, and I lived there by myself for almost two years. I really came to enjoy my own company. For the first time in my life, I was happy being by myself. I found it liberating.

Margaret and I had fallen in love, but she would not move in with me. In fact, she wouldn't openly acknowledge that we were dating until after my divorce. She was raised in an old-school Lebanese Maronite Catholic family, and that was unacceptable behavior.

I never bought into all those old-world principles. What with my '60s-era morality, I had rejected the ancient ways as a matter of political defiance. But all of a sudden, at this late stage of the game, I started to see some wisdom in doing things according to old protocols. It gave everyone involved a chance to think through the process, and consider fully the consequences of the decisions being made.

In this case, first, let the old marriage officially end. Then date each other. Then, if all goes well, consider officially uniting. Then and only then, formally ask for the hand of the one you love and hope she agrees. And that was what I did.

Margaret and I were married on February 23, 2003. The priest did the ceremony in Aramaic, and it took place in the Lebanese

Maronite Catholic Church. It was a beautiful day, and just our close friends and family were there. Margaret's father gave away the bride with pride and dignity. My relationship with him has grown beautifully over the years.

Margaret told me that she was not going to be my answer. That she would not, and could not, fix me. If there was any fixing to be done, that would be up to me. This was a level of maturity and mental health I never knew existed. I loved her even more.

ONE OF THE OTHER BENEFITS of living by principle was rebuilding my relationship with my mother. For too long, I had ignored her because I was consumed with my grandiose ambitions and failures. I sucked at remembering her birthday, and I could go years without seeing her. I had not been a dutiful son. She didn't deserve that, and now I was determined to atone as best I could. She, above all, deserved better from her son.

Mable was living in St. Augustine, and was semiretired. She had been taking in foster kids for the state. She loved having a lot of kids around, but she was getting older and having trouble keeping up. I started going down to visit her every birthday and holiday, and began actually being a son to my mother.

Over the last few years, she had developed an intestinal condition that caused her excruciating pain, and she was finally going to deal with it surgically, which went badly, and after that she was placed in a full-care facility against her wishes. My sister Peggy lived nearby, as did my stepsister JoAnn, who was the daughter of Mable's last husband, Jack, who died in 1988. But neither could provide the degree of care our mother needed. Against her formidable will, Mable resigned herself to life in a nursing home. I continued to travel to Florida every holiday and birthday to spend time with her. On these visits we had great talks, and I brought her up to speed on my newfound clear-headedness. We reviewed our lives together. I would take her out to the International House of Pancakes, and we drove around St. Augustine and talked endlessly.

Her condition deteriorated with the early stages of dementia and renal failure. After one difficult trip, I talked it over with Margaret and Kathi. We decided it made no sense for Mable to be isolated in Florida. So, the three of us moved her to Los Angeles so we could all spend whatever time was left with her. She lived in a full-care nursing facility across the street from our office, and I spent most every morning with her. She often didn't know exactly who I was beyond a nice man who came to see her every day and brought a doughnut or flowers. Her appetite diminished. Eventually she entered hospice care. Her long painful journey was nearing the end. Kathi and I spent time with her as she descended into her memories, telling us that her mother, father, sisters, and brothers had come by for a visit. We made sure she wasn't in pain.

We got the call early one fall morning in 2005 that Mable was gone. We went to her bedside to say our goodbyes. Decades before, she had donated her body to science, and a transport from Loma Linda medical college came to collect her remains. Pragmatic to the end.

The Bodies for Science program is essential and unbelievably beautiful, and after two years of study for two medical students, Mable's ashes were returned to us. We spread them over her roses in the backyard of her stepdaughter JoAnn's house in Florida, as she'd wished.

Bob Timmins and I continued to develop our relationship over the years. He was my treasured friend and confidant, and I loved him dearly. He was my backstop when things got complicated. We might go months without talking, but whenever I got tangled up, he could help me find a way through. He remained my cherished brother and teacher until his death in 2008.

About six months after Bob's death, I went into a deep depression. I knew a psychology student who said this was not unusual when we suffered the loss of someone important. Now that Bob was gone, the little snags piled up and boom, I was in a black hole of meaninglessness. My friend suggested a therapist he knew, and

I jumped into the work. Dr. Judy Kann has helped me through the peaks and valleys ever since, and I deeply appreciate her guidance.

Change continues to be a challenge. The adjustment to different phases of my life has been at turns easy and smooth, or painful and overwhelming, and everything in between. Changing my life has been my greatest challenge, but the result is that I get to live a decent life.

Finding a way to live where drugs and alcohol are no longer necessary has allowed me to live a manageable life. I don't have trouble with the police or drug agents anymore. I don't end up in violent confrontations with people. I have not returned to criminal court (except to speak at drug court graduations). It doesn't mean I get to win a Grammy or an Academy Award; it doesn't mean I get wealth and recognition. What I get is a manageable, civilized, honest, useful, and productive life.

After 15 or so years, I hit a wall with recovery orthodoxy. I found too many black-or-white positions that didn't comport with the many shades of gray that make up human behavior. I also found that the fundamentally Christian core ideology discounted nontheism with a condescension that amounted to intellectual dishonesty. Over time, I found these and other issues unpalatable.

After so many years away from drinking and drugging, I needed to take more into view to see the whole picture. I have resolved to not throw the baby out with the bath water. There is much that is good in the orthodox approach that can be very effective, especially in the early years. Just as there is something to be said for the positive effects of some religious practices. But in both cases, I have no belief in the supernatural and the patently false. I am a skeptic and try to align myself with philosophical and scientifically provable truths. Mine is, without a doubt, an ongoing, living life process.

I am a fortunate man. I have had many great teachers who have helped me when I asked them to. I enjoy the moments that hit me as exquisite, and grab a kiss from joy as it passes by. I have found no grand, ultimate answers, just a lot of small, but important, course adjustments to be made. I expect to remain a student all my days. I do believe, to quote one of my heroes, Charles Bukowski, that "kindness is just about the best we can do."

CHAPTER 36

PROBLEMS OF ABUNDANCE

In 2003, Becky Tyner, Rob Tyner's widow, and artist Gary Grimshaw agreed to license MC5 image rights to the Levi's corporation without my approval or an accounting. This could have been a mistake of epic proportions, but Margaret envisioned a way to make it work. After some creative thinking and skillful negotiation, she arranged to have the three surviving MC5 members—Dennis Thompson, Michael Davis, and yours truly—along with some special guests, join together to play the music of the MC5 in a one-off performance at London's 100 Club. The event would be filmed and recorded for DVD release, and it would be a free concert for the fans. All sponsored by Levi's clothing, which had just released a line of MC5-themed apparel. I liked Levi's, which at the time were still manufactured in the United States.

At first, I was a little wary of the plan. It was a lot to consider. I called Charles Moore to see if he and tenor sax man Ralph "Buzzy" Jones would join us, and they did. I was happy to have Charles on the gig because he had worked with the MC5 and was still one of my best friends and musical mentors. I knew having him there would uphold the MC5's commitment to moving the music forward.

We went about filling out the band with singers Dave Vanian from the Damned, Motörhead's Lemmy Kilmister, and the Cult's

Ian Astbury. Nicke Andersson from Sweden's Hellacopters would play second guitar, and Primal Scream's Gary "Mani" Mounfield was our deejay for the night. The rehearsals prior to the show in London were enjoyable, and it was fun to be playing with Dennis and Michael again after so long. We had stayed in touch intermittently over the decades, and I took pleasure in their company. They were both rusty, but they seemed to be playing pretty well, and I felt good about the show's prospects.

The club was packed, and when we hit the stage, I was blown away by the response. The fans roared their approval; they were as excited as I was. We played well, the show was an artistic success, and we did a lot of press. I was happy to see Dennis and Michael get their pictures in the papers and recognition for their time in the MC5. Everyone had a wonderful time in London. We all went home with a few bucks and some new Levi's fashions.

After that success, the idea of more shows came up. Margaret and I figured three American dates were possible: Detroit, New York, and either Chicago or Los Angeles. We floated the idea to my agents, and in 72 hours they came back with a world tour offer.

Promoters jumped at the possibility of booking this version of the MC5, and I was stunned. Margaret knew this would happen and took it all in stride. The first thing I needed to do was talk with Dennis and Michael about it. This was going to be a much bigger commitment than a one-off performance, and I wasn't sure they understood the rigors of going on the road at this level. Touring could be rewarding artistically, personally, and economically, but it would also be very hard work.

My question to them was: If it wasn't going to be fun, then why do it? I didn't think this was an unreasonable position to take. I had a thriving career as a recording artist, producer, and film composer. I had been playing, writing, recording, and touring since the MC5 imploded, and by this time I didn't need the money. I had work that I liked that was meaningful, and I really enjoyed playing with the musicians I was working with in Los Angeles.

I was pleased when Dennis signed on. He seemed happy about the possibilities. When I met with Michael, he confided he didn't like playing with Dennis, and I told him, "If you don't think this will be fun, let's not do it." His response was a bitter: "I need the money." Not the answer I was hoping for. He then reassured me that he was cool with everything and wanted to do it.

The wheels started turning and the dates came in. Margaret began the work of organizing the tour. I recruited Marshall Crenshaw on guitar, and Mudhoney's Mark Arm as lead singer. Our U.S. booking agent managed Lemonhead singer Evan Dando, and lobbied to include Evan on the tour. I didn't know him at all, but his enthusiasm was high and he had a good voice, so I agreed to have two lead singers. The idea was not to *be* the MC5, but to celebrate the *music* of the MC5. The last thing I was doing was attempting to fool people into thinking this was the MC5. I came up with the moniker DKT/MC5. It would immediately distinguish between the original and this new band with Dennis, Michael, and my surname initials added on.

We opened the tour in Toronto, and naturally, because of my time in prison, it was a major headache getting into the country. I had to post a large cash bond for the 24 hours I would be in Canada. Rehearsals went well, but I did have to gently communicate to Dennis that he may not survive the tour playing every song balls-to-the-wall. He needed to reel it in and relax behind the kit. After all, we weren't teenagers anymore.

I used local horn sections in the major cities. Charles Moore had prepared me with horn charts. I found excellent young players who worked well most of the time. I would rehearse them at the sound checks. The horn sections added the free jazz dimension that was part of the MC5's mission.

The next night was the big test in Detroit. We were playing the Majestic Theater on Woodward Avenue. The theater was a very big room, and it was sold out. This was trial-by-fire for this new incarnation. The hometown crowd loved the music. Our older fans were happy to hear these songs again, and the new fans screamed and hollered like only Detroit audiences can. For me there was one rough moment onstage when Dennis's tempo noticeably slowed during "Let Me Try." I nudged him and he responded with a heart-felt "fuck you." He apologized the next day on the bus.

I had begun to notice that Evan was out of sync with the rest of us. He was spilling his drinks all over the stage, and never seemed to know where he was supposed to be or what he was supposed to be singing. I stopped his onstage drinking and made sure he had a set list, and things seemed to settle down a bit.

As the tour went on, some aspects got better and better. I loved Mark's performances, and I get a music lesson every time I play with Marshall, who killed it on guitar.

Evan was starting to miss sound checks, and it seemed like he was in a fistfight every other night with someone in the crowd. He was also hitting garage sales along the tour route and filling the bus up with crap: books, coffee pots, dishes, all manner of junk. His manager and his wife were with him on the tour bus, so I left them to wrangle him.

The tempo problem was addressed on the bus as the new, all-grown-up DKT/MC5 were able to talk as adults. Dennis agreed that the tempos were uneven. The next day I was in a music store, and ran into my friend Chris Ballew from the Presidents of the United States of America. I mentioned I was looking for a click machine for touring, and he told me they had found a new gizmo, the Beat Bug. It was a small LED meter like a watch face that sat on the snare drum and showed the tempo the snare was being played at. Genius!

Dennis and I clocked all our songs' tempos, and made a master list for him. Now all he had to do was hold it to the prescribed beat. This gave him the freedom to improvise and play fills, and return to the correct tempo. Problem solved. He started referring to it as his tachometer. Very Detroit.

The stage mix was another problem needing a solution. I secured an endorsement from Aviom. They produce an extremely useful system of individual mixers for studio headphones that could be adapted to in-ear monitors for live performance. The Aviom system worked beautifully. Everyone could set their own in-ear mix to hear just what they wanted, at the level they needed, without affecting anyone else.

I happen to be a big believer in in-ear monitors. My hearing is damaged from a lifetime of working in absurdly high sound pressure levels, and in-ears help me enjoy my work and protect what's left of my hearing, especially singing. I'm no Marvin Gaye, but I like to sing. And when I can hear myself, I can harmonize competently and blend with the other singers. Singing is one of the most fun things I do in music. With in-ears, I usually end up singing better by the end of the set, as opposed to being hoarse at the finish, which was how it used to be.

Now that the technical challenges had been solved, the music got better and we started to function like a band. We had a good road crew, and we were rock & rolling across the United States in our big green tour bus, doing 30 shows in 30 days.

We worked our way across the country and when we hit Dallas, the original MC5 bassist, Pat Burrows, arrived at sound check. I had spoken to him a few times over the years; I'd made my apologies and we were good with each other. We had talked on the phone earlier in the day and I was looking forward to seeing him, but he didn't stay for the show. Sadly, I got word a year later that he took his own life. We didn't get a chance to say goodbye.

When we went to Australia, Deniz Tek from Radio Birdman took over on second guitar, and the situation with Evan Dando came to a head. He had disappeared into the crowd after a festival gig, and didn't make the flight to New Zealand for our shows there.

When we reconnected back in Australia, I called a band meeting to let Evan know he would not continue the tour beyond Japan. I explained that he could do whatever he wanted in his life, but not on this tour any longer. And, if he needed help for drug, alcohol, or any other problems, I would get him help. He blew up, insisting he didn't have a problem. He threatened that if he read in the press that drugs got him fired, he would know who'd said it.

We carried on to Japan's Summer Sonic Festival in Tokyo and Osaka, and Evan was sent home. To his credit, he wrote me a year or so later and apologized for his behavior. I wished him well.

After a short rest, DKT/MC5 was off to Europe for the summer festivals and club dates across the continent. We added the incredibly talented singer Lisa Kekaula from the Bellrays, with Nicke on guitar, along with Mark, and we three grizzled veterans. It was extremely fulfilling to play big festivals like Reading and Leeds, and to have thousands of rock fans singing along with MC5 songs that were written and recorded decades before their birth. This was something I never in a million years thought possible. We traveled in a luxury tour bus and stayed at four-star hotels, dined in fine restaurants, and everyone went home with a decent paycheck. To my mind, things could not have been better.

Yet, Dennis and Michael didn't seem to share in the enjoyment. They remained isolated from one another, as well as the other musicians in the band. At sound checks, musicians usually work out arrangement problems, learn new songs, or improvise and play for the fun of it. I noticed that I could play with Michael, or I could play with Dennis—or all three of us could jam—but Dennis and Michael never, ever jammed together. A rhythm section that could not play together was not a happy rhythm section.

As the tour went on, I could feel resentment building. They didn't like the fact that Margaret and I were calling the shots. They were correct; we did make all the important decisions. The professional relationships that the tour was built on were Margaret's and mine, and I was the bandleader and musical director. I found the resentment discouraging because I knew I wasn't the power-crazed kid I once was. I have been working with musicians all my life, and I treat people with dignity and respect. The mutual respect and camaraderie I have with other musicians is one of my most valuable possessions. Margaret and I financed these tours and were responsible for everything that happened on the road. If something went sideways, it was on us, not on Dennis or Michael. Even so, they became openly hostile to both of us.

It seemed to me that, for two guys who had been utterly out of the world of professional music for 30 years, to return to the appreciation and money as we did, was pretty nice. To be back in the band and perform our music for fans around the world was an unexpected gift for all three of us. I found it amazing and almost unbelievable that we were experiencing more success than we'd ever had. They were also equal with me in terms of income. Margaret and I did all the extra work, and I wasn't even taking the leader's share, which by American Federation of Musician's standards would have been double.

I understood their attitudes. Bandleaders are always in a double-bind position. Sooner or later musicians resent their leader. It's predictable and unfortunate, but it's a fact of life in bands. They don't see, and have little appreciation for, the hours the leader must put in to assure that employment is forthcoming. Whether you're a superstar writing and producing the next record, or a local band booking the next wedding gig, it's never resolved, and remains a tension to be lived with. It's especially tough when you start out as kids with a one-for-all-and-all-for-one attitude. Ultimately, I wasn't too rattled by my old band mates' complaints, and rolled with it all. I was looking for a deeper meaning from the effort, so I made it a point to honor Fred Smith and Robin Tyner, by name, at every show.

Touring is, by its very nature, hard work. It's a young man's game. I wasn't old, but I wasn't young, either. I think that's why it's called middle age. If you're the Rolling Stones or an emerging new band, the work is essentially the same. You must get your body to the next gig; you must perform the music with enthusiasm, while maintaining an irregular schedule of sleeping, eating, and all the other basic functions of life. All in constant motion.

I know why young people love touring. It can be exciting, with unbelievable fringe benefits—and it was when I was in my 20s, 30s, and even into my 40s and 50s—but after a couple of weeks of it, I longed for my own bed and regular routine back in LA. It's not as hard as hot-tar roofing in Brooklyn in the winter was, but it's no stroll in the park, either.

If it sounds like I'm complaining, I'm not. The invitation to play my music around the world wasn't the only valuable thing. Meeting new people and seeing how people live on this planet was important to me, too.

Our promoter in Ireland was my friend David Holmes. David and his partners in Belfast set up the DKT/MC5 gig, and they did a fine job of it. They introduced Mark and me to a former IRA member who gave us a vivid tour of Belfast's neighborhoods, trouble spots, and cemeteries. It was illuminating.

The Belfast show was the finale of that European tour, and the crowd was one of the best we played for. They were a skeptical bunch at the start and stood with their arms folded, giving us the "show me" attitude. I like crowds like this because I can, and do, "show them." They went nuts: roaring cheers, people dancing with abandon, and everyone having a ball. Good stuff.

After Ireland, a return round of European dates was booked. "Handsome Dick" Manitoba came on to sing, and British guitarist Adam Pearson from the Sisters of Mercy took over on second guitar. Lisa stayed on, and we rocked our way through the final dates. DKT/MC5 had run its course, and it was time to let it go.

The intervening years have been productive and rewarding. I have been fortunate to build a full-time career scoring film and TV, and, with a rhythm section of Eric Gardner and Doug Lunn, I've worked all over the world. We played well together and had a fine time doing it.

Tom Morello has become a cherished family friend and comrade in social justice work. In 2009, we did a few excellent Justice Tours, where we did a day of activism and a day of rock in cities across the country. "Fight the Power, Feed the Homeless, and Rock the Fuck Out" was our motto. We both come from bands that were politically conscious, and we have tried to make a difference in our work. One of my character defects is my cynicism, and Tom always breaks me out of it with his unbridled enthusiasm, intelligence, and energy.

After recording some tracks on her new record in 2011, I did a wonderful summer tour of Europe with the great chanteuse Marianne Faithfull. On a night off in Berlin, she agreed to have dinner with me. I had to call my wife and brag, "Can you believe I'm going to dinner with Marianne Faithfull?" It was fascinating to hear her recount the '60s from her perspective. Looking over at her singing every night, I couldn't help but marvel at her resilience. She was a walking history lesson of popular culture. The other musicians in the band were world-class, and we all played together beautifully. It is one of my cherished memories.

Later in 2011, Margaret arranged a final DKT/MC5 appearance at Guitare en Scène in Chamonix, on the Swiss-French border. This is a premier festival, and everyone was happy to re-up for it. Alice in Chains singer William DuVall was an excellent addition to the lineup. He has an incredible voice and was a deep MC5 fan, so he understood what the band stood for and was able to internalize our mission. Plus, he was tall, dark, and handsome, with a huge Afro. He was perfect in every way.

Sadly, Michael Davis's health was failing. Movement was difficult for him, and he couldn't stand for the performance. He leaned on a stool as we played for a sold-out festival audience. I went with the flow, and enjoyed everything about the trip.

When we finished the show, I went back and helped Michael walk up to the front of the stage, where we took our bows, arm-in-arm. I had a feeling this was important for Michael, and I wanted him to absorb the full appreciation of the fans. He was grinning like a Cheshire Cat, and that made me happy.

His condition continued to decline after that last gig. When I heard he had made a turn for the worse, I tried to go see him, but he told me not to come. I told him I loved him, and he said he loved me. On February 17, 2012, Michael Davis died at 68 in Chico, California. Michael had lived hard and played hard like the rest of us, and it took its toll. Those final years together as DKT/MC5 were bittersweet.

I settled back into life in Los Angeles, and took classes at UCLA to upgrade my musicianship. I was hired to score a documentary film, *The Narcotic Farm*, for PBS. Ironically, the film's subject was

America's first attempt to deal with addiction as a medical and social problem. The story centered on the U.S. Public Health Service
Hospital in Lexington, Kentucky, my alma mater. I also narrated the
film.

Knowing the history of Lexington intimately, I decided that the
score had to be jazz, played by jazz musicians. It occurred to me
that I could reimagine some of the cues I'd written into songs and
record an album at the same time. I called my old friend and collaborator Charles Moore to brainstorm with me, and together we
wrote and arranged the music. These writing sessions were the best
of times. Charles was not only a professor of music at UCLA, but a
great raconteur and an even better listener, as well as a formidable
jazz trumpeter. We assembled a band that included jazz piano prod-
igy Tigran Hamasyan, Phil Ranelin from the legendary Tribe on
trombone, Ralph "Buzzy" Jones on tenor and bassoon, bassists Doug
Lunn and Bob Hurst, and drummers Brock Avery and Eric Gardner.
It was a dream band; a stellar lineup of musicians well-versed in
playing free.

The sessions were a ball, and the final result, *Lexington* by Wayne
Kramer and the Lexington Arts Ensemble, was released in the spring
of 2014. I was shocked when it went to #6 in the *Billboard* jazz charts.
I figured there would be pushback from the rock fans because of my
use of horns and pianos, but I was wrong. They embraced it.

Charles and I were gratified and inspired by the success of the
record. We had agreed to begin work on a follow-up when he died
unexpectedly later that year. He was my dear friend, partner, and
teacher for almost 50 years.

CHAPTER 37

JAIL GUITAR
DOORS

As we rode up from Manhattan to the picturesque town of Ossining, I remembered that Sing Sing was the prison that movie gangsters in the '30s and '40s referred to as "up the river," as in up the Hudson River from New York City. To say that I was having complex feelings would be an understatement. Entering this iconic penal institution would be the first time I'd been in a prison since I'd left the Federal Correctional Institution in Lexington, Kentucky, in 1978, as prisoner 00180-190.

Sing Sing is intimidating: 20-foot stone and concrete walls, with gun towers every few hundred yards, it stretches over 130 acres. This penitentiary carries the history of American punishment inside its walls, and has been the scene of some of the worst abuses. Six hundred and fourteen men and women were executed there until the abolition of the death penalty in 1972. Today would be a considerably more positive event.

To its credit, New York's Department of Corrections has been attempting to make up for the tragic mistakes of the last 50 years, the massacre at Attica being foremost for me. Their willingness to let a bunch of debauched rock musicians and political agitators into one of their maximum-security prisons spoke volumes about their resolve to move corrections into the twenty-first century. New York has decreased the population of its prisons and closed many, while simultaneously reducing crime rates. They have created a system of drug courts, nonviolent courts, and mental health courts to cope with the complex challenges many of us face in life. It's not perfect, but today, New York is doing better than many states.

I had lived in denial for decades about my time in prison. Of course, I talked about it some, and even recorded one light-hearted song about it, but I'd never really looked inside my heart and faced what it meant.

Sometimes, with certain people, I bragged about it, but as a rule my experience was so far beyond most people's purview that talking about it made me feel like an alien. Most of the people I came into contact with had never experienced anything like a prison term.

Conversely, when I ran into someone else who had done time, I usually overdid it with an inappropriate level of fervor. I never addressed my shame and fear. I believe I was afraid of what happened to me and how it changed me, and I wanted to believe that I had everything under control. And yet, here I was, going back into a prison, and I was nervous about it. Of course, this was an utterly different circumstance, with none of those original fears—but really, why was I doing this? Why go to all the effort needed to round up these rock stars and wrangle them onto a bus at 8:00 in the morning after a big New York City gig the night before? I had wanted to do something to confront mass incarceration for a long time. This was going to be my start.

My mind was racing, as if something buried deep inside me was bubbling up. I was going to either cry, laugh, or puke. It wasn't intellectual; it was emotional. I was both afraid and engaged. It was happening, and I had to go through with it.

The previous night in the dressing room of the Nokia Theater in Manhattan, Billy Bragg and I were talking about acoustic guitars. I had been doing more solo acoustic gigs, and I was struggling to get a decent onstage sound out of my guitars. His guitar was colorfully painted with slogans like "Stay Free," "This Tool Kills Time," and

"Jail Guitar Doors." Billy told me he'd founded an independent initiative in England, to provide guitars to prisoners for rehabilitation. He'd named it Jail Guitar Doors.

I hadn't known anything about this when I invited him to come to New York to perform this show. I just knew he was a brilliant singer-songwriter, and that he supported social justice around the world. I hadn't even thought about the song "Jail Guitar Doors" in decades.

Billy explained that he founded Jail Guitar Doors UK to celebrate Joe Strummer's life's work. It was Joe and the Clash who first inspired Billy to pick up the guitar and raise his voice for justice, so he named his initiative after their song.

"It's an old Clash B-side. You ever heard it?" he asked.

"Yes, I know the song," I replied. "It's about me."

He said, "Whad'ya mean?" And I told him the story of the Clash writing it about me when I went to prison back in the '70s. He looked at me with a blank expression on his face.

"What's the first verse?" I asked him.

He thought for a minute, sputtered, and his face turned red. "Bloody fucking hell, I completely forgot. It *is* about you!" We both cracked up. (For the record, there are also verses about Peter Green and Keith Richards, who were having trouble with the authorities, too.)

As the night progressed, we continued to talk prison, rehabilitation, politics, and the transformative power of music. But emotions were intensifying in me. We played that night for a few thousand ecstatic rock fans at the annual benefit concert for the NYC charity Road Recovery. We were joined onstage by my old pal, Iggy Pop, and he was superb.

We rocked the house. It was one of those rare nights in music when everything falls together beautifully. Everyone sounded good, looked good, and it was for a good cause. At the end of the show, Road Recovery's founders Gene Bowen and Jack Bookbinder walked out onstage with three prison officials and presented me with a set of Sing Sing cell-door keys. I was knocked out. The symbolic value was not lost on me. The keys to freedom! All my musician friends surrounded me, everyone smiling big smiles; happy not only for me, but for all of us who pulled together to do the work we did. As Tom Morello put it, the night was "well and truly rocked."

I have learned the value and meaning of service as a way of life, and it partially defines me. One of the ways I grow and heal is by being of service to my fellow man. The Buddhists say, "To be selfish and wise, do something for someone else and you will benefit, too." I could say that almost everything good that has happened to me over the last two decades has been a direct or indirect result of helping someone else. This is more than just an ancient axiom. It is a design for successful living. The reward is in taking the action itself.

This is my route to durable fulfillment—doing for others, and accepting the accomplishment with humility and pride in a job well done. This is how I rebuild the self-respect and dignity I lost on my trip to the gutter.

So now, here we were at Sing Sing to meet and perform for a group of long-term, violent felony offenders who had made a commitment to positive change. On the bus with me were my friends: Don Was, Tom Morello, Boots Riley, Etty Lau Farrell and Perry Farrell, Daniella and Gilby Clarke, Jerry Cantrell, Matt Pinfield, Handsome Dick Manitoba, Dave Gibbs, Carl Restivo, Eric Gardner, and, of course, Billy Bragg. It was a big day for everyone: technicians, artist managers, prison staff, prisoners, and the musicians. We all took a giant leap of faith.

Most of my colleagues were grim-faced through the sign-in and security briefing process. There was no joking or cutting up, which is unnatural for any bunch of musicians.

The concert was held in the inmate dining hall. Our crew had set up the gear on the floor, and we did a quick line check before the inmates were escorted in. I had given some thought about my speech to the men. I knew I had to be rigorously honest. I wanted them to know that I identified with them, and that it was possible to successfully return to the free world. Afterward, the men asked questions, and we had a few good laughs over some of my missteps.

Tom, Handsome Dick, and others in our group shared their own challenges. We had a good conversation together.

Billy opened the musical concert with a very powerful solo acoustic performance. He sang his own "I Keep Faith," as well as the Bob Marley gem "Redemption Song." When he got to the final chorus, the men spontaneously sang along, and I was moved to tears. Between songs, Billy talked about the power of the guitar as a tool for self-expression. He said that the donated JGD guitars were not gifts, but a challenge to the men to use them as tools to express themselves in a new and nonconfrontational way. These ideas rang true for me. He was talking about the inmates, but he was talking about me, too.

After Billy finished, the rest of us strapped on our electric guitars, plugged in, and rocked Sing Sing. Each performer squeezed the most out of their songs, and the fellows responded with cheering and whooping and hollering. We finished with a rousing version of "Kick Out the Jams." In the end, they gave us a standing ovation.

The prison officials, particularly Deputy Warden Leslie Malin, felt things were going so well that she approved an aftershow meet-and-greet. We all sat at tables, talked with the guys, and signed shirts and set lists.

On the bus back to Manhattan, Margaret, Billy, and I continued to talk about Jail Guitar Doors. At one point, I told Billy, "What you're doing in England is great. But I'm an American, I've done time, and I'm a musician. Maybe I could take this on in this country. Maybe I can be a bridge between the musicians on the outside and the musicians on the inside."

"Right," he said. "Because I was just about to task you with it. You're the only one who can do it because you've been inside, and you know how the system works." This was the moment to tie together some of the big-ticket themes of my life—love, music, prison, service, social justice, and political activism—into one neat package. So right then and there, on that bus, Jail Guitar Doors USA was born. Over the past three decades, I had watched with dread and anger as prison populations skyrocketed. More people just like me were going to prison for longer sentences under worse conditions. Now, I could do something to mitigate the damage.

Between 1975 and today, people would be sentenced to terms of up to 25 years for the exact same offense I pled guilty to. In some cases, life without the possibility of parole sentences have been imposed. These punishments hardly fit the crime.

Back at the hotel that night, nearly every musician pulled me aside to tell me their feelings about what they'd experienced. To a man, each was deeply struck by the fact that the inmates they'd spent the day with seemed to be "regular guys," and that it could have been any of them doing time inside. But instead they were protected by celebrity, wealth, luck, or any number of resources the prisoners didn't have. Handsome Dick was especially unsettled by the fact that he was returning to his abundant life in Manhattan, while those men returned to their cellblock cages.

EPILOGUE

Fatherhood eluded me for a long, long time. I had started thinking about it in the late 1980s. Not that I was a prime candidate for parenthood—I wasn't. But it would enter my thoughts from time to time, mostly in the form of baby dreams.

Margaret and I were in complete agreement from the start that we wanted a child and we began our quest the old-fashioned way. We were diligent and consistent, yet no urchin appeared.

A purely coincidental meeting with a friend one afternoon proved to be crucial. She and her wife were facing the same parenthood challenge, and they had found an attorney who specialized in adoption. We hadn't considered this yet, but I was already in my sixties. I told Margaret, "If I'm going to be a papa, we'd better get this show on the road." Our attorney, David, had been helping families find each other for almost 40 years. He was a combination of lawyer, family counselor, and spiritual guide.

I'd had deep, long-standing misgivings about fatherhood. Clearly, I didn't have the best track record, and for a long time I wasn't convinced that I could overcome my character defects and shortcomings sufficiently to be the father I wanted to be. I had been driven by self-seeking wants all my life, and now the idea of being accountable for another human being shook me to my core. My truncated experience with my own father didn't imprint an intuitive grasp of how to be one, and I had spent my whole life avoiding the subject. My concerns grew as the possibility started to come into view.

One of the social workers we met with during the process asked what I wanted for my child. I told her I wanted our child to know he would always be safe. I wanted our child to know he could make mistakes and it wouldn't be the end of the world. And I wanted our child to know there were boundaries that I would hold him to. She said, "So, you want to be the father you never had." I burst into tears.

My greatest fear was that my child would follow my footsteps into addiction, prison, and rock & roll. I know ultimately that I will not be able to control these things, but that's my fear. Margaret and I discussed it endlessly. We talked to friends and strangers who had traveled this road.

We decided to move forward. We had a deep desire to be a family with a mama and a papa and a child. We worked through our myriad feelings and fears, and concluded that we believed in ourselves enough to trust that we'd be good parents. If we didn't do it now, then when? We wanted our child, and nothing was going to stop us from finding him. We were ready, willing, and able.

David introduced us to a young couple who were searching for a devoted mother and father because there was a baby coming. The two women hit it off and became close. When our baby was ready to arrive, we were right there to welcome him into the world. He went straight into Margaret's arms and never left.

His name is Francis Maron Kramer. I loved the rhythm of it. Francis was the name of one of my dearest friends, and Margaret wanted to honor him with a namesake because he is family. We believe that family are the people who love and support us. The rest are just relatives. Plus, we discovered that Francis meant "one who is free." What better aspiration for our boy? Maron, his middle name, comes from St. Maron, patron saint of the Maronite Catholics. This name was his connection to Margaret's culture and traditions. I figured later, when he's a little bit older, I will turn him onto Chuck Berry, Sun Ra, and Aristotle, so he'll get to know my culture and traditions. And when he wants to know more about his ancestries, we will support him.

I wanted to experience fatherhood as a grown-up. I wanted to be a man who could meet all the challenges of full-on adulthood. A fully realized man who could weather the range of emotions, and persevere with dignity and a little grace. A man who could care for others before himself. A man who did what he said he was going to do. A man who could be depended on. I couldn't wait to change dirty diapers, do midnight feedings, and rock a baby to sleep. I wanted to do everything that parenting required of me, and more. I believed I was ready to do this at last.

Francis will be five years old with the publication of this memoir, and he's bursting with enthusiasm for life. He brings me joy every single day.

THE BEATS OF MY LIFE break down pretty simply: childhood, the MC5, crime, prison, sobriety, service, and family. I have tried my best to illustrate some of the major peaks and valleys truthfully and accurately. Putting it down in a linear fashion has been enlightening, and has helped me understand myself and what happened in these first 70 years.

There is much that can never be resolved, like the loss of so many people. My dear friend and partner of over 40 years, Mick Farren, died two weeks before my son arrived. He had moved back to England for the benefits of the National Health Service. Living in America, he couldn't afford the medications he needed for his emphysema. He had been ill for a while. We wrote a lot of great songs together, and had many great adventures. We raged our way across the continents. He loved performing in bands, and died on-stage playing a club date in London on July 29, 2013. He was a great writer and a great friend.

I have a good life today. Most of the time, I get to do the kinds of things I like to do with people I like to do them with. I adore my family. I am fulfilled in my work. I am at peace with my past. I am content to remain a student. My definition of success is being able to continue.

I created most of the hurt in my life. Most, but not all. Some of it I put squarely where it belongs, on the War on Drugs, which has caused me immense anguish. It is a catastrophic failure of public policy. Like most of the 2.3 million people now incarcerated, I didn't need prison; I needed help.

This "war" is a misguided political atrocity that has been destroying families for generations. Drug prohibition has killed more people than drugs ever could.

I still live in the tension between the angel and the beast, and that is my lot as human. This struggle will continue until the day I depart. Mine has been a painful and beautiful experience, and I wouldn't change any of it, even if I could.

ACKNOWLEDGMENTS

I would like to extend a special thanks to my terrific editor, Leslie Wells. Leslie brought her immense skills to bear and transformed my manuscript into a book. I also have deep gratitude for Peter McGuigan, Ben Schafer, and Margaret Saadi Kramer for their additional editing.

Luc Santé encouraged me at the onset and many of my favorite authors—Jerry Stahl, Adam McKay, Nick Tosches, Mick Farren, Mike Doughty, Eric Spitznagel, Kat Kambes, Rob Roberge, Ken Hartman, Adam Davidson, Jen Banbury, and Aristotle in particular—sustained me through the process and gave me inspiration and support.

Thanks to all at Da Capo Press for faith in me and my story.

INDEX